CONFESSIONS OF A MURPHY'S LAW CHILD

Surviving Child Abuse, Racism, Poverty,
and Trick-Ask Ideology

DR. FRANKLIN TITUS THOMPSON

Published in October of 2022

Print ISBN: 978-1-66785-774-9
eBook ISBN: 978-1-66785-775-6

Front cover art concept by Church Mouse
Back cover artwork by Vociferous

Printed by Book Baby in the USA

Selah Sound, Inc.
Titus-Vision Publishing
8451 West Center Road
P.O. Box 24242
Omaha, NE 68124
531-225-0907

Website:
Omahachangeagent.com

TABLE OF CONTENTS

ACKNOWLEDGMENTS

THANKS GOES OUT TO THE PEOPLE WHO HAVE HELPED ME TO SUCCEED IN life despite having to navigate difficult terrain. A very special thanks goes out to my wife, the talented and beautiful Beverly Bray-Thompson, for believing in me and supporting me when many others chose not to. I love and adore you. To my children, Kelly, Ivy, Franque, and Jasmine, thank you for providing daddy with inspiration and a reason to continue pushing through when times get rough. Lastly, much appreciation goes out to Omaha Public Schools educators Ordra Bradley, Grace Davis, Gene Haynes, and Bernice Nared. Your love, intervention, and non-traditional approach kept scores of young people from falling through the cracks of society.

"There is no greater agony than
bearing an untold story within you."

– Maya Angelou –

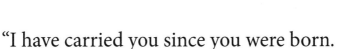

"I have carried you since you were born.
I have taken care of you since birth.

When you became old, I did the same.
When your hair turns gray,

I will take care of you. I made you
and I will care for you."

Isaiah 46:3

INTRODUCTION:

GET THE FUNK OUT MY FACE

THEY CALL ME CHURCH MOUSE FOR SUNDRY REASONS. RACIST WHITES SAY I am "one of those uppity educated Blacks who do not know their place." Misinformed hood homies believe I am "an enemy to my own race." I guess I am too Black for one group, and not Black enough for the other group. In addition, so-called friends say that I am the classroom geek who grew up to be an "adult-square-pants." Supposedly, my personality lacks the "jiggy" factor that was popular among 1960–70s hipsters. Because I live by religious Kingdom principles, some people say that I am devoid of being fresh and exciting. If in fact things such as regular church attendance, not smoking "da chronic," [1] believing in family values, treating women with dignity, not yanking on the family jewels, mastering mainstream English, adopting a bipartisan mindset, voting for the person and not the political party, and striving to recapture lost historic Black culture mean that I am not a real soul brother, then, well, I am guilty as charged.

I don't buy it, and neither should you. I will not apologize for being an eclectic moderate conservative thinker who follows a spiritual path. A moderate mindset is a wise thing. Likewise, God reached out and cared for me when others kicked me to the curb. Every successful move I have made in life is due to God's direct intervention. "Do not allow this one to fall through the cracks," the Good Lord commanded as He dispatched His angels to watch over me. God did not abandon me when most others did. Because of this fact, I am willing to take a bullet for Him any day and anytime. If that makes me a social dweeb or a nerd, well, you'll get over yourself.

The name Church Mouse was given to me during the 1970s, when most urban Black teens were searching for ways to navigate tough political, social, and identity issues. Many of my peers chose responses such as anger, despair, separatist ideology, alcohol, drugs, crime, and the hot pursuit of materialism. I chose education and spirituality during a time when Blaxploitation [2] personas ruled the day; thus, I was branded a nerd. The name Church Mouse has stuck, but it was not the only moniker given to me. Others include Black Opie, Uncle Tom, RINO [3], Poot-Butt, White Boy, Mr. Odd Ball, Uppity Nigger, and Affirmative Action Boy. Whatever, hater bitches. For years, critics of all persuasions have unsuccessfully tried to describe me. It has been nothing short of nauseating, even comical at times. For better or for worse, I am what they made me to be: an American solo dancer. A soldier who successfully grew up in a silo with little help.

It is important to highlight the fact that *this book is not for everyone*. If an American tale about rising from the ashes is not your cup of tea, feel free to drop back ten yards and kick this mother function over the crossbar of life. Nonetheless, my story has significance for kids who hurt, and for those who raise themselves. This story also helps adults who are navigating a hard past. Some of you have been wandering in a desert for far too long, and it is time to come home.

Murphy's Kids. What a strange moniker. It corresponds with the so-called Murphy's Law that states if a series of things can potentially go wrong, they will. As incredible as it sounds, there are some kids who, from the day they are born until they leave this earth, encounter more than their fair share of bad luck and misfortune. It is as if a vixen were attached to their spinal cord. Most children learn to adapt, but far too many acquiesce. They become victims and turn to the dark side. A few choose to die and take innocent lives with them. I choose to fight the powers that try to hold me down. If you have a desire to combat child abuse, this book could be your huckleberry. If you are unhappy with the typical Black/White, Democrat/Republican, up/down, day/night, and devil/angel style of binary thinking that permeates our society, feel free to jump on board this freedom train. If, however, you are more into things such as making everything about you, letting children drift without direction, playing games about power and privilege, sustaining the status quo, setting political traps for one another, or "bumpin' to da beat and smackin' dat ass all up and down the dance flo'," this literary effort is probably not for you.

This is not a typical memoir. It doubles as an anthem for the abused and misunderstood. At times, this story is fluffy and PG-rated, but most of the time it is written in an urban realistic style—raw and unapologetic, with a purposeful emotional and lyrical flair. There are times when my story gets downright ugly, but never is it X-rated or fabricated. Yes, my views jump back and forth across the political divide like a kangaroo hooked on Ritalin, but I am not spastic. I am black-coffee-woke and eclectic. Thirdly, I admit I commit a cultural sin by airing dirty laundry. To members of my family and ethnic group, I have but one message: Do not run from the monsters that vex you. Stare your demons down until they no longer have power over you!

Groups offended by this account might include atheists, Proud Boys, Make America Great Again patriots, left-wing liberals, Pollyanna thinkers, language police types, Marxists, and group-think-only Black folk. That leaves dolphins, penguins, snow cone ladies, and kids who raise themselves as my main audience. That is good enough for me. I am aware that my cavalier approach might cause book sales to suffer and political support to suddenly dry up, but I also know that broken people have a real chance to heal by reading this effort. So, if you fear that my message is not PC (i.e., politically correct) enough, you might want to stop, drop, and roll. Sail on, good soldier. There is no shame in taking a pass if you think my approach is too avant-garde.

This is a bare-all-facts story about how I overcame child abuse, racism, the American brand of poverty, and stinking thinking. I share that story utilizing a colorful and ethnic flair. Ebonics, 1965–95 urban slang, and salty street vernacular flow like a river in this book. Ministers, religious friends, and English teachers please forgive my linguistic fall from grace. I am sorry that I do not use the typical church or college professor language to tell my story. No, dubious speech is not an innate part of Black culture, although some comedians and "gangsta" rappers would have you believe otherwise. Hail Mary full of grace, "da funk, and the crunk [4] are wit me." And, if by chance you are one of those who abuse children, Yah Mo [5] just might be there to bust a cap dead off in yo brazen ass! Please forgive my mouth, Father God. "Loose my tongue," King Jesus, and set me free. Some folks say I expose too many ethnic and culture of poverty insider revelations. I am what I am, and it is what it is. Let's keep it real and relevant.

I do not use emotional flare and spicey language to create a buzz. Rather, it is an integral part of surviving the culture of poverty, warts, and all. The story of overcoming obstacles cannot be told using the Queen's English nor conservative Nebraska language. The usage of the "N" and "B" words will probably not sit well with literary purists. I use the words of the urban streets as if they are a sedative. Black people are constantly doing a balancing act of when to hold and when to fold in the card game of life. Whenever faced with blatant forms of racism, I react professionally. But the more subtle and institutional forms of racism are trickier to navigate. Sometimes you take a diplomatic approach, while other times you reply with a snappy "Get dat funk out my face, G!" Ebonics can help a Black man stay out of jail, while also providing much needed emotional relief. The therapeutic benefit of speaking Ebonics is a fascinating discussion.

Most readers understand racism, poverty, and child abuse. Those are basic concepts taught in sociology class. The concept of trick-ask ideology, however, might be elusive to some. I use the term to classify folks who are not sincere in their human relations efforts. For example, a White conservative once asked me, "What gives Black people the right to take *our jobs*?" Really? Black liberals often lament that "We don't own the boats and planes that bring dope into this country. Why do we blame the poor drug dealer who's just trying to survive?" Am I missing something? A racist republican once asked, "Why can't the majority of Black people act like you and the other few good ones?" An air-headed democrat might ask, "What is so wrong with letting rap artists call women out of their name? How is that lowering the American bar?" Please.

Trick-ask ideology. It is as real as baseball and Mom's apple pie. But do not confuse the term with "Ole Trick Ass," the pseudonym I use for Satan, the prince of pain. That mother function does not give a rat's ass about you or me. His heart is made of stone. There are readers who will not like the religious metaphors that I use. I posit that we cannot separate child abuse and racism from the spiritual realm. A Bible passage from Ephesians 6:12 reads, "For we wrestle not against flesh and blood, but against principalities, against powers, against the rulers of the darkness of this world, against wickedness in high places." There are times I fight with my fists, my pen, and my vote. Most of the time, I utilize the Word of God as my main weapon of choice.

At times, this story is dark and depressing. One hard-luck scenario follows another without much opportunity for the reader to come up for air. I apologize for this, but I refuse to change my approach. For kids who hurt, sorrow is a reality they navigate daily. Softening that storyline so that audiences feel safe and warm does not prepare educators, counselors, and other help-professionals to work with at-risk children. Some readers might need to toughen up. It is also important to mention that the anecdotes provided in this story are not intended to be monolithic depictions of all Black people. No single person can speak for his or her entire race, gender, or family. Still, the general themes presented here have an authentic ring for Americans of all colors and backgrounds. This story is simply one Black man's interpretation of how Murphy's Kids navigate disadvantage.

This unorthodox autobiography is written to read like a novel. It resembles the 1970s TV sitcom *Good Times* on steroids. Pain and sorrow abound, but in the end victory rebounds. It is told from a third-person point of view out of therapeutic necessity. The number of emotional breakdowns I endured while recounting my story are too numerous to count. To help deal with the pain of reliving a sordid past, I chose to draft my story from a detached position. Pretending that I was a neutral observer reporting from the outside looking in helped me to experience a level of objectivity I would not have been able to capture had I followed a first-person narrative.

Writers like me take a huge risk by publishing tell-all tales that bare their souls. The reaction can be one of either feast or famine, as in: "Thank you for shining new light on a problem that is too often overlooked" vs. "Ah poor baby, do you want me to give you a cookie?" Revenge is toxic; forgiveness is golden. It would be easy for me to quietly ride off into the sunset and celebrate my retirement years. Truth is I may have pushed others away because there was a heavy cloud that hovered over me. I apologize now that I look back on that reality. Still, I am reminded of the lyrics of an old gospel song: "Something's got ahold of me, and it won't let me be." That something is about protecting vulnerable kids and promoting positive human relations.

Something is out of sync. Political ideologues argue over topics such as critical race theory (which is often misunderstood), while kids die daily in the streets. Turn on any credible news source and you can see that violence, school shootings, and suicide rates are on the rise. Consult any reputable academic resource and one will find that Blacks, especially males, fall statistically near the bottom of the "doing well" totem pole. Only the homeless, certain refugee groups, and Native Americans do worse. And not all traditions are the enemy. Black homes need fathers. Period. End of sentence. While it is true that there is room for competing paradigms to peacefully coexist, pundits who want to rewrite the last ten thousand years of Black existence in the name of a fragile liberal agenda are playing with fire. Yes, I am an ally of intersectionality viewpoints, but not at the expense of altering history just to make PC folk feel warm and fluffy.

Some of our children are in big trouble. The top ten reasons people choose suicide to deal with life's problems are severe depression, traumatic stress, bullying, social isolation, a sense of hopelessness, being a burden to others, experiencing a great loss, having to endure chronic pain or illness, substance abuse, and failure to control impulsivity. [6] The most salient factor that correlates with mass shootings at schools and rising gun violence in general is the shooter's previous history with brutality. Violence breeds more violence. Other risk factors include child abuse, social isolation, bad role modeling, poor anger management, LGBTQ status, and a desire to exact revenge. [7] The easy answer to explain away the problem is to say that certain people suffer from mental illness. While this may be true for some cases, the literature also identifies a secure family setting, love, and engaged mentoring as the antidote to keep kids from going dark.

Our children are not born mentally ill. Neither are they innately endowed with a desire to take the lives of others and themselves. Violence is a learned behavior, and many times the misbehaviors of children are a simple cry for help. But at what point do we stop labeling them as monsters and social misfits? *At what point do we stop throwing rocks at our own creations?* Rather, let us teach parents, educators, ministers, help-professionals, and law enforcement personnel the warning signs that help to catch the problem *before* children fall through the cracks of society. Yes, we can make a positive difference if only we engage our kids in loving and meaningful ways. Nevertheless, the miracle of this story is that short of providing shelter and food, *children do have the wherewithal to successfully raise themselves.* This is a sad and shocking statement, but there is hope. Murphy's Kids can make it in life even when "the village" does not fill in the gaps where parents and society fail. They can learn to become like Houdini.

Despite the fact that racism and politics are openly addressed in this book, the main focus is to identify counseling and survival strategies for children who hurt. This story is 90% true, with a sprinkling of added coloring. Occasionally I take writer's liberty by adding creative input to a vignette to help spice things up. Sometimes I combine the stories of several kids into one collective portrayal to show how some view their pain as a shared experience. There are times I use a vivid imagination, and I invoke spiritual exegesis for special effect. The views presented in this text are not meant to replace conventional race and human relations practice and thought. Neither do I feel that my truth is the only or the most accurate truth. It is a piece, however, that is sorely missing from the general discourse. Let's provide our children with 360 degree truth.

Sir Church Mouse Devoid of Crunk and Funk—that is the full rendition of the putdown moniker assigned to me by "homies from the hood." Silly little Ebonics haters. It seems as if everybody is gunning for an HBO (Home Box Office) comedy special these days. If the truth is told, you could combine a dozen or so of my loudest critics, and they would still not measure up to the Black experience nor the insight and wisdom I possess in one eyelash. I might even be a prophet. But more than likely, I am just a little squirrel running around trying to find a nut. A humble little country boy with a passion for truth and honesty. Chances are, I am not the only one.

Lastly, it is important that readers reserve judgment about the overall message of this book, as well as the messenger, until the entire Church Mouse saga has been told. That story might take several publications to completely unfold. Only then will the reader be able to assess whether they are willing to accept my particular call to change agency. Oh yes, one last thing: I want it to be known that I respect "the crunk" and I am definitely not devoid of "da funk." In fact, I am a creator of funk music and culture in both justified and uncut versions.

My Achilles heel is that I am thirty years ahead of my critics who are perpetually in catch-up mode; thus, unfair name-calling and misrepresentations persist. Despite the egregious lack of apologies, I dedicate my life to love and serve everyone—even those who cut my wings. They say a sucker is born every day. Call me grape flavored. Still, a true critical thinker can easily make a case that I am one of the most woke and "keeping it real" Black men alive. Each reader is left to decide for themselves whether this statement is accurate or not.

CHAPTER 1:

ENIGMA

THERE SAT CHURCH MOUSE IN THE EARLY WINTER OF 1992 AMID A THRONG of graduate school hopefuls, a thirty-nine-year-old African American male slumped over a grueling standardized achievement test that he was not ready to take. Possessor of three college degrees and a cumulative college GPA of 3.8, he knew his entry into the doctoral program in education administration at the University of Never-Ending Opportunity (UNO) was imminent. Despite his lack of preparation for the test, he prided himself in being a catch-up artist—a talented kid who had an ability to quickly cover lost ground. "Lawd, let me cop dis one last swig," [8] Church Mouse playfully exclaimed as he prepared his mindset for entry into the hallowed halls of academe. Like it or not, here comes Black America preparing itself for leadership roles.

Church Mouse was a kindhearted, easy-to-please, simple guy; a country boy who derived immense pleasure from the little things in life. Funk was his favorite genre of music, and fatback and hominy grits was his food of choice. For many a southerner these were magical ingredients for the stomach and the soul. When Church Mouse moved up north, he carried southern culture with him. You can take the boy out of the sticks and bushes, but you cannot erase the Carolina influence from a country boy's DNA. Keep it jiggy and keep it funky, country boy.

Earlier that morning, his wife, Banana Babe, cooked him a large helping of his favorite dish. She threw on a Bootsy Collins funk CD, and Lord have mercy! We are talking about the kind of stuff that makes your body jerk uncontrollably as if one were being filled with Casper the Holy Ghost. [9] Hallelujah, somebody! Somehow the image of food and music always finds its way into conversations about Black people. The practice among younger Blacks is beginning to fade but make no mistake about it: soul music is king, and soul food is still the reigning queen. The simplicity of seeing a couple of neck bones swimming in collard greens juice is enough to give a Black man courage to hit Ole Lucifoot [10] "dead in his mouf." Slap a soul brother a glass of red Kool-Aid to go along with his corn bread and candied yams, and he might start playing Parliament/Funkadelic's hit song "Atomic Dog" on a Cajun musician's accordion. Canine bruthas (brothers) in the house, let America hear you bark!

A true soul sista (sister) knows what her man needs to make it in this opaque world. He needs funk music, grits, a rack of bacon, and Jesus on the main line. A little female dessert on the side might also help to top off the deal, if you know what I mean. Sorry, religious readers. Church Mouse may very well be highly favored, but he also gets easily distracted by the finer things of life. More importantly, a real Black woman understands the problems that come with living in a nation full of illusory beings. She knows that every now and then her man needs a pump, a bump, and a James Brown [11] grunt in order to make it. Good God! Soul power. Papa don't take no mess. Now take your man to the bridge but be careful not to "hit him" the wrong way. Brothers get a serious attitude when you hit them on the downbeat, instead of on the one.

Church Mouse lived a curious life of highs and lows, a life of curses and bountiful blessings. Like "Indian Summers" in December. Parents you barely remember. A thin line between love and hate. An odd mixture of daylight and darkness. A deafening experience with isolation mixed with showers of blessings from above. Like liquid pain mixed with doses of granular gain. So-called friends working hard to drown you, while the Good Lord lovingly resuscitates you. Hit me on the one before you crush my dreams. But what did it all mean?

Church Mouse did not adhere to the stereotypical street rules of what a Black man was supposed to act and sound like. His independent and spiritual mindset often caused him to be rejected by his peers. Conversely, the White Man kept his racist knee squarely on Church Mouse's neck. No matter how expert he became, Church Mouse always had to play second fiddle to a White person who was jumped over him via a job promotion. Sometimes his trainees became his new boss! Church Mouse was the genius behind many company innovations but guess who took the credit and received the bonus. It wasn't funny then, and it's not funny now.

Church Mouse is an enigma. His name was given to him as a sign of disrespect. During the summer of 1972, friends—both Black and White—were upset that he made the choice to accept Jesus Christ as his personal Lord and Savior. Back then, there was open hostility against people who chose religion as a viable option to combat the various social ills that permeated the land. The pro-spiritual song lyrics of R&B artists such as Marvin Gaye, Staple Singers, and Curtis Mayfield had not yet fully taken root within the Black community. In today's hip-hop world, church is "da bomb" and Jesus is "da homie." Back then, however, sex, drugs, liberal ideology, and astrology were the magic pills that were sold to young people as a cure-all. These vices were easily embraced, and yet they failed to bring about the desired outcomes people were searching for. While it is true that many born-again believers brought ridicule on themselves, criticism against them was, nonetheless, overdone. The assassination of civic leaders, Vietnam, and the Watergate scandal did little to inspire belief in the institutions of humankind. People like Church Mouse needed something more than just palm readings and charlatans to believe in.

Church Mouse was a social reformer who believed that the views of Black conservative leaders like Frederick Douglass, Harriet Tubman, Booker T. Washington, and Jackie Robinson had relevance for today's world. And yet, he was a huge fan of Barack and Michelle Obama. Did that make him a confused flip-flopper, or a wise sage? Like Solomon of the Bible, Church Mouse possessed a large measure of erudition, but his gift was also a curse. While it provided him with incredible insight, it seldom brought him acceptance from his peers. The rule of the 1970s ghetto was to dumb down and act cool. Strangely, that practice served as a therapeutic response to centuries of racism. Smoking, drinking, partying, and acting badass helped many Black folks erase the sting of slavery and Jim Crow. The rise of leaders such as Muhammad Ali on the critical hand and Superfly on the superficial hand was easily predictable, but too many Whites of that day had blinders on. Americans are good at throwing rocks at their own creations. Likewise, Church Mouse had one sustaining problem in life: he was born thirty years ahead of his time. This fact placed his detractors—both Black and White—in constant criticism mode. As a child, his daily prayer to God included the plea, "Lord, please make me slow, dumb, and happy so I don't have to hurt anymore." His petition was ignored as his gift continued to grow.

The twentieth century was a time of incredible mixed signals for Black people. They were told that in order to succeed they had to think and act White, but when they complied, they were not allowed to join this nation's exclusive clubs. In addition, the mid-1950s was a time when inebriated parents began entertaining the idea of switching roles with their children. Most Black parents did not commit this crime, but far too many of them did. Unfortunately, many disadvantaged kids had to master the art of raising both themselves and their parents. The net effect on Black families was that way too many children ended up skipping their childhood.

Million-dollar smiles hid the gangrene infestation of a society gone wrong. A symbolic representation of a way of life heaven will never bless. Here, oh Lord, is our sacrifice: hurting kids with wide eyes and porous hearts. Remarkably, not all of these children became lost to the streets. Resilient Black, Brown, and Red kids grew up to be this nation's best products. Still, too many of them succumbed to the pressures of the ghetto and ended up embracing the culture of poverty as if it were a seductive lover. Alas, we discover that the accumulation of material goods is no substitute for spiritual healing. Only God, loving parents, and positive self-esteem can heal the lacerations that were inflicted on the children of poverty by the keepers of the material gates.

Spit into the wind, Church Mouse, and dare the excretion to find its way back. Surround yourself with more of yourself and pretend that the hollow cavern entrenched between your Adam's apple and tailbone really isn't there. Or at least, say that it's a temporary anomaly; a fissure of ghostly characteristics. Inhale the American Dream. Bellow like U.S. Congressman Steve King, the great icon of the misinformed. Yes, there are great thinkers located on the political right, but republicans like King badly miss the mark. Revel in the words of his alt-right comrades, but also fear the liberal lunatics of this world. Advocates on the far political left speak about socialism and love as if humankind is good enough to pull that experiment off. Pundits on the far political right speak about a thousand points of light bursting onto the skyline of a warm summer night. They proclaim that ever since the election and reelection of Barack Obama as the forty-fourth president of the US, racism has dissipated into a melting pot of an ever-evaporating past. They pop their buttons and beam brightly as they incorrectly make that assertion.

Press your smoke-colored lipstick against a Black man's open wound so that he may stagger with dignity. Kiss his wife while she is blindfolded. Run your hand up and down her ebony thighs. Slide your tongue across her lips and breathe dysfunction into her soul. Place your hands on the rear end of her man's oppression and rotate him to the tune of God Bless America. Whisper sweet nothings into his ear, and then send them both to their final resting place. There Black people will find peace and solitude, or at least, they tell us so.

On the day Church Mouse sought to enter his grad school program, reality came crashing in on our star child. Verbal abilities and ethnic creativity can color the academic world for only so long, then "bam!" The truth begins to set like a bowl of vanilla Jell-O in the icebox of Western civilization. "What the hell is this shit!" exclaimed Church Mouse as he opened the math portion of the Pre-Professional Skills Test (PPST) educators must take for state certification. The religious fundamentalist, immediately embarrassed by his primitive outburst, quickly repented. Church Mouse wanted to believe his response was spontaneous, that it emanated from the bowels of a simple misunderstanding. Chances are the response sprang from a much deeper origin. A familiar place. A familial root. You can mask the impact of living in "da hood" for a while, but the truth will always come out in the rinse cycles of life.

Everyone knows it is easy to be a hypocrite in the land of multiple Bibles. Pray for peace and understanding at church on Sunday morning, while insisting that Michelle Obama is a Black Panther in disguise by sundown. Or go on television and talk about caring for poor people while secretly planning to downsize the labor force that sustains their very existence. Or kill foreign women and children in the name of liberty and God, while allowing industrialist friends the opportunity to feast on the spoils of war and colonialism. It's your basic sleight of hand trick. We all do it to one degree or another. Church Mouse is no different than the rest of us. Maybe we are all more transparent than we'd like to think.

Church Mouse grew flushed with embarrassment. "The devil made me say those words," he whispered to an onlooker. You can't go wrong when you blame Lucifoot for your missteps. We share no part in the creation of our problems, so says the myth. A nearby Black student glanced at Church Mouse and shrugged her shoulders in disgust. Misery loves company. Telepathic communication is the glue that binds Black folk together in a common struggle. One glance is worth a thousand words. Meet my best friend, Shaniqua Sims. We have only known each other for a full sixty seconds. We are homies in the struggle, and you best believe we've got each other's back. Right on for the revolution, regardless of whether or not it will be televised.

Church Mouse thought he was good to go. In fact, he entered the room with a cocky attitude. He saw himself as talented enough to skip the review sessions that so-called slower students needed to take. Older Black women refer to that kind of thinking as "smelling oneself." Church Mouse had always been at the top of his class, but now, his ship was sinking fast, and the usual magic act he relied upon was quickly dissipating. The smoke and mirrors of his scholastic preparation began to evaporate right before his eyes, leaving only a paper-thin academic foundation behind. You can't coax a fox to come out of its hole if there is no vermin to feed it. You cannot fake the funk if you've never experienced the sensation of slapping your grandma because the sweet potato pie she baked melted in your mouth like honey. (An important side note: Readers who are devoid of funk may not want to attempt this dangerous stunt.)

Lying there before Church Mouse was a brand of math he had never encountered. It was not that his previous educational opportunities hadn't offered advanced course offerings, nor was it because Church Mouse wasn't willing to take honors math and science courses. The answer to his predicament rested in a simple truth: his parents and high school counselors never pushed him to pursue advanced course offerings. Even if school officials had wanted to do so, they were consumed by the incredible amount of energy it took to keep young revolutionaries from tearing down the school building—a common occurrence during the late 1960s and early 1970s.

Here are a few important questions educators must ask themselves: At what point do you run out of time and energy when dealing with the demands of troubled children that grace our inner-city schools? Do teachers have limitations, or do they possess special powers like Iron Man and Wonder Woman? To what extent must educators do the job that parents refuse to perform? And at what point should churches and community groups help resolve the growing problem of violence and academic disadvantage? Can religious folk make it into heaven singing about starry crowns and streets of gold, while children die right outside their church doors? Is Church Mouse a phony? Is he really a closeted liberal trying to pass himself off as a conservative? Is he in need of a good dousing of right-wing political repro-gramming? You best believe that candidates willing to give him a good ole fashion GOP shakedown are in no short supply.

What connection does Church Mouse's current condition have to his sordid past? Did he receive one too many blows to the head from his stepmother's trusty weapon, the kitchen broomstick? What about the lashes from her lethal tongue? Do words leave welts like that from an extension cord whipping? What about the impact of a father who was unplugged, dis-engaged, and absent? How can things like chitterlings smell so bad, yet taste so good? Is funk better uncut or justified? Will cartoon character Wile E. Coyote ever catch the Road Runner? Is there enough meat on its tiny bones to satisfy dude's hunger? Which of these boys is the dumbest: Elmer Fudd or Yosemite Sam? At some point, a true soul brother must ask the important questions of life.

Stop whining, Church Mouse. Yo smack is whack! [12] You uppity sub-urban Blacks like to pretend that you live in high cotton while eating fatback and greens on the down low. No G, you're nothing but a squirrel running around trying to find a nut! You're just a pissant. Nothing more than a pawn in this game called life. A pig wallowing in fermented slop. Awaken from your inebriated state of conservatism, my drunken and miseducated one. And when you finally come to your senses, you will correctly surmise that someone has slipped a mickey into your drink. You will discover that you have been sipping on fool's gold.

Buck up, you sanctimonious sellout. Save yourself from your histri-onic babblings. Quit making baby history. Every time I see you, I witness you crying. Would you like to have a little cheese to go with your whine? You diversity folk complain too much. Stop waiting for someone to pull your punk asses out of the fire. Pull yourself up by your own bootstraps, for goodness's sake! So what if you came from an abusive family. So what if you came from a crime-infested neighborhood. So what if your teachers passed you along and did not properly prepare you for the rigors of college. Small inconveniences such as having a Twilight Zone zip code shouldn't stop Black kids from becoming Rhodes Scholars. Look at the Asians, America's model minority. They come to this country and succeed despite all odds. "Why can't Blacks, Mexicans, and Natives do the same?" asks the old guard. And the uncritical portion of the conservative drumbeat goes on and on, while the brainless side of the typical liberal dance continues.

By his sophomore year of high school, Church Mouse began to give in to the intense peer pressure many kids face as they navigate the inner city. Driven by the fear of rejection, your boy began to crave social acceptance like a hooty [13] gasping for oil. The more he acquiesced, the more academic excellence evaporated. Luckily, his infractions were small and not of the "half-ass" variety. He could have chosen more debilitating behaviors such as selling drugs, dropping out of school, pimping women, and selling out his historic Black culture. But Church Mouse could not stand the thought of giving Lucifoot, the king of jackasses, the pleasure of seeing another brother fall. Completely selling out was something Church Mouse just couldn't bring himself to do. There is a line that even hurting kids won't cross if they are truly God's property.

Unfortunately, Church Mouse responded to the culture of poverty by relying on practices all too familiar to disadvantaged youth—decreased attention to academic affairs accompanied by an overreliance on creativity and smooth-talking abilities that allow a young person to slip and slide through the education system. Rumor has it that teachers can easily be duped by the practice. Everyone knows that a student can obtain a high school diploma without knowing his/her times tables. I mean, what do you think they make iPhones and laptop computers for? And please do not be an African American student with a 4.0 GPA during the early 1970s. An urban myth posits that Blacks who study too much and speak mainstream English are "trying to act White." Mercy Lord. Ghetto lies sometimes camouflage themselves in sagging pants with a little bling-bling (ice) and ching-ching (cash) on the side: "There's a party over here, ain't shit over there." [14] Learned helplessness is so fascinating when it is uncloaked.

Keep it real, C-Money (Church Mouse). Dazzle your undergraduate professor with some fancy footwork. Use the ole verbal machine gun approach to set up a cognitive smoke screen. Break it on down with a one-two step. What it be like, C. Mesmerize your teachers with guilt and emotion, and then presto: you're out of there with a certified bachelor's degree! But entry into the graduate and professional levels of higher education is a horse of a different color. It is the White Man's last stronghold, and it does not appear that the keepers of his gate are planning on relinquishing control anytime soon. At the mere sound of his voice, one by one, young would-be minority scholars drop like roaches encountering dichlorodiphenyltrichloroethane (DDT) on a sweltering summer's night. Black males in particular become spastic, shaking as if common sense is exiting their bodies.

Tell Banana Babe to "cook dem chillen" [15] some hominy grits so they can build up their resistance muscles! If you don't, they might find themselves slain in the Ghetto Ghost, a shirt-tail relative of the Holy Ghost. Make sure you lay a large handkerchief on passed-out women so that their undergarments do not show when they fall to the floor. When they regain consciousness, they will find themselves stuck with over-inflated academic reputations, low GPAs, low wages, and relationship problems. Sound familiar? This scenario is far from describing the views of a few disgruntled minority revolutionaries. No, this is a colorless saga—a story that rings authentic for thousands of students from all ethnic backgrounds. Black male status, coupled with a myriad of social problems, appears to accentuate the problem to the nth degree.

The math section of the PPST proved difficult, and for the first time in his life, Church Mouse was willing to concede that the higher education deck was stacked against people like him. Or, at least, that standardized tests only measure exposure to the dominant literary canon and not actual intelligence and the academic potential of an individual. "Pull yourself together and stop writing such nonsense," the writer told himself! Church Mouse is no closeted liberal. When the physician slapped the newborn into existence, the child turned to the physician and said, "Give me another one for the Gipper, doc."

Yes, indeed he did. From the moment of conception, young Church Mouse used the blood from his umbilical cord to sign his name in the annals of conservatism. A moderate conservative, yes, but from day one, he depended on no one for a handout. How could any child depend on help from people who were absent all the time?

Church Mouse was battle-tested and conservative-tough to the bone. The mere thought of people associating him with the views of left-wing liberals might mean that the semi-sanctified one was turning into a (gulp) democrat. Heresy. Blasphemy in the holiest of temples! One step forward and two steps back. Everyone knows that Black babies are born to be liberals. They all talk the same, think the same, and vote the same. They even drink the same red sugar drink. Abort this puppy before someone puts him in charge of running things. Maybe we can convince Church Mouse to do the honors himself. The simple solution is always the most efficient one.

Suffering a greater than usual sense of entrapment, Church Mouse hurried to his car and inserted the key. He looked in the rearview mirror and noticed that his face was unusually swollen. "There is no way my poor test performance will fly with this fine institution of higher learning," he whispered. "The jig is up. I have topped out. I've gone as far as my abilities will take me," he said. Topping out was not so bad if Church Mouse could honestly credit his failure to a lack of ability. It is not meant for every student to get a master's degree. No rule exists that says all birds must flap their wings and fly. Some birds just waddle around on the ground and move their wings in pretend fashion. Ghetto birds have even been known to catch a jitney [16] to arrive at their destinations. Sometimes life boils down to chicken-fried decision-making.

But something did not add up with this scenario. Something just did not pass the smell test. Years of academic success had convinced Church Mouse that he was a member of the scholarly elite, and yet after today's pathetic performance, he felt like he was the doorkeeper of the learning disabled. Deep inside, Church Mouse knew he had more ability than what his test scores would reveal. The feeling of academic failure was not a totally virgin experience for your boy. After graduating with honors from high school, he struggled with the demands of college during his freshman year. Hooray for inner-city high schools who pass kids along without properly preparing them for life. Can you say, "inflated academic self-worth?" Needless to say, the university experience jarred his familiar, but mistaken, notion of upward mobility.

So, what is the answer readers might ask? The solution is legendary: In order for Black students like Church Mouse to succeed and reach the same destination in life as their White counterparts, they will have to ingest overcompensation as if it were a pot of gourmet coffee. They will have to learn to make work their drug of choice. They will have to burn a candle all night over a term paper that better-prepared students easily waltz through. They will struggle over the simplest of grammar rules that should have been learned in grade school. Fight the power and shake the cobwebs out of your system, ghetto and barrio children. But do not forget your roots. Act cool and floss a little, but also stand up straight and talk White. Make sure your homework and term papers don't utilize the verb "be" in sentence structure. Become one of those "good minorities" who prove themselves worthy in the eyes of the keepers of the academic gates.

And, if by some chance you buckle under the pressure—if you decide to become part of the rising cadre of young people we so easily label as an angry minority citizen—don't fumble the ball. If you are going to be half-assed, go all the way with it. If a Black Man is on his way to hell, he might as well go there wearing gasoline underwear and smoking a fat cigar! Fire up the chronic, C-Money. They say weed is the perfect cure for college jitters, but it is also rumored that it makes you hungry and sleepy. Feel like skipping class today? Dig it! But before you doze off, grab a midday sandwich and a Twinkie, and watch a nostalgic video. A Blaxploitation flick will do just fine. Let's see, will it be *Trick Baby, Boss Nigger, Blackenstein, Blackula, Sweet Sweetback's Baadasssss Song,* or *The Legend of Nigger Charley*? Any one of these enigmatic, D-rated cinematic blasts from the past will do. Sip on Ripple,

Mad Dog 20/20, or Boone's Farm [17] wine, and then pour some on the ground for fallen homies. What kinds of choices did easily sidetracked Blacks make regarding the future of their race and their children? Were they aware that it was all part of the Ku Klux Klan's design for Black extinction? Yes, these words are explosive, but they are accurate. French-kiss the nuance.

A feeling of anomie overtook Church Mouse as he popped the car's gearshift into reverse and backed out of the school parking lot. On one hand, he was angry because he realized he had been cheated out of a proper education. Yet, he clearly understood that his life turned out to be noticeably better than the lives of his siblings and peers. One man's snare can become another person's springboard. Mixed blessings conjure bittersweet memories of the way we dreamt ourselves to be compared to the way we now see ourselves looking backward into a mirror.

Post-chapter mentoring tips for educators and policy makers. Achievement tests mostly measure exposure to the dominant group's literary canon. They are *not* accurate indicators of intelligence and ability. There are several types of intelligence—no one more important than others. Also, it is important to not force all learners through one educational funnel. Not all students belong in an academic college track. Stop closing vocational oriented schools and programs. They are still needed. It is also important that educators recognize differences in learning styles.

Post-chapter survival tips for children who are bullied and misunderstood. Be true to your own set of beliefs and don't worry about following and pleasing the crowd. Yes, this can lead to social isolation and loneliness, but you must first and foremost learn to love, respect, and believe in yourself. Very few people or groups of people possess all the truth. Blacks need to allow for more diversity of thought and individuality. Contrary to popular myth, *there is no one way to be Black*. True Black culture is rich, varied, and multifaceted. People who tell you differently are lying. Stay independent-minded and embrace an eclectic view of life and politics. More importantly, learn to become the ultimate Renaissance man and woman like our ancestors modeled. Do this even if your homies and relatives reject you for it.

CHAPTER 2:

GET ON THE GOOD FOOT

Besieged by a sense of failure following his collision with the graduate school entrance exam, Church Mouse did what many frustrated African American males tend to do: they get in a car and drive around in circles. Around and around the Black community, Church Mouse looped. Like a needle stuck in a flawed vinyl record, the beleaguered man relived his failure until he turned the ordeal into a blues song. Academic love on the rocks. Sir Church Mouse in search of a blues band. Has anybody seen his background singers, the Blue Notes? Play me one of those sad country songs, C-Money. My baby done left me, and now I no longer have someone to write my term papers. What did I ever do to be so black and blue? [18]

Deep inside Church Mouse churned an inexplicable feeling yearning to express itself, but he had no clue how to get it out. It was as if something else needed to take place before fate would allow him to move on with the rest of his day. A haunting voice inside his head began to whisper, "Surround yourself with more of yourself—surround yourself with you." The voice lingered like a sinister refrain from an "everything-goes-wrong-for-a-brother" movie. He tried blocking out the interference, but the voice just would not go away. What did the words mean, and where did they come from? Was it a word from heaven? Was it a message of narcissism?

Style and emotion can be the opiate of some (though not all) Black folk. The jazzier the sound, the sweeter the potion. The darker the berry, the thicker the notion. Invest your money in education, stocks, and savings bonds, not on spinning rims and jewelry, C-Money. To be fair, we must acknowledge that some of the appeal of emotional problem-solving might be connected to survival: you do what you must do just to make it to the next day. Picking one's poison is a skill not enough oppressed people have yet conquered. To "The Man" in charge, it translates "heads I win, tails you lose." The hallowed halls of academe don't give a rat's rear end about liberal interpretations of the root of social dysfunction. They believe in science and data collection.

Yes, it is true that in today's society much of the blatant forms of racism are starting to disappear, but it is trying to make a gallant comeback in recent years. "Stay in your place and don't compete with me," members of today's Proud Boys organization decry. "But if you insist on entering my sanctuary, always remember that '"I am the Lone Ranger, and you are Tonto. I am the head person in charge, and you are my lieutenant,'" they say. "Better yet just ignore pursuing leadership opportunities altogether. Instead, entertain my group with a coon routine and make us feel good. Do a tap dance or dunk a basketball. Stay in your lane. Tell us one of those funny Rudy Ray Moore [19] jokes," that voice demands. Unfortunately, too many citizens White and Black comply. While these words are caustic to some, they were the norm in the not-so-distant past. In some circles, they still describe a portion the world today.

Listen to the haunting specter of self-doubt surging through the streets of broken glass and boarded-up houses. Close your eyes and try to imagine the dissonance created when silence is shattered. What it be like, C? Contemplate the meaning of the bass guitar thumping on the one (i.e., the downbeat). Feel that wicked drum kick. Lock that nasty rhythm guitar in the pocket. Pay close attention to the hidden meaning of the lyrical groove. I've got new glasses. Pause for a moment and ponder what is really taking place. And if you listen close enough, you will discover that the music of today's inner-city world sounds like the stuff of warfare. Attention Jazz, Blues, and R&B: it is time to step aside and let a new kid take over. Trap music [20] will take you to a whole new level. Good or bad, it is here to stay. In America, knowledge is freedom. Freedom to empower others for positive change. It also means freedom to be wrong.

In addition to driving around town in circles, some frustrated minority males relieve their stress in one of three other ways: (a) drop out of any and everything, (b) get high, or (c) play sports. It is rumored that the talented few can successfully perform all three at the same time. To help ease the stress of what he had earlier endured, Church Mouse decided to go to the gym and play basketball. Drugs and quitting were a nonstarter for the human relations warrior. He had enough skill to hang with a recreational crowd, but he was far from being adept at excelling in basketball. But the game of football was a different story. While he was proficient with the pigskin, the finer points of the round ball easily escaped him. More importantly, he desired the physical workout most middle-aged men need to stay healthy. Besides, getting together with the fellas to blow off steam can be therapeutic for a frustrated civil rights warrior. Question: Are Black republicans allowed to call themselves freedom fighters? Do any of them make the grade?

Enter Pookie Johnson. Johnson was a friend and classmate with a checkered past. He was an indescribable soul. Many have tried to define the essence of Pookie only to find themselves raving and babbling at the same time. Despite his lack of formal education, he was highly intelligent and gifted. Pegged in his early years to have great leadership potential, Johnson seldom applied himself. He was a born politician and might have gone far in that arena had it not been for botched career moves and bad decisions. With wit and wisdom as sharp as a razor's edge, he possessed an uncanny ability to sway people to do things they normally would not do. He was North Omaha's finest. He possessed the kind of ability that could persuade conservative radio talk show hosts to support increasing welfare benefits to the poor. Now, that's real power!

Pookie Johnson was an immensely popular person. This was especially true with women, for he was beautiful to look at. His look was likened to a Greek sculpture carved out of broken glass, then smoothed over by the heat that emanated from the fires of inner-city unrest. He had both a rough and a soft side to his personality. Most notably, he carried a special place in his heart for the underdog. He was one of the few superstar types who respected and cared for the not-so-popular kid, a trait for which Church Mouse highly respected him.

Johnson was also a gifted athlete from a family of gifted athletes— urban icons that left a mark on the record books of local high schools. Pookie was a trophy that your sister might set on a mantle to admire. He was every- thing many of his admirers wanted to be. At the same time, Johnson repre- sented a few things many of his critics despised. Pookie was a pill—the large kind that is hard to swallow. Despite his charm and high intellect, at times he could also be a wise-cracking, no-homework-doing, fast-talking, jive-assed hustler. Pookie Johnson was Colin Powell, Marion Barry, and Goldie from *The Mack* [21] all rolled into one.

It is safe to say that Johnson was emotionally challenged. He har- bored a rage that almost reached supernatural proportions. Even Lucifoot himself had to occasionally step aside and let Pookie have his way. A mys- terious and complicated soul Johnson was, but don't be fooled; he was no anomaly. He was but one of many from his generation who suffered the symptoms of a spiritually lacerated soul brought on by racism, miseduca- tion, learned helplessness, and the culture of poverty. In many ghettos of America, Johnson's character was the norm, not the exception. At his core, Pookie was a good man. Whenever possible, he preferred resolving conflicts peacefully. Shedding blood without the use of a weapon was the ultimate test of manhood in most ghettos. Negotiating was the better tactic, but good ole fisticuffs often became the order of the day. Doing battle the old-school way was a rite of passage for most Black males. There was no need for weapons. It was the code of the ghetto—a '60s and '70s thing.

Engaging in physical battle with Johnson was risky business, and emerging victorious over him was even more dangerous. If you were lucky enough to actually win the fight—an occurrence that seldom happened—there was always a bevy of kinfolk and loyal followers willing to take out the most insignificant soul at the blink of a Johnson's eye. If Pookie did not pound you into the ground himself, a bevy of followers were all too eager to complete the task on his behalf. You might as well take your ass whipping the first time and move on with your life. Johnson was passion personified. Entourage identified. He was both hope and despair. Pookie was love, but he was also calamity. Above all, Pookie Johnson was a walking time bomb ready to go off without any prior warning.

That was then. Twenty years had passed, and Johnson was only a mere shadow of his former self. Oh, sure, he still possessed a Greek body, an athletic muscular tone, and that intense look of conquest about his demeanor. He still had a remnant of that searing look in his eyes—the kind that cuts through flesh—but Johnson was now a wandering soul. Sadness ruled his face—a look Church Mouse had never before seen. He peered inside his friend's soul and witnessed a void of terrifying depths. An abyss from which rebounded waves of social commentary. A paradise lost. A life unfulfilled. A past unreconciled. A childhood struggling to get out. A keg of dynamite aching to explode.

Enter a lighted match. Mr. Johnson had chosen Church Mouse to be on his basketball team. The two gentlemen were the elder statesmen holding court that day. Johnson also invited a few Chinese foreign exchange students to play. The opposition mostly consisted of younger African American males who wanted to showcase their talent. The expectations of each group were not the same, however. Unlike the elders and the exchange students, the young bucks did not come for cardiovascular exercise or conditioning. They came for one thing only: it was all about showtime! What started out as an innocent escape from the world of rules and regulations quickly turned into a live documentary detailing an inner-city ritual known as ghetto ball.

The rules of ghetto ball are similar to those of hockey. Elbows, toes, and inflated egos—anything goes. Think about the explosive ingredients in the mixture of a typical game of ghetto ball: frustrated, non-directed Black males descending on a basketball court, the reek of testosterone piercing the air, peacock feathers spinning like airplane propellers, foul language piercing the atmosphere, and a belief—real or imagined—that you have been socially wronged by a character known as "The Man." Somebody owes you something, and you plan on collecting your booty by any means necessary. Ghetto ball paired with a mindset for reparations is a volatile mix. Prepare to get your lip busted and your ego bruised.

Some Black males take on whole new personalities when they play the game of street basketball, ghetto style. They open their heads and empty decorum onto the ground. They speak in riddles and talk the language of fallen angels: "Boom, boom, boom, sucka—I just took yo ass to the hole, punk mutha fucka! Now what you gonna do about it, little bitch?" Church Mouse stood in awe each time the ritual unfolded itself as if he were witnessing it for the first time. The rancid words spewing from the mouths of the players sounded like . . . Well, to tell you the truth, they sounded like today's Trap music! Friends wanted Church Mouse to adopt the language as a means to validate his "Black card," but he could never bring himself around to that mindset. The language of the streets made him cringe each time he heard it. The words seemed so harsh and so devoid of life. So poverty-stricken. And yet, they sounded familiar. Familial.

Buffalo chips. Minority males ought to be able to play a friendly game of basketball without the pointless posturing and fighting that often accompany the game. Machismo turns sour when it's taken too far. G-ballers should not treat athletic competition as if it were a battleground. Here's a word to the wise: If women can learn to communicate beyond grunts and exotic handshakes, so can males. Try it sometime, guys. You might be surprised at the results.

On this day, the wannabe superstars took turns trading incompetence and insults. Each player threw up a bevy of shots, but very few of them went in. Squabble after squabble ensued. The lack of fine-tuned basketball skills served only to heighten the general frustrations each player carried around on his shoulder. Two of the Black players took it beyond acceptable limits and began arguing over every minor point of contention. And if you don't know what that conversation sounds like, "it goes a li'l bit sumthin' like dis:"

Player 1: Foul!

Player 2: Dude, ain't nobody even touched you.

Player 1: Man, you been killing me all day long wit dem long-ass fingernails you got. Where you from, Hackin-Sack, New Jersey, or suh-in?

Player 2: Nah man, I'm from Show-up-a-Sad-Ass-Nigga, New York.

Player 1: Oh, so you got jokes, now? Well, bring yo big bumpy-ass nose over here so you can get faced-up. I am the Hoops Master from the Midwest, and I'm about to take yo ass to school, chump.

Player 2: Say what? You gonna school who? Nigga, please! [22] Yo jump shot is so weak, I'll throw yo shit all the way back to dat raggedy-ass house yo mamma live in.

Player 1: Keep on talkin' against my mamma 'cause you 'bout to get yo feelings hurt when I bust this pill [23] off in yo cry-baby ass.

Player 2: You ain't gonna bust nothing but some bubble gum, little sissy. Comin' up in here handing out weak insults.

Player 1: Pass me the pill, y'all. Let me take this East Coast chump to the hole.

Player 2: Will somebody please give dis bitch da pill. He likes to talk shit—let's see what he can do wit it. Show me what you got, sissy. (Player 1 then dribbles left, crosses over behind his back, drives right toward the basket, and puts up yet another missed shot.)

Player 1: Foul again, nigga!

Player 2: Mutha fucka, that's bullshit!

Player 1: Fuck you.

Player 2: No man, fuck you. If you gonna call small-time fouls, you need to go over to that other court and play wit dem girls. You ain't nothing but a pussy anyway.

Player 1: Say what? Pussy? The only pussy I seent was last night when I crashed your ole lady's crib . . .

From here the reader can easily imagine how the rest of the conversation quickly digressed toward the abysmal.

At first, the ritual followed its usual, predictable path. There was nothing unusual about this particular game of ghetto ball. As long as no one stepped over the line of no return, the game flowed like milk and honey. Testosterone levels were high. All the predictable "mutha-fuck," "bitch," and "punk-ass" word combinations were securely in place. Male peacock feathers were in fast propeller rotation mode. Yes, there were a few stare-down moments thrown in for added flavor, but there were no serious breaches of normal ghetto etiquette. Quite frankly, the average inner-city spectator would have been bored and dozed off, unless, of course, you were someone like Bishop T. D. Jakes or Evangelist Junita Bynum watching the spectacle. Ministers like that would have taken a switch to those boys. Yes, indeed they would have.

Suddenly, a small detail went awry and one of the players stepped over the acceptable line. He committed a hard foul against Pookie that was intentional. "So what you gonna do about it, old man?" the offending player snarled. Johnson bristled. *Oh, no*, thought Church Mouse to himself. *Why did he have to go and say a dumb thing like that?* The kid did not understand.

He did not really realize what he was up against. He had no clue that the simple game of ghetto ball was about to evolve into a nuclear explosion. The kid circled his prey and continued to trash-talk. Pookie Johnson looked at him and sneered. "You better check yourself before you wreck yourself, fool. You need to do like James Brown and get on the good foot," Johnson warned. "Still quoting old-school lyrical lines, I see," the young kid responded. Shut your pie hole, dude.

Well aware of Pookie's past, Church Mouse knew his classmate was not wrapped too tight. Earlier, Church Mouse had peered into his friend's eyes and clearly understood that he had evolved beyond flesh and blood. He was now a spirit—a lost soul of wandering allegiances. Johnson was not one for turning the other cheek. He had revolutionary blood in his veins. If pushed too far, Johnson could give Islamic terrorists a run for their money.

The tide quickly changed when the young man started chest-bumping Johnson. Pookie's eyes turned hot-iron red like that of a utensil freshly drawn from a blacksmith's kiln. His voice took on an added eeriness as if being filtered through an audio effects processor. With fist tightly balled, Johnson let out a wild, animal-like roar and kicked the ball with such force that it ricocheted off the wall and the ceiling. The young man jumped back and looked at Church Mouse in bewilderment. "Wuz up wit your boy?" he asked the semi-sanctified one. "He be on drugs or suh-in?" Silly little Ebonics boy.

By then, the activity in other parts of the gym had come to a halt, and every eye was focused on the action at the far northeast corner of the facility. Although Church Mouse knew very well what was about to transpire, he conned himself into remaining hopeful. Surely, angry revolutionaries go through a mellowing process after years of maturing, right? The current ruckus was only part of the usual game of ghetto ball—just another facet of the ritual—Church Mouse told himself. It was all wishful thinking, my dear suburban assimilator.

Not wanting to be shown up in front of his friends, the young challenger stepped up his verbal assault. Pookie obliged and entered into a verbal exchange known by most inner-city residents as the art of handing out snaps, selling wolf tickets, or playing the dozens. [24] Gettin' jiggy wit it, y'all. Back and forth the insults flew. They swirled about Church Mouse's head like paper dolls bristling in a wind preceding a fierce storm. From the combatants' mouths tumbled a series of sordid phrases such as shit face, mutha fuck, bitch-breath, punk-ass, and other made-up street concoctions. Much of it carried little meaning. Each man spoke the words as if they were standard entries in Webster's Dictionary, and no one thought the phrases were wrong. When the culture of poverty invades the marrow of a person's bone structure, it alters their vision. It makes thugs look like role models. Porcupines like furry bunny rabbits. The Grinch like Santa Claus.

Charges and countercharges flew back and forth like NBA players running up and down the basketball court. It was verbal warfare at its finest, ladies and gentlemen. The signifying monkey has left the building. And if you were wondering, yes, there were a couple of jokes aimed at mothers and other relatives sprinkled into the mix. If you can't take a "yo mamma" joke, then get out the kitchen. Trying to remain legitimate, Johnson made mention of things such as, "Young dudes of today need to do a better job of understanding the Black struggle," and "At least I know how to keep a job." Those comments brought a smile to Church Mouse's face. They added a measure of legitimacy to the otherwise contorted game.

But suddenly, the conversation turned ugly with the introduction of the following statement made by the kid: "Can't you afford some Clearasil (i.e., a brand of acne medicine) for dem nasty-ass bumps on your face?" That insult was followed up with "You need to buy suh-in for dat dragon in yo mouf!" Suddenly, the ante had just been upped. Pookie met the challenge with a retort about the player's crooked teeth. The coup de grace of all African American insults, however, was launched in desperation by the young buck once he realized he was losing the verbal wrestling match. He hesitated, then unleashed the lethal "Why don't you put a comb to dat nappy-ass shit on the top of yo head?" Katie, bar the door—dem is fightin' words, folks. Commenting on a Black person's breath was one thing, but when you introduce hair insults into the mix during the early 1990s, that meant you were taking the fight to a new level. If and when you open that door, retaliation takes on a whole new look. This was before the legislative efforts of the early 2020s, when Blacks reclaimed the right to wear their hair in nontraditional styles.

Afros, konkalines, processes, perms, jerry curls, wave nouveaus, Mohawks, and bald hairstyles. For ungrounded Blacks, identity was closely tied to the style and texture of their hair. Too many folks linked their self-worth to the chemical ingredients in a bottle, a can, or a plastic tube that was obtained at a drug store. Symbols of self-esteem purchased with the almighty dollar. In God, we pontificate. Unfortunately, a portion of that sentiment still remains within various elements in the Black community today. Hair texture, skin color, and the language of African Americans—these were the last three vestiges of so-called historic Black shame. Limited space and time do not allow for a deeper analysis of this explosive topic but trust the warning—you don't want to touch on any one of these topics during an argument.

"Are you sure you want-summa-dis?" Pookie Johnson asked his assailant. "Are you prepared to meet your maker?" The second statement was not what Church Mouse wanted to hear. It reminded him too much of Johnson's volatile past. For example, there was one time back in high school when a certain female classmate pushed Pookie too far, and he retaliated by picking up a school desk and hitting her with it. The damage was serious enough that her mother came up to the school looking for him carrying a loaded pistol. Luckily, the school principal successfully intervened and made her put her pistol away.

The young G-baller did not understand this part of Johnson's past. He did not understand that Pookie was wrapped very loosely. The kid kept ignoring important cues until Johnson got fed up and yelled, "I've been waiting for this moment all my life. Are you prepared to die? I am. Come on, li'l punk-ass nigga. Me and you, let's do this thing right now." "This is definitely going in the wrong direction," Church Mouse muttered.

When Johnson went inside himself, it was as if his physical strength quadrupled in power. But he was not the only Tech High School graduate who possessed this unusual trait. It was a trait that permeated the hallways of Nebraska's most celebrated and feared high school. Even the girls were super strong, and many of them could beat up a boy. Several people in succession tried to stop Pookie as he rushed toward the young combatant, but it was all for naught. He tossed each person aside as if they were nothing more than papier-mâché dolls. Church Mouse, too, was one of the disposables that got tossed aside. Afraid of what might happen, Church Mouse convinced a bystander to slip out of the gym and alert campus security.

The young buck and his friends had never witnessed anything like this. They came from a younger generation where boys fight cowardly with weapons, instead of with bare fists like the warriors of old. Although this generation watches TV reruns of the famous prizefighters the likes of George Foreman, Joe Frazier, Ron Lyle, and Earnie Shavers, they truly don't understand the devastation one left hook to the body can do to the average twenty-first-century kid. Even the source of strength for the combatant's hero, Mike Tyson, was not fully understood by his generation. They don't understand how poverty and abandonment turn regular everyday guys into the Hulk. Young people of that decade did not know much about crusades against social injustices. Thirty years later they embraced a radical form of protest, but 1990s kids were mostly a materialistic bunch. They were more familiar with the battle of a different kind: the imaginary battle of video games.

Young people of the twentieth century did not comprehend the historic emotion behind a Chocolate Thunder (i.e., Darryl Dawkins) basketball dunk, a Wilt Chamberlain 100-point game, a Jim Brown touchdown, or a Johnny Rodgers punt return. They conned themselves into believing these feats were done with smoke and mirrors. They made themselves believe that the athletic competition of the '60s and '70s was subpar, thereby making the accomplishments of former sporting greats appear larger than real. "How can a small 180-pound athlete like Oklahoma Sooners running back Joe Washington literally fly through the air a full seven yards without his feet touching the ground?" they asked. "All that nostalgia shit is nothing more than old-school hype," the younger generation convinced itself. "TV producers must be doctoring older films to make athletes appear to be more spectacular than what they really were," the youthful excuse reasoned. Father, forgive them, for they know not what they say.

Suddenly, the young man began to acquiesce in a manner he thought would best resolve his impending doom. "Hold on. Let's make peace. Let's talk this thing out," the young man suggested. Johnson smelled death, and the moment afforded a glorious opportunity for the completion of his morbid quest. "It's too late for talk," Pookie snarled. Church Mouse noticed Pookie eyeballing a volleyball pole, the kind with the heavy metal base at the bottom. "You wanna dance with the devil," Pookie asked. "Come on. It's time for one or both of us to meet that mutha fucka!"

"This is not good," Church Mouse muttered. He knew that this situation was headed in the wrong direction, the same as the desk incident with the female classmate back in high school. Needing to intervene quickly, Church Mouse picked himself off the floor and rushed over a second time to block Johnson's advance. Again, ping-pong, ricochet-rabbit went the lightweight contender to the floor. "Enough of this mess. I know what I've got to do," the semi-sanctified one snarled. Church Mouse knew what time it was, and he knew what needed to transpire. There was no time for polite speeches about bootstraps or "a thousand points of light." All the fancy things the academy and conservatives taught him suddenly were nothing more than dust in the wind. A close friend was hell-bent on self-destruction, and it was time for love to show up. It was time for Church Mouse to lay down his college degrees and all the suburban sophistication he acquired during his post-college years. It was time once again to be ghetto fabulous.

More importantly, it was caring time, and that meant reconnecting with his turbulent past. It meant that Church would have to revisit a lifestyle he had long ago buried—one that he had almost forgotten about. Like an enmeshed family, 1972 Omaha Tech High School classmates have a storied reputation for banding together when one of their own needed help. With most Trojans, there was no middle ground. You either fight, or you make love. Build or destroy. Embrace or burn down. Eat Mama Jo chitterlings or expensive caviar. Tech High students made those kinds of decisions with ease on a daily basis and were masters at justifying either choice.

For years, Church Mouse desperately tried to forget the details of his hard-squabble past. He had grown ashamed of his poverty roots. He made himself believe he could hide behind his new-found suburban conservatism. In addition, he was a Jesus Movement–styled, born-again Christian who didn't believe in violence and the ways of the world. But like Siamese twins, the ghetto and he were joined at the hip. God's surgical knife separated them at conversion, but there was still an umbilical cord attached. No longer able to resist the lure of his past, Church Mouse opened the flood gates to an array of hidden memories and emotions. Growing stronger by each second, they made him hungry again. Old instincts never die, even for a sanctified rodent.

Bent down on one knee, Church Mouse began calling on the spirits buried deep within. These were the same demons Pookie Johnson and other Tech High graduates wrestled with. They had names such as "Emmett Till," "Middle passageway," "Take your ass to the back of the bus," and "You can be a respected sidekick, but a White man must always be the one out front and in charge." The proverbial "single-parent family" ghost was the angriest of those spirits. It is especially lethal when that dude convinces fathers of Black homes to drop out. Yes, these are strange names for spirits, but they were as real as American dirt. Over the years, Church Mouse had done a decent job of keeping his demons sedated, but now he found himself pouring coffee down their throats in hopes they would quickly sober up. He needed their supernatural strength if he were to have any chance at saving his friend from self-destruction.

With the same searing look Johnson earlier displayed, Church let out a sinister roar that shook the gymnasium. Hello, darkness, my old friend. Nice to make your acquaintance again. "What is going on here?" whispered a bystander who watched the bizarre behavioral display. "Who the hell are these guys?" one of the opposing players asked.

These guys were members of the most notorious high school graduating classes in all of Nebraska's education history. These guys are Omaha Tech High Trojans, class of 1972. Along with the classes of 1971 and 1973, they formed the backbone of the Black Power Movement in Omaha, NE. While it is true that North Omaha parents and politicians led the overall movement, it was the young people from Tech High School who ignited the fire of protest. They were the foot soldiers that brought about much needed changes in North Omaha. Most of these kids never experienced a true childhood. Students like Pookie Johnson and Church Mouse were too busy changing the Omaha social and political landscape to have had time for something so normal. They were part of an inner-city brigade that helped Nebraska come to grips with its hypocritical stance on racism, poverty, and White privilege during the late 1960s and early 1970s. A similar group of young revolutionaries would not grace the American scene again until fifty years later, when Minneapolis police murdered George Floyd.

Early 1970s Tech High School students were part of a larger national movement that instructed young Black children not to hate the color of their skin, the shape of their nose, or the size of their lips. They emulated African American heroes like Muhammad Ali and Malcolm X—warriors who became living water to scores of dehydrated souls. Sacrificial lambs for the sake of Black pride and cultural sanity. Johnson and Church were prodigies of sorts—part of a remaining few who understood the true meaning of the phrase "I am my brother's keeper." Today, many refer to them as bleeding-heart liberals. Some claim they are old Marcus Garvey radicals—a dying breed. A few might even say they are fossilized relics of a bygone past.

Feeling his own power rapidly increasing and seeing that Johnson had picked up a heavy volleyball pole as if it were a mere paperweight, Church Mouse knew it was now or never. Either he was going to deter his friend from his morbid quest, or the six o'clock evening news would be reporting another Black-on-Black homicide. Johnson began to tilt the volleyball pole in a fashion that made it clear he was planning on ramming its point into the young man's body—an outcome that would produce a bloody mess. As Pookie picked up steam, the Church Mouse of yesteryear suddenly appeared. Welcome home, Mighty Mouse.

Unlike previous intervention attempts, Church did not allow himself to get thrown to the floor. Instead, Pookie Johnson ran into a brick wall—an old friend who had much love and respect for him had finally showed up. At first, it took Johnson by surprise. Where did Church Mouse suddenly acquire all this superhuman strength from? Was it a mirage? Was it Caribbean voodoo? Was it a gift of the Holy Ghost? Earlier, Johnson had gotten his way with every person who tried to intervene. Now he was being thwarted by a dude he considered a mere choir boy. "What's going on here?" Pookie asked himself. "Yes, it is true that this is a fellow Trojan blocking my path but isn't he just a third-string warrior?" wondered the puzzled titan.

Again, Pookie struggled to break free from Church Mouse's grasp, but no dice. Like an immovable object, his friend stood firm blocking Johnson's advance. "I can't let you do this," Church Mouse sternly replied. "You and I come from the same hellhole. We have wrestled the same demons, and we've fought many battles together. I don't mean to disrespect you, but all of this is leading you nowhere. Put the pole down. Let's gather up our shit and get the hell out of this bitch. It is time to go home," Church Mouse said with a fractured voice. Startled, Johnson glared at his classmate for a brief moment and then attempted yet another countermove to overpower his friend. Again, he encountered a brick wall. Zilch. Nada. Air ball. Then Church Mouse calmly bent over and whispered in Pookie Johnson's ear, "I need you to be around so you can help me organize our first class reunion. You won't be able to do that if you're sitting up somewhere in jail."

Almost immediately, the red glare in Mr. Johnson's eyes subsided. The genuine concern of an old friend must have finally struck a chord in Johnson's raging soul. Apparently, brotherly love was something that Pookie lacked in his life and receiving a good dose of it from a caring friend may have provided an important piece to his sudden awakening. Or perhaps the reminder of his failure to organize a class reunion was a factor in explaining Johnson's sudden change of heart. Although Pookie was voted class president, he had let many years go by without fulfilling his post-graduate leadership obligation. The twenty-year milestone was approaching, and Johnson's graduating class had the dubious distinction of being Tech High's only modern-era group never to have organized a formal affair. It was a perplexing thing to explain. Graduating classes from eras before and after Johnson's group were spirited and well organized. It was as if a ghost of despair descended upon the building during the 1971–72 school year and settled not only into the brick and mortar of the building but also into the bone marrow of the student body.

An earlier ten-year reunion effort offered an opportunity to remediate the problem, but disagreement sprung up among committee members over whether to invite the few White students who made up only 6% of the graduating class. Apparently, not enough time had passed for old wounds and student divisions to heal. Church Mouse voiced his objection fervently and pleaded that the group's mindset must evolve, but the committee simply ignored him. Who takes advice from a conservative Uncle Tom who lives in the suburbs anyway?

A group of dissenters outside of the planning committee sprang up when it was discovered that the noncommissioned officers (NCO) club at the local air force base was suggested as the site for the official dance. Unfortunately, there were a few classmates who complained about "not being able to smoke marijuana because the event would be held at a venue located on federal property." Say what? These are thunderous confessions, ladies and gentlemen. The inclusion of this information is not intended to put Tech High graduates on blast. It is, however, symptomatic of how the culture of poverty erodes normalcy. You can sometimes hide stinking thinking by way of social engineering aerosol sprays. For true healing to occur, the smaller details of the culture of poverty story must be revealed even when it is embarrassing.

Yes, folks; it is true. Despite the many heroics and accomplishments of the Omaha Tech High School classes of 1971, 1972, and 1973 there were some graduates who never moved beyond their prison walls of reacting to the daily racism they faced. While this was not the case for all Tech graduates, it was true for far too many of them. The curious combination of legitimate social change students mixed in with thug types who could care less about the Black Revolution was one of the signature hallmarks of the three Tech High graduating classes. The class of '72 in particular was a textbook example of that odd mixture. It was as if daylight and darkness simultaneously existed throughout the building. Singer Sly Stone wrote a song in 1971 about mothers who had to love both the child who went to school to learn and the one who went to burn. It's a family affair, and Tech High was a close-knit family of revolutionaries, geniuses, nerds, athletes, thugs, wannabe pimps, musicians, beauty queens, and everyone else in between.

As the years went by and people grew older and wiser, much of the trifling mindset among Tech graduates dissolved. In addition, once they got started, the class of 1972 went on to sponsor the most successful and popular of the various inner-city reunions. The events became so popular that students from other schools eagerly attended. Class of '72 dances were the bomb. At the ten-year mark, however, ghetto-fabulous thinking was in full effect and students struggled with creating the unity they needed for success. The fact that some Trojans wore their at-risk persona like a badge of honor provides a chilling commentary on inner-city life in urban areas during the civil rights era. It is a predictable consequence of poverty, racism, and being ignored.

Johnson never attended those failed reunion meetings, neither did he organize any alternate efforts of his own. Still, the task of bringing his peers together to heal wounds from the past was important to him at least on an intellectual level. Earlier in the week, Pookie had informed Church Mouse that he was beginning to feel that he had let his fellow classmates down. He suddenly realized that not attending to his responsibility due to landing himself in jail over a silly little thing like a basketball game was juvenile, to say the least.

Suddenly, the tide quickly turned. Johnson looked at Church Mouse, then smiled and said, "I'm not going anywhere, Mr. Preacher Man. I'm gonna stay right here and shoot free throws with my friends from China." *Shoot free throws?* Church Mouse thought to himself. *How boring! Why not shake hands with the opposition and finish the game we started? Or better yet, why don't you sit out a game and let the rest of the players continue? Even a game of h-o-r-s-e would be better than a bunch of stiffs spinning around in a circle shooting free throws.* Just then, Johnson conjured up his powerful hypnotic abilities and aimed his telepathy straight at Church Mouse: "You really want to shoot free throws with us, don't you?" Pookie suggested to the spellbound classmate. "Yes, I do." Church Mouse nodded mechanically.

Church Mouse was now putty in the hands of the demigod. The stunned crowd gazed on with amazement at the bizarre turn of events. "Boff you mutha fuckas is mental," cracked the young punk. "I'm taking my crew over to this other court, and we're gonna play real basketball like normal folk do." "Leave us!" Church Mouse snapped. "I guarantee you don't want to be around if both me and my friend go off at the same time," he warned.

Pookie Johnson puffed up like a blowfish with pride. He was happy to see a third-string Tech High soldier step up and take charge of the situation. "My nigga—now that's the warrior that I know! I knew you had it in you, Choir Boy. I guess even Jesus knows how to thump every once in a while," Johnson snickered. Church Mouse rolled his eyes and played off the wise-crack. But yes, come to think of it, the Lord does possess the wherewithal to clear out the gym with one snap of His finger. He can throw down with the best of them. If ever in doubt, call Jesus up on His cell phone and diss [25] His mother. Blacks aren't the only ones who despise yo mama jokes.

By this time, the demons had subsided in both warriors. Johnson was back to his enigmatic self, and Mighty Mouse was eager to distance himself from his alter ego and get back under the safety arch of his suburban canopy.

And yes, he hung around and shot free throws with Pookie and his foreign exchange friends, who were too frightened to go against Johnson's wishes. For about ten minutes, the beleaguered men shot free throws and not a word was uttered among them. Front rim, back rim, side rim, no rim. Some serious bricks [26] were thrown up on that day. There stood Johnson's brick-heaving brigade taking turns drawing air and iron. And the reasons for such poor display of athletic ability, you ask? Was it a lack of talent, or was it a case of emotions getting in the way? Six-to-one, half-dozen-the-other, it was a mixture of both.

Because they did not want to upstage Johnson, his Chinese friends were probably missing shots on purpose. Perhaps it was part of the cultural exchange orientation they received before departure from their motherland: never outshine your American hosts. Most of all, stay low and keep cool when encountering wild-eyed urban homies. Even if you possess a black belt in karate, there is no kung fu on earth that can disrupt the path of a bullet launched from John Shaft's big-ass gun. [27] And contrary to early 1980s Hollywood myth, neither Asian nor Black people possessed the ability to catch bullets with their teeth. [28]

Church Mouse was the worst of the offenders. He never caught the rhythm of the stroke. Having to deal with his earlier academic failure, and now having to babysit Pookie Johnson, took him way out of any effective mindset for athletic competition. By then, too many emotions were welling up inside his soul. Hiding behind a conservative middle-class facade was the way Church Mouse hid from the pain and sorrow of his past. On this day, however, the tactic backfired. No amount of cosmetic cover-up could mask the gaping wounds of his past. Church Mouse knew the calm exterior he allowed others to see was a front that masked underlying turmoil that constantly churned within. Face up to it, C-Money. Don't run from it. And, what about Pookie's lack of performance? Well, let's just say Johnson was a burned-out soul who struggled to find his niche. In 1981 he unsuccessfully ran for Omaha City Council. In 1998 he sponsored a successful camp for underprivileged kids. In 2005, he walked the streets of Omaha with ragged clothing and a wooden staff as if he were Black Moses. Plethora was his alias.

The exploits of Pookie and Church Mouse soon faded, but the sound of hard shots coming flat off the rim of life is a story that continues to replicate itself over and over in America's Black community. We live in a politically correct world where this kind of storyline is no longer in vogue. Times have changed, and we have twice elected a Black president. There is no longer a need to have separate Black and White beauty pageants, many folks say. The world has now acknowledged Black beauty. Men of all colors want to French-kiss it now. Yes, phase one of the civil rights era is gone, but please answer one simple question: What happened to the magician's rabbit that was made to disappear? Did it transform itself into a white elephant? Did it end up on someone's dinner table? Was it all just a dream that blew away once Bill Clinton and the liberal countercultural movement burst onto the scene to cancel out Reaganomics?

What is it about the land we live in that makes it so easy to crank out the Pookie Johnsons of the world? Surely kids like him do not just drop out of their mother's womb with a mindset to hurt others. Yet, somewhere along the way, many of our children become seriously derailed. At-risk kids of all colors are coming out of the woodwork these days. Poor Black, Brown, and Red males were always susceptible, but now middle-class White males have forged to the front of the high-concern line for domestic terrorism and blowing buildings up. Some of these children grow up to be dysfunctional parents, who raise yet another generation of even higher-risk offspring. Has anyone noticed that the bar continues to be lowered per each decade? And the pattern takes place while the rich get richer, and the poor get poorer.

———————————————

With the help of a caring friend, Pookie Johnson successfully weathered the storm without serious incident. The young buck and his partners were once again having fun playing regular ghetto ball on the other side of the gym.

The exploits of a couple of civil rights warriors from yesteryear slowly began to fade, giving Church Mouse an excuse to return to his polished, suburban self. But could he really go back? Could Church Mouse ever be the same after encountering two major episodes in one day? Was he really a member of the suburban elite he pretended to be? Could he simply "shake off that inner-city funk" and return to his world of warm cappuccino and Maranatha Christian music?

Get on the good foot, Boy Wonder! Your stank is in serious need of justification. It is time to expose your fake and trade it in for what's behind door number three. Face up to your destiny, C. Pain and happiness exist in a circular round. Sorrow and ecstasy together abound. Your past is your present. You and the ghetto are one: inseparable and joined in suck-face position. You can run all you want to, but you cannot hide from "da hood and what it represents in your life." No amount of higher learning, assimilation, conservative politics, or religion will be able to mask the emptiness that lies within you.

To be void of contour is your defining character, Church Mouse. To toil and spin is your destiny. Or at least some people have led you to believe so.

Post-chapter mentoring tips for educators, counselors, and members of the judicial system: *Don't be so quick to throw away so-called troubled children.* This includes both the vulnerable ones and the ones that raise hell. Some of the latter are only following the bad examples set for them by the system and/or wayward adults. Some of our world's greatest leaders took a while before they blossomed. Even when certain early behaviors are not ideal, persons who are lost still have a chance to rebound and make something of themselves. Like St. Paul of the Bible, these individuals can be reclaimed and polished up for effective service to their community.

Post-chapter survival tips for children who hurt: Attention minority students who suffer from racism, poverty, bullying, and child abuse: You must learn to master two worlds – your own ethnic culture and that of the dominant group. If you do not, you will lose. Learn to securely plant a foot in both worlds and become adept at the art of code-switching. Don't be surprised that most White students will not have to perform this additional task. Don't be angry that you will have to give twice as much effort to arrive at the same place in life as your White counterparts. In America and Europe it is called White privilege, but in other parts of the world it is called majority group privilege. Embrace the inherit unfairness and learn to manage it. No, it is not fair, but it is a global reality. God will keep score on your behalf, and things will ultimately be reconciled in the end. You will be rewarded for your diligence. I believe you can do this. I have faith in you and your ability to be fabulously patient, steadfast, and resilient.

CHAPTER 3:

DIRTY LITTLE SECRET

SENSING THAT CHURCH MOUSE WAS DISTRAUGHT, HIS WIFE, BANANA BABE, searched for something clever to say that would cheer him up. "Boy, you look tore up from the floor up," she teased. "It's been quite the day," responded her weary husband. "In more ways than one, I threw up some serious bricks today. Not only did I bomb the graduate achievement test that I took this morning, on top of that I also ran into some homie problems. Did the counselors at Central High School push you guys to take upper-level courses?" Church Mouse asked his wife. Banana Babe nodded yes. "I thought I could get by on natural ability today, but I guess that plate of fatback and grits you cooked for me this morning wasn't potent enough to energize my academic muscles. Maybe I should have 'axed' yo uncle to knock a hog in da head. [29] I could have used summa dat Louisiana funk dis morning," he joked. Banana Babe chuckled.

Church Mouse quickly turned the conversation to a more serious note. "I don't remember Tech High School teachers and counselors stressing the importance of taking higher math and science classes," he said. "They probably did, but I just can't remember them doing so. Today showed how deficient I was. It is as if I am not the honor student people have been telling me that I am. And to top it off, I had to keep Pookie Johnson from going crazy on this one kid we were playing basketball with. Had I not intervened, things would have gotten very ugly," Church Mouse informed his wife. Fully aware of Johnson's reputation, Banana Babe shook her head in agreement. "What is it about my graduating class that makes us so brilliant on one hand, and yet so volatile on the other hand?" Church Mouse asked. He pulled a chair up to the kitchen table and eagerly awaited his wife's response.

Seeing that Church Mouse was experiencing elevated levels of anxiety on multiple fronts, Banana Babe responded by playing the dozens—a tactic used by African Americans not only to assess an opponent's mettle but also to help ease the stress of living in the ghetto: "You know what they say about you Tech High thugs. Y'all were so busy fighting, getting high, and getting laid, y'all must not have taken the time to learn anything," she quipped. "After all, it was your graduating class that brought about the closing of the junior high portion of the school. All that fighting y'all did was the reason my parents transferred me out of Tech and sent me over to Central High," she scoffed. Banana Babe was not being disrespectful. Making wisecracks about cantankerous Tech High students was a fun way to throw friendly shade on peers that you, nonetheless, loved and respected.

Jackleg funkology. Reverse Black female psychology. Soul looks back and wonders how I got over. [30] Ah, yes. Omaha Technical High School during the late 1960s and early 1970s—Nebraska's best-kept human relations secret. Several stories can and should be written about Tech High's opening in 1923, the school's glory years (1930-60), the era of social and racial unrest (1968-74), and lastly the days when the school made a great rebound before it was finally closed in 1984. Church Mouse attended Tech during the days of the Omaha Black Revolution era. It was a time when the school made the local newspapers for all the wrong reasons. That period should not be the only one chronicled, but don't ignore it either. Many tales have been written about Tech High School, but it is mostly about the great athletes that graduated from there, such as Bob Gibson, Bob Boozer, Ron Boone, Fred Hare, Johnny

Rodgers, and several other greats. That needs to change. Both the glory days and the troubled years need to be told.

The Midwest: a place where cows roam, football players bench-press one another, and corn grows as tall as a scarecrow's eye. It is a place where coaches turn out athletes with no necks and muscles in their fingers. In Nebraska, babies are born with huge biceps and highly developed six-packs. Male toddlers have been known to set discus and shotput records. Even the women of Nebraska are special. If in doubt, check out their volleyball and softball players.

Some religious folk claim that the Midwest is also the home of America's moral compass, second only to the southern Bible belt. A few have made the claim that there is no racism in the Heartland. Surely the birthplace of kindness doesn't experience cultural and economic inequity. Nebraskans are too busy harvesting corn, herding cows, and scoring touchdowns to ever find time to indulge in the greatest of sins. Praise the Lord and pass the barbells! Nebraska is a place where the boys are the squarest and the girls are the fairest. Rumor has it that most Nebraskans, like coach Tom Osbourne, speak in a monotone voice. That voice has a pious quality to it. Even the curse words of the Midwest sound innocuous. Dadgummit.

We often hear about the Joe Clark stories detailing the problems of big-city urban schools on the east coast. [31] We are familiar with the Jaime Escalantes of the world who breathed life back into the empty souls of barrio kids in Southern California, but Omaha, Nebraska? [32] "Isn't that where the Bible was unearthed in a recent archeological dig? Isn't that where they filmed *Mutual of Omaha's Wild Kingdom* television series? Isn't that the flat state with rows and rows of cattle and corn? Aren't the only Black people in Nebraska the ones who are recruited from out of state to play on their football team?" [33] Omaha is a textbook city for studying the northern pattern of race relations, but that is a story for another time and place.

───────────────

Prescription drugs may not pose the same type of danger that illicit street drugs do, but they can be equally harmful if utilized improperly. This is especially true when the abuse is innocent. Just when you think yourself to be safe, chemical calamity can sneak up on you like a zombie in the night. Prescription painkillers can help you erase things you want to forget about. More importantly, your escape carries the approval of a physician's chicken-scratch signature. In your hand lies a license to cheat. You are now free to cast judgment on low-life junkies and drug pushers. Those people are the real problem. Prescription drug abusers just happen to be misguided choir kids who accidentally fall off a church pew, so says the myth.

Church Mouse was no criminal, and he certainly was not a drug dealer. He was not a manipulator of the truth nor a con artist. No. But he did fool himself into thinking he was safe. He was a quiet soul suffering under the weight of a confused society. Can you blame a soul brother for needing something extra to help him get over the hump? Church's reliance on prescription drugs was his way of hanging onto a sliver of hope that soon he would awaken from his nightmare—that someday someone would finally slip the boogeyman a mickey.

Several critics have argued that Church Mouse is his own worst enemy, that he was too conservative, too stubborn, and too serious and archaic for his own good. Others say he was born on the wrong planet, or at least during the wrong century. If Blacks were allowed, King Arthur's round table would have suited him well, but the urban ghettos of the twentieth century? Boy, please! According to street standards, his level of ghetto stank was not strong enough. True historic African Americans care about setting a high standard, but not your average hood homie. [34] "We don't want to hear your lectures about accountability, and we certainly don't care about your conservative politics," his critics bemoaned. According to popular sentiment, even if Black people forget to engage in the political process, as long as they join the Democratic Party, that should take care of their civic duty. Whether or not they actually vote is another story. "And we sure don't need all that talk about attending church. If we acknowledge 'The Man Upstairs' and embrace a Christmas, Mother's Day, and Easter (CME) religion, that should suffice," claims the misinformed. Controversial? Yes. Inaccurate? You decide.

Although Church Mouse was no liar, he did not always provide the full truth. Very few of us do, especially if detractors are constantly riding you like a fat Mama Jo tick. He was able to convince his wife that when he went into three-day hibernation periods, it was the result of physical and mental exhaustion—a simple case of working several jobs and needing serious downtime. Although the explanation was partially true, his ailment was also the result of a dirty little secret: Church Mouse was addicted to prescription painkillers and anxiety medication. At one point in his mid-twenties, he popped Valium like it were candy. He was not proud of that fact, but it helped him make it to the next day.

Over the years, Church Mouse learned to deal with the stresses of life by pleasing others and by overworking. He relied heavily on prescription pills to help him manage stress. As his body built up a tolerance to the medication, he found himself taking heavier doses to cope. That, in turn, made him moody and tired, which put him out of commission for extended periods of time. It was a cycle he desperately needed to break, but he could not do so until he learned more about the world and himself. Prescription drugs provided him with temporary respite so he could put up with the next round of buffalo chips society kept dishing out. An unintended consequence of the medication was that it made him irritable and manic depressive. Today, it is recommended that the usage of Valium not exceed two or three months, but for whatever reason, doctors back in the 1970s allowed patients to be on it for extended periods of time.

But make no mistake about it, Church Mouse did not need an artificial stimulant to throw him off his game. There was enough insanity going on in the 1960s and 1970s to convince even the wisest of saints to wander off the beaten path. Sadly, manic depression became his close confidant. Church Mouse hovered with ease along the borders that separated the will to live and a desire to throw in the towel. It is a struggle that many aspiring difference-makers face. It is a territory many change agents know all too well. This is a difficult and embarrassing fact for Church Mouse to admit, but to truly help children who hurt, the full truth must be shone.

Church Mouse was good at hiding his secrets from others—loved ones included. The fact that they, too, relied on heavy meds to combat monstrous health issues made it all that much easier for them to overlook Church Mouse's secret. It is hard to notice someone else hurting when you're caught in your own debilitating vice grip. The group that Church Mouse was able to fool the most was doctors. "I can manage it. I know how to regulate my intake," he convinced local physicians. And why wouldn't they believe him? Church Mouse was all that the ghetto was not—all that the White establishment held in high esteem. He was clean-shaven and conservative cut. The ultimate professional. A churchgoer. A role model devoid of liberal whining. America's poster child.

Here is an important question that must be answered: Do lies remain untainted if they stand behind the American flag? Are they unblemished if we say them in God's name? If you sin for the greater good of mankind, will your transgression only land you in Purgatory? Church Mouse was sanctified-slick. He knew how to walk the walk and talk the talk in such a way that suspicion was deflected away from him. On the outside, he resembled the Rock of Gibraltar. He had an image to uphold. And how does one accomplish this? By pounding on one's chest and staring the devil straight in the eye. By deflecting reality, and by dreaming.

Close your eyes, my semi-sanctified one. Dream about a past that you try to run from. Dream about a life that never was. Your real name is not Church Mouse. It is Black Opie, and you live in *Mayberry R.F.D.* [35] When you awaken, try to function as middle class as you can. Pretend that the world is sane. Act like the American dream is for everyone without encountering difficulties. Fake it by claiming the power structure genuinely cares about you. Pretend that every Black person who calls you "soul brother" genuinely has your back. Ignore attempts by clueless folk who make sport of trying to pigeonhole you into what a "real Black person" is supposed to act and look like. Heaven forbids that you should do homework and attend church. And do not react when they call you "White Boy" for taking school seriously. Never let them see you sweat. When the world throws hot butter on your grits, parlay that negative experience into a food festival. Surround yourself with more of yourself, and pretend you are an everlasting battery that goes on and on and on—a veritable supply of inner strength. Do not be surprised when people bring hoards of their problems to you to solve, while very few of them address your needs. They secretly think you are Batman, so you probably will not get the attention that you deserve. They mean no harm—they're just human. And don't be surprised when they make up stuff about you out of thin air! It is the way of the world. It sucks, but you will get used to it.

Party your pain away and smoke your sorrow into oblivion. Drown you demons in champaign and pop a pill to relax. Jump up on life's dance floor and drop it like it's hot! Pop that booty so that cool people will think you are popular and urbane. Bark like a fraternity Q-Dog. Americans feel more secure when men in charge act like an alpha male. Pimp a few hoes on the down low. Persevere even when your batteries run low. And when you begin to disintegrate right before the eyes of those who claim they love you, concoct a lie and spit in a tin cup like a tough guy chewing tobacco. This is the storyline of the accused—the anthem of the abused.

Cloud your needs with double talk, C-Money. Remember the rules of the inner city: You can never afford to appear vulnerable and wanting. Your role is not to be embraced but to serve and protect the weak. During times when you have a need, mutter something about bootstraps and a thousand points of light. Recite the line that says God helps those who help themselves. Click your heels three times and salute the flag when you say it. Somehow, someday the respite you need will magically produce itself. Above all, learn to be there for others even when your gas tank is low. If you don't, people will punish you for not caring. The words of guilt from a selfish generation will hook you, for it is in your nature to please them even when they don't deserve it. People will demand that you work yourself to the bone, for most of them only look out for number one. No, not everyone in your life is guilty of these infractions, but the number who are is alarming. There is a chance that they might not even be aware of it. There is a rumor going around that you possess superpowers. Straighten up and fly right, Clark Kent. Now, spin your illusion, Holy Ghost Junior, and let the miracle unfold.

Learn the art of taking Bible verses out of context and using them against others you are trying to co-opt. It is the American way. Throw in a couple of jerky body movements to make it seem spiritual and other-worldly. Talk like televangelists do. Pretend that God is the leading star of a reality television show. Give him spicey lines to read. Conduct your affairs like uncritical politicians conduct theirs—by making up reality as you go along. Manufacture imaginary clones that will meet the needs of significant others. Learn to be there even though you really are not. Presto! Swear that your kids will walk a different road than you did, even if it kills you.

"Will it be one or two pills this time?" Church Mouse asked himself. "Piss on it," he whispered. "That big bowl of hominy grits Banana Babe fed me today will dilute a triple dose of over-the-counter meds. Besides, I've got a cast-iron stomach and I can handle anything. I am the ultimate alpha male. I am the Mack—the BIG PILL!" Church Mouse boasted as he pounded his chest. Then he capitulated. With eyes wide shut, Church Mouse unwisely took a Valium pill, along with two over-the-counter sleeping pills. He convinced himself that grits and fatback would nullify the potency of the medication. Silly little Holy Ghost Boy. A simple lesson in Chemistry 101 would have straightened out that bit of misinformation.

But today was no ordinary day. It was a day of reckoning—a day of destiny. As sure as his once youthful head was now rapidly balding, Church Mouse was destined to revisit a time and a place that seemed far, far away. And yet, it was as close as the bird resting on the oak tree outside his bedroom window. Please don't beat Church Mouse up for being human. If you find that you must chastise your boy, at least peck him lightly like a woodpecker with a headache. [36]

Take a fantasy voyage down memory lane, Church Mouse. Revisit your past in cinematic imagery. Misery loves company. Success breeds contempt. Dream about the victories and the defeats. Nostalgia conjures bittersweet revelations of the way we were. Sleep, my son. God has ordained that you must face up to what you have been running from. It is time to revisit all the things—both good and bad—that have shaped and molded you. Close your eyes and concentrate on the task at hand. And if by chance you are fortunate enough to awaken from your medicated slumber, grab hold of your children and shield them from the incredible onslaught of Satan, that cold-blooded Sith who wants to have them erased from planet earth. He is cold-hearted and there is no mercy in him. If you are trapped in a burning building, he would walk the other way. He behaves this way because his heart is made of granite stone. Darkness is where he finds his delight. His allure is like Las Vegas strip lights, and too often we play the part of his fool.

Post-chapter mentoring tips for parents, educators, ministers, and help-professionals: We need to do less talking and a whole lot more listening to kids who are hurting. They reach out to us, but their cries often fall on our consumer-oriented deaf ears. They don't need lecturing; they don't need to hear your personal stories. They need love, laughter, and healthy alternatives to counterbalance the madness they face. And it is not just the traditional bullied kids who are vexed. Some kids have special sensitivities and personalities and don't easily fit into the world's classification of being normal. Think Elijah McClain, the Michael Jackson styled kid from Aurora, CO, who was killed by police in the spring of 2020 because he wore a germ mask and "looked suspicious." These kids need a kind ear, mental rest, and a sanctuary to escape to. They need quality downtime to decompress. Do not judge them as being strange or eccentric. Rather, give them enough space to be uniquely different from the so-called norm. It is especially important for the Black community to embrace an eclectic view. Our collective survival depends on it.

Post-chapter survival tips for children who do not fit the typical cultural norm: There will be times when you will be the only one who understands you. You must find the will and the courage to stay in the pool of life, even when others do not care if you drown. This is not the greatest news to hear, but it is real. Learn to trust your gut. It is important to find alternatives to a chemical solution to your heartache and pain. There are no shortcuts to healing. It will be nice if you have someone to go through it with you, but don't bet your lunch money on it. Most Murphy's Kids will have to face their demons alone. Unfortunately, there are very few short cuts in life and mulligans are rare. You must adopt a "refuse-to-lose" attitude. Be extra careful that you are not substituting one form of a crutch (i.e., drugs and alcohol) for a different type (i.e., bitterness or martyrdom) that can cause a whole new set of problems you don't need. Be independent-minded and remain strong! Yes, these directives are difficult to do, but I believe in you.

CHAPTER 4:

SPRINKLE A LITTLE STANK ON MY P-FUNK

THE DECISION WAS A TOUGH ONE FOR YOUNG CHURCH MOUSE TO MAKE. IF you are going to shoplift food items from the local convenience mart, you might as well take something of nutritional value. Sugar Babies, potato chips, and a can of pop will not cut it when your body craves vitamins and much-needed protein. The impecunious child longed for solid nutrition that would hold him over until wrestling practice let out. He needed something of substance to satisfy the hunger pangs until he received his nightly meal of beans and rice. It was 7:40 a.m., there was no breakfast that morning, the school's tardy bell was about to ring, and he desperately needed to scamper away with a stolen morsel or two.

It was in the early spring of 1971, and Church Mouse knew this crossroads all too well. Each time he approached it, he worked out what he thought was a defensible rationale. "God knows this isn't real stealing," he reasoned. "He knows I will pay back my debts," the semi-sanctified child convinced himself into believing. "I can't stand it when classmates tease me about receiving free lunch meals from the federal government. I just hope the word has not gotten back to the pretty girl I've got eyes for. Good thing we don't have the same lunch period," he whispered to himself. "If she finds out that my family are welfare and food stamp recipients, she'll drop me as if I were a bad habit," Church Mouse concluded.

Like most Black people in the 1970s, Church Mouse outwardly identified as a democrat. In his heart, however, he was conservative to the bone. He was a democrat in name and function, but he didn't always agree with every tenet and philosophy most liberals embraced. He preferred Malcolm X's emphasis on self-reliance and cultural dignity. Fiscal conservatism was also semi-attractive if it was done in a manner that did not ignore social justice issues. He knew that his stepmother pimped the system by "cooking the family books" to make it seem as if she and her husband were poorer than what they really were. Most Black families did not cheat the system, but Beulah was accomplished at it. Unfortunately, most White people zero in on the guilty few and assign blame to the entire group. An investigation of this phenomenon at a deeper level is worthy of an analysis, but that is a topic for a different day and time. At East High School, it was a social death sentence for a student to receive subsidized lunches. Church Mouse took verbal abuse from the school's middle-class Blacks who were mostly uppity in their mindset. Church Mouse was in their cultural crosshairs. Free and reduced lunch students were referred to as "welfare babies." It was hard on poor students who craved social acceptance from their peers.

During the early 1970s, Denver East High School students—both Black and White—had little, if any, tolerance for poor and disadvantaged students. The college prep school drew from affluent neighborhoods, while neighboring Manual High School catered to the Five Points and other poorer sections of town. Although East High (housed in a building older than dirt) was in the inner city, a suburban mentality, nonetheless, ruled its hallways. Unfortunately, its African American population acted more elitist than did the school's White students. It is amazing how bougee Blacks easily forget that they share similar cotton field origins. Church Mouse was young and had not yet learned the art of telling haters and perpetrators how and where to step off; thus, he cooked up an unrealistic way of handling elitist peer pressure.

Church Mouse meticulously kept track of his IOUs by writing them down on small pieces of paper and storing them in his wallet. To one establishment he owed fifty cents, to a second store it was a dollar, and to yet another seventy-five cents. Like clockwork, he took whatever babysitting or yardwork money he could garner and faithfully went to each establishment he owed money to and secretly paid them back. Quietly, he would place the money on the ledge of the customer service counter or on a cash register in an unopened aisle. Other times, he would insist that a teller gave him too much change, thus forcing them to take back a portion of it. As long as he was consistent about repaying his debts, Church Mouse felt that God understood his "shop borrowing." Often, he would paperclip a small note with the words "thank you" written on it to a dollar bill. He seldom accounted for the fact that most cashiers coming along to open a new aisle might not forward loose-lying monies to management. Once Church placed his reparations near an official receptacle, he conned himself into believing that he was free from obligation and guilt. Well, at least in the eyes of the Lord, he thought he was absolved. No, Church Mouse was not proud of his twisted ethics, but he felt Jesus would honor his intentions.

Church Mouse's ability to cover up his little game was slicker than hot snot on a frozen doorknob. One might even say it was dipped in American ingenuity. The plan was simple and effective: enter a store and legally purchase one bag of chips while sneaking a variety of other items into his coat pocket. When lunchtime rolled around, Church Mouse would hang around outside with the cool kids and show off his contraband to friends. Sometimes they would share in the spoils, which made him popular. He pretended to be a middle-class kid willingly choosing to spend his money on junk food because "school-prepared lunches were so horrible." The fib was readily accepted in those days because ragging on school lunches was the in thing to do.

The thin-as-a-rail child had an undernourished look about him. His friends often teased him about it. Genetics played a big part, but poverty and lack of a proper diet were also reasons for his thin physique. Church Mouse also possessed a high-strung digestive system that caused him to metabolize food at a mega rate. For whatever reason, Church Mouse was constantly hungry, and he often looked the part. But one thing was always clear: he never failed to turn over all monies for his redemption. On weekends, he worked extra hard to atone for his shop-borrowing. Mostly, the subsidized school lunch ticket stayed at home, tucked away under the mattress in his bedroom. The few times he did use it, he made sure that he jumped in a line that only had White students. He hated it when the cashier would take too long to punch his card. When you attend a prestigious college prep school, there is a certain reputation one must uphold. At Denver East High School, being a welfare student was not sexy or cool. Yes, the game was clever, but it was also unwise, especially on a day when the planets were not in alignment.

The Lord was always there at the right moment to cover for his protégé, but not on this particular morning. God's alarm clock must not have been working properly. That is what you get when you buy goods from a suspect angel standing on a corner selling wares from under a trench coat. Wuz up wit da janky hookup, G? You gonna leave a brother hanging like that? Surely, the Almighty must have understood that only reputable vendors can be trusted. Sears, Roebuck, and Co. easily come to mind. Wares produced by "Pookie Nem, Inc." usually don't come with a legitimate warranty. Or maybe the day went sour because the special arrangement Church Mouse thought that he had with the Lord never existed in the first place. Poverty has a way of distorting a person's thinking. It can sometimes act like a drug on the nervous system. Or, perhaps the child's imagination just got the best of him. I mean when you stop and think about this scenario, it is somewhat of a stretch to believe that God would set an alarm clock every morning to help a confused child steal junk food from local convenience stores. Next thing you know, Church might try to convince readers that God plays the lotto.

The Good Book says that God is omnipresent, but on this day, home-boy must have partied too long and hard the night before. Too bad He did not give his protégé the assist he needed. A large, burly policeman grabbed Church Mouse by the collar and slammed his face onto the checkout counter. His nose began bleeding profusely. Quickly, the officer led the frightened boy to a storage room at the back of the store. Church Mouse was so stunned by the swift turn of events that he momentarily lost his ability to speak. After the initial shock wore off, the beleaguered teen withdrew into himself, put his head down, and began to block out his surroundings. With each passing moment, Church Mouse grew increasingly light-headed as a trickle of blood traced his face. The store manager grudgingly offered him a wad of paper towels.

Images and sounds began to swirl about his head as if those yelling at him were paper dolls bristling in a wind that preceded a fierce storm. Growing more disoriented by the moment, the young lad found it difficult to decipher the questions being thrown at him. As the policeman led the hand-cuffed child out of the store, fellow classmates entered and began pointing and snickering. One of them was the girl he had been trying to impress. She rolled her eyes in disgust and pretended not to know him. When it rains, it pours. As the squad car pulled away, Church Mouse leaned against the window and gazed into the sun's glare bouncing off the concrete.

For the good times.

———————————————

Like an altar boy attending a convention for pimps, hookers, and whores, Church Mouse stuck out like a sore thumb when he entered the juvenile detention center. With lunchtime swiftly approaching, a few of the rougher kids in detention began whispering among themselves about the new geek who had just arrived that morning. The frightened child quickly concluded that in order to survive his unfamiliar environment, he would have to feign being badass. Church Mouse surmised that he needed to manufacture a dose of "ghetto stank" that he could call on to help ward off bullying that he was bound to encounter. If only he could tell some girly jokes or fabricate a few character traits that would make him appear more street worthy—something that might help him win favor with the alpha dog of the group.

Young Church Mouse spent the better part of the morning rehearsing over and over in his head how to act more street worthy. He imagined himself contorting his fingers and walking with a ghetto limp. To increase his believability, he whisper-practiced talking foul-mouthed. *How about the proverbial "mutha-fuck" and "bitch" combination that mamma often uses?* he thought to himself. We are talking jive-ass transformation 101 here, ladies and gentlemen.

Wait a minute, did Church Mouse just say "mamma"? Yes, unfortunately he did. Standing all of four feet, ten inches in high heels, his stepmother, Crazy Beulah, was an intimidating figure who possessed the swagger of a marine and the mouth of a sailor. In most inner-city homes, it is the father or the wayward uncle who is the family character you must keep an eye on. In Church Mouse's family, the situation was flipped. Some might say that is a sexist view. Beulah was queen bee of rancid funk. She was a stone-cold badass. Church Mouse had big shoes to fill. Could mamma's choir boy replicate the same effect as she? He softly rehearsed over and over as he nervously pranced around the one-person detention cell and yanked on his crotch. "I'm a bad mutha fucka. I'm so tough, I'll kick Dolomite's ass!" the conflicted child nervously whispered. [37] What do you think, readers? Was his funk routine stank enough?

Lunchtime arrived in record time that morning. Needless to say, Church Mouse's get-tough-quick plan to impress his peers failed miserably. It is hard to fool professional con artists, even when they are only young apprentices. A strait-laced cat like Church Mouse cannot suddenly change his stripes. He can't just walk into the lion's den one day, light up a fat cigar, and start shooting the breeze without stirring up some level of suspicion.

Church Mouse's all too mechanical approach immediately alerted the teenage warlords seated at the lunch table that he was an imposter. Teasing soon gave way to target practice—a slap on the head here and the taking of a few French fries there. One inmate confiscated Church's carton of milk and dared him to take it back. A second inmate called him a "pussy" and challenged him to do something about it. After lunch, a hood homie pushed him to the ground during recess time. Church Mouse was quite adept at defending himself. He could have whipped any of the boys in a fair one-on-one fight, but because he feared group retaliation, he deduced that it was safer to just put up with the bullying.

The ultimate insult came during a pick-up game of basketball. Church Mouse had the audacity to miss an open shot from close range. He did not draw iron, nor did he hit the backboard. Zero. Zilch. Nada. Goose egg. Missing a shot that badly was one sure way for a young Black male to quickly lose face with peers. The rule in the hood is that a shooter must at least hit something when the pill (the ball) is launched. Although Church Mouse was an accomplished football player, a good boxer, and a half-decent wrestler, the finer points of the game of basketball escaped him. The rough and tumble sports came easier than the finesse stuff. On this day, he didn't even throw up a brick. Church Mouse shot an air ball—the ultimate shame for a young soul brother. Then in an unwise attempt to cover up his clumsiness, young Church Mouse yelled at the ball as if it were a person. He blurted out a phrase his mother would have been enormously proud of: "Get yo bitch-ass in da hole, you stupid mutha fucka!"

There laid every boy—teammate and foe alike—sprawled over the pavement, laughing their heads off. It was 100% participation. A few laughed because the ball didn't draw iron. Others laughed because your boy tripped over his feet as he launched the pill. One or two laughed because of Church's ludicrous attempt at trying to pass himself off as a tough guy who cursed a lot. The alpha male burst out in laughter because of the overall comedic value of the moment. Church Mouse showed that he was the ultimate nerd, clumsily trying to fit in. Physical and verbal sparring was a vexing yet manageable thing for a brother to bear. Public humiliation, on the other hand, was kryptonite to a boy trying to survive the era of super cool. You dig?

With the ball clutched under one arm and egg all over his face, Church Mouse slowly wandered over to the nearby chain-link fence, pressed his forehead gently against the matrix, and whispered, "I just want to go home." It was the first time in countless years that Church Mouse actually wanted to return to the place of sanctuary he had grown to fear and despise.

———————————

Speaking of the home that Church Mouse grew up in, it is only proper at this point to provide readers with an overview of what that home looked like. It was not all bad; there were positives and good times. Still, the situation was light years away from being a healthy and normal home. Unfortunately, the airing of family dirty laundry cannot be avoided here. After many years of considering the pros and cons of opening that door, Church Mouse decided that the story of overcoming obstacles was bigger than protecting the secrets of a few family members and friends. It was with much trepidation that Church Mouse made his choice, but the product of telling a survival story is enhanced albeit at a cost to personal and family privacy.

Although the two families that Church Mouse belonged to ultimately found ways to become places of relative love and stability, during the early years of his upbringing they were textbook examples of dysfunctional homes. The mis-parenting that took place in both homes improved as time progressed and each sibling grew up and became wiser for it, but during the formative years of each sibling's childhood experience, full moons and werewolves appeared to party in synchronicity. Although the adults of the two homes were good people, they had serious shortcomings regarding their parenting skills. It is quite likely that the problem was generational. Their parents, too, may not have said and done everything they could and should have. Fighting Jim Crow segregation and navigating manufactured poverty may have had a lot to do with that.

Each of the twelve children was negatively impacted by racism, poverty, child abuse, neglect, and learned helplessness, with some members experiencing greater degrees of trauma than others. The Omaha side of the family consisted of Church Mouse's biological mother, Rainy Eyes, and three maternal siblings. Rainy Eyes lived a sorrow-filled life of bad decision-making, tough luck, and failed dreams. Her biggest setback in life came when physicians wrongly diagnosed her medical condition for several decades and prescribed to her the wrong medication. White doctors had convinced her that she had narcolepsy, when, in fact, she suffered from diabetes. As a result, her elderly days were spent dealing with total blindness and kidney failure brought on by years of medical misdiagnosis. Equally unfortunate was the fact that she lost her two oldest children in a divorce settlement from her first husband. During the 1950s, it was unusual for women to lose custody of their children to a man. The impact and public humiliation of that loss stayed with Rainy Eyes until the day she took her last breath.

Rainy Eyes was the consummate disengaged parent. The three children she raised often complained that their mother was absent in mind, body, and spirit. She often left her kids alone at home or in the care of others, and many times, they had to scrape for food the best way they could. When she was at home, she was emotionally unplugged from her children. Because of depression, she cried a lot. Her children were forced to make up the rules of life as they went along. This led to some successes, but also, a lot of predictable mistakes were made. Sadly, the father of the kids was absent. A janky boyfriend who hung around made matters worse. The culture of poverty was an inconvenient reality for Rainy Eyes. The fact that her kids made it to adulthood despite not being given much to work with is a testament of their personal strength and resiliency. Hats off to the Omaha kids, despite a few mistakes they made along the way.

The oldest Omaha sibling, Dubious, was a popular person in North Omaha, but he constantly stayed in trouble with authorities and battled with constant bouts of manic depression and substance abuse. Being the child that his mother's divorce was centered around had a negative impact on shaping his behavior and worldview. Like his older brother, he could be a kind and giving soul, but only on his terms. Brown Sugar, the middle child, lived a roller-coaster existence of highs and lows. She experienced more than her share of abuse and neglect. She did not always make the best decisions and had a habit of picking the wrong men to date. Early in life, she had the potential to become a debutante, but the ghetto made her hard and cynical. It took Brown Sugar until her late fifties to find positive karma. Her lifetime goal was to raise a healthy family in a safe environment and be a happy grandmother—normal things that escaped her childhood. The youngest sibling, Vociferous, was the perfect kid. He was Rainy Eyes' favorite child. As he grew older, however, he became like a crossword puzzle. It was as if he had twin personalities. He had a unique ability to be both daylight and darkness at the same time. And yet he was the most caring and giving of the siblings. Not having a father in the home may have impacted him the most. Despite his unpredictability, it was evident that Vociferous was a gifted specimen with unlimited potential. He may have been the most talented of the kids.

The South Carolina portion of the family—the one that raised and nurtured Church Mouse—consisted of his full brother June Bug, their biological father, the King of Ghosts (aka the Road Runner), his second wife, Beulah, and seven new siblings, who more than likely were all adopted and/ or "creatively captured." The father of the home was a loveable guy but an alcoholic and absentee family member, nonetheless. He was far from being a bad person, but he sucked at the job of being an engaged parent. The mother of the home, Crazy Beulah, was an enigma for all time. She is like no other person to ever walk the planet. One or two lines cannot accurately describe her majesty. It may very well take a couple of volumes to fully explain her essence. We begin that effort in this chapter, but we will have to keep coming back to that task over and over throughout a three-book saga.

The two oldest children—Nefertiti (a surrogate mother to Church Mouse) and June Bug (the rebellious child)—were independent types who were strong enough to build a successful life despite their parents' shortcomings and archaic ways. Church Mouse (the family do-gooder) was not as opportunistic, however. He was an overly sensitive mama's boy and a people-pleaser to boot. He was a late bloomer and did not find his voice until he reached his mid-forties. The fact that he looked like his father encouraged Beulah to be extra hard on him. She rode him like a Mama-Jo tick on a possum's underbelly. She often warned that she would make sure he did not turn out to be like his "criminal brother and his hoe daddy." Not a good sign for any child. Church Mouse was also a teacher's pet and the best student in either family. This combination did not go over well with siblings, nor did it pass the smell test with most kids in the hood. They felt that Church Mouse was acting White. WTF (what the James Brown funk)?

The rest of the South Carolina family included younger brother Slim Jenkins (the lost child), younger sister Sunshine (the favored child), twin sisters Temperament (the wounded child) and Silhouette (the invisible child), the Marvelous One (a special needs child), and Conflicted (the youngest, cutest, and yet most compromised child). Each sibling was a jewel in their own right. Each has their own spin on what it was like growing up in Beulah's crazy house. Most of the siblings were challenged by the mis-parenting in the home, but a few may not have been.

Claiming that the children turned out to be troubled because the mother was the sole negative influence in their lives would be a major misstatement. Yes, Beulah was a big pill to swallow, but she did not ride solo. Beulah and her children clearly suffered the effects of southern and northern racism and poverty. But they were also adversely impacted by the father's alcohol problem. And if you believe in the accuracy of the Children of Alcoholics (COA) research, you must conclude that the impact was a lasting one. According to that research, we know that the drinker in the home is not the only person who suffers from the disease of alcoholism. Negative impacts touch the lives of all family members.

The literature identifies the following COA roles played by various family members in most alcoholic homes: (a) Enablers – those who cover up for the alcoholic; (b) the overachieving child or the Family Hero; (c) the

Scapegoat – the child on whom family anger is displaced; (d) the Lost Child – the withdrawn sibling who lacks self-esteem, assertiveness, and direction in life; and (e) the Mascot – the person in the family that provides levity and humor as a way of diverting attention away from the real problems generated by alcoholism and related issues. During the 2020s, a separate body of research that went under the label of "Narcissistic Parents" (NP) produced conclusions that are similar to the COA findings. Church Mouse concluded that each family member took on the characteristics of one or more of the COA and NP roles. It is not the purpose of this manuscript, however, to assign those roles to specific family members.

Church Mouse easily played the hero role. However, it was hoisted onto his shoulders by older adults in the family without his consent. One might also conclude that Church Mouse may have possessed some sort of divine guidance, as if there were an invisible hand guiding his every move. Beulah's mom, Grandma Queen, would often tell Church Mouse that God had a special plan for him, but she never explained what she meant. Whether the sentiment was true or not, it was something that created much tension and jealousy between Church Mouse and his siblings. June Bug and Sunshine especially despised the goody-two-shoes image of Church Mouse. Because it brought him much pain and social isolation, Church Mouse despised the designation. He became the solo dancer of the family by forging an independent path that was not defined by popular norms nor the expectations of others.

Church Mouse was extraordinarily ordinary in the spiritual sense of the word. Although heavily scrutinized and often criticized, he had little say in how he turned out. From the beginning of his time on earth, his steps appeared to have been ordered. It was almost as if Church Mouse was preordained to be a wilderness walker. "Let us make a choir boy," God, the Father said to his crew. "And upon his shoulders will rest an urban test of survival. If he succeeds, we'll call him faithful. If he fails, we will call him human," said the Holy Ghost. "Bet," responded His Son, the Lord of Hosts. And then a new creation came forth. But no instruction manual was provided. There were no batteries, and no guidelines or instructional videos were included in the packaging. There was only a screwdriver and a few loose parts to be assembled. Some people say that God has a sense of humor.

Church Mouse was easily the most compliant of Beulah's nine children. The twins were also low-key and obedient in their personalities, but not as conservative and kiss-up as their older brother was. Anyone who took the time to observe the situation could easily see that heaven hardwired Church Mouse slightly different from the neighborhood norm. No, he was not a special case, but he also wasn't typical. There is no shame in stating that fact. Again, it is what it is, and Church Mouse is who he is. Haters need to get a life and work on their own stuff.

Interaction between young Church Mouse and Beulah was strained. A love–hate relationship describes it best. During the young lad's early years, mom and son were like ace boon coons. [38] Buddies to the max. But, by middle school, the child grew to fear and despise his second mother. By the time he became a high school student, all Church Mouse wanted to do was find a new home. Despite repeated physical and emotional abuse, he remained one of Beulah's most loyal and trusted children. Too bad she never caught a clue.

Crazy Beulah: Ah, yes, the eighth wonder of the Gullah world. Her name alone causes demons to tremble. Over the years, the question of which of the nine children were actually her own biological offspring never fully got fleshed out. Church Mouse's educated guess is that Beulah was unable to bear children, thus she overcompensated by taking in kids that other people threw away. Some of her adoptions were of the bootleg variety, however. Church Mouse is not 100% sure, but the addition of the twins to the home may have been more of the "creative capture" scenario than a benevolent adoption story. It was typical for mothers in the Deep South to have birth certificates, names, dates, and other important vital statistics altered so that children could not be traced by their biological parents. Sometimes it worked, but it often backfired. As adults, it was not unusual for complete strangers to walk up to Beulah's children and introduce themselves as long-lost siblings. This caused much consternation in the family. The fact that Temperament and Silhouette survived abandonment by their original parents, abuse by Beulah, and neglect by the King, in addition to southern racism and poverty is a testament to their personal strength of character. Lesser women would have folded and crumbled. All hail to the resilient sisters for not giving up when many factors were not in their favor.

If it is true that Beulah was barren, it partially explains why she could be super sweet one minute and completely out of her mind the next. It is quite possible that Beulah was mentally and emotionally compromised and did not fully realize the impact her condition had on her children. She very well may have suffered from a multiple personality disorder. If so, few doctors in segregated Mount Pleasant, SC, took the time to diagnose and treat those kinds of medical conditions for Black folk. In their minds, "all niggers were mentally deficient." At times, it really did appear that Beulah had at least three personalities: gentle and loving saint, a conniving witch on a broom, and a determined Black businesswoman with a Napoleon complex. There may have been a few others. Beulah's volatile temper and reputation for unpredictable behavior were legendary. It prompted people from the neighborhood to invent nicknames for her. They came up with various titles, such as "Dat Mean Ole Lady," "Da Grits Witch," and "Bad-Ass Soul Sista Number One."

Crazy Beulah. That was the nickname that ultimately stuck. She earned the moniker one summer day while driving down Venning Road in the Four Mile section of town. Encountering some children playing in the middle of the road, she blew her horn and yelled, "Next time I blow my horn and y'all don't move out the way, I'm gonna run yer little asses over!" "Dat lady crazy," responded one of the scampering kids. Thus, the name, and the legend, was born.

It did not matter to Church Mouse that Beulah was not his real mother. He knew she had love for him, albeit a strange, Twilight Zone version of it. And despite the physical and emotional abuse she dished out, Church Mouse still gave her credit for not totally abandoning him like his two biological parents had done. He swallows hard each time he admits this fact, but don't be fooled: the relationship between mother and son was a vicarious one. The child's desire to rebel against Beulah's authority, however, was not your typical story about a teenage boy "smelling himself." [39] Church Mouse was by no means a perfect child, but he was a good son. One to be proud of. He was obedient and thoughtful. He was courteous to others. He did all his chores and always said, "Yes, mam" and "Yes, sir." He regularly attended church, he excelled in school, and he didn't disrespect women or use foul language. He was a goody-two-shoes nerd.

Beulah never caught the rhythm of the parenting stroke. For reasons still unclear, the relationship between mother and son became needlessly strained. Most of Beulah's friends understood her son better than she did. When they advised her to ease up, she found ways to brush off their advice. Beulah erroneously believed that she saw traits in the little guy that reminded her of her husband's suspect character. Day by day, Beulah grew more convinced that she needed to exorcise a playboy spirit that she assumed Church Mouse inherited from his father. Unfortunately, Dad was not around to protect his son. Beulah also feared Church Mouse was turning into a problem child like his older brother June Bug. Daily, Church Mouse prayed that his absentee father would return and rescue him. It never happened. Silly little dreamer. Ghosts do not have the wherewithal to save themselves, much less a Murphy's Child in need of rescue.

A meaningful relationship between Church Mouse and his biological mother, Rainy Eyes, never materialized. Even when Church Mouse became an adult, she acted as if she did not trust her second son. For reasons unexplained, she kept him and younger sister Brown Sugar at arm's length while being semi-attentive to the other three children, albeit still not sufficient enough with them either. She believed Church Mouse harbored ulterior motives, and that his love was fake. Up to the day she passed, Church Mouse never felt appreciated by his biological mother. He does not remember ever eating a meal prepared by her. She never attended his school graduations. Not once can he ever remember her saying the words "I love you." If she did, it was when he was a baby, and his memory did not go back that far. Come to think of it, he is not sure his father ever uttered those words. Nothing from nothing leaves nothing. The sum total of the zero game is something inner-city kids are forced to play. Conversely, Beulah said those precious words all the time, but you were never sure which personality you were speaking to.

Critics might disagree that life in the 1960s Deep South and the 1970s northern ghettos of America was as toxic as Church Mouse portrays it to be, but scores of others would agree. Each sibling has his or her own version of both the family story and their recollection of fighting racism and poverty. Some of those accounts might view events similar to Church Mouse's recol-lection, while others will differ with their interpretation. To each his reach. As siblings grew older, a few engaged in lively debates over which family setting—Omaha or Mount Pleasant—was the most toxic. The result of those debates typically ended up being one of those six of one, half dozen of the other type of conversations. The older Church Mouse became, the more he began to realize the blessings of not being raised by Rainy Eyes. Still, he never got to a place where he was willing to bet the mortgage on the benefits of hanging out with Beulah's crazy ass.

Upon the passing of all three parents to the next life, each sibling had to make a crucial decision about how each mentor would be remembered. The difference in the various approaches each child took is the stuff gradu-ate-level counseling psychology textbooks are made of. Rainy Eyes' legacy remains foggy. Regarding Beulah, some kids have swept all negative mem-ories under the carpet and sanitized her reputation. The older each child grew the saintlier Beulah became. Mother Theresa had her rosary beads, and Beulah had her extension cords. Hail Mary full of grace, Moses' staff and Beulah's broomstick were one in the same. Strike a pose and pass down your commandments. A few siblings blamed Beulah for 100% of things that went wrong in their lives. The chances of those kids finding peace and joy are slim to none.

To be sure, not every family member wanted this book to be published. Some viewed the decision as counterproductive to the goal of forgiving and moving on with your life. Church Mouse contends that until all his siblings receive some type of professional counseling, they will not be totally free from the psychological and emotional prisons they inherited because of being raised in dysfunctional homes. Some of the damage done is easily recognizable, but a lot of it is at the unconscious level and hard to get at. If unaddressed issues keep popping up like a stubborn mushroom, there could be a lot of pill-popping and restless nights ahead. For the few kids who weren't targeted as much, it will be easy for them to be judgmental of those who were. Whether or not counseling intervention can counteract the effects of Beulah's voodoo, the King's run and drink behavior, and the egregious sin of omission perpetrated by Rainy Eyes remains a question that only heaven can answer. Yes, it is true that living with Beulah and her absentee husband was not all bad. In fact, there were good character traits that were passed on to each child by all three parents. This is true despite the kids having to navigate ripe buffalo chips on a daily basis.

Nevertheless, the net impact of living in Beulah's strange abode was not healthy physically, mentally, or spiritually for most of her kids. Yes, the Road Runner and his two peculiar wives may have been good people, but they did not ace parenting 101. Depending on which child you speak to, the grade awarded to each parent fluctuates somewhere between B and F. In the eyes of Church Mouse, Beulah's grade was the lowest among the three parents. There is a 50% chance, however, that she was not psychologically and emotionally well enough to fully comprehend the damage her nuclear ways had on her children. Whether her radioactive persona was due to the residual effects of racism and poverty, old-fashion stubbornness, the embracement of a cavalier and toxic lifestyle, mental illness, or all of the above is a question for the ages that may never get answered. Still, if an everyday neutral person had a one-on-one session with Beulah, they could easily come away with the impression that she loved her children. The King was negligent and absent. Rainy Eyes was disengaged and extricate. Beulah was ever present and accounted for, but she had the strangest brand of love known to humankind.

One night during January of 1971, the usually reserved Church Mouse found a need to go nuclear. As a junior at East High School, he began feeling the pressure of growing up and facing adulthood, as most teens do. This could not happen if he continued to hang on to the apron strings of women all his life. Neighborhood males of the day had a saying that if you were going to be a real man, you had to "show yourself legit by letting go of your mamma's tit." Yes, it was a crude way of describing an inescapable reality most inner-city boys face, but it was real talk. It was a way of life in most 1970's ghettoes.

Church Mouse was more than willing to be the responsible young adult others wanted him to be. He gladly wanted to embrace the tenets of principled living. It was in his DNA. He was as good a candidate as there ever was to prove the point that not all Black males go buck wild when given a little freedom. Church Mouse made a serious mistake with the earlier shop-borrowing incident, but that was an anomaly—a move brought on by poverty, desperation, lack of self-esteem, and the mixed political signals of the day. Despite an occasional setback here and there, the kid had the right stuff to succeed as a true leader. Everyone but his mother understood that you give a kid like that a little room to grow and develop. One day they will make a bunch of money and turn around and bless you with a new house and car if you nurture them properly. Growing up under Beulah's roof with her archaic rules only served to sidetrack Church Mouse's growth. Either mom had to change, or her son had to go. One of these results was predestined.

Because Beulah's estranged husband was out chasing women across America, and older siblings Nefertiti and June Bug were living out of state and raising their own families, Mom came to rely heavily on her third oldest child to fill the role of the man of the house. Being a parent figure to his younger siblings kept Church Mouse from attending important school functions and extracurricular activities that would have prepared him to be the leader he was hardwired to be. Taking on a heavy domestic role in and of itself was not such a dreadful thing if Beulah would consider meeting him halfway. Her old-school philosophy was over the top, and the net effect of her disciplinary style and lack of communication skills made her son far more serious and conflicted than what was normal or healthy.

The few hours Church Mouse spent away from home participating in football, wrestling, and school leadership activities sent the Crazed One into a tizzy. It meant that younger siblings Slim Jenkins and Sunshine might have to babysit the smaller children as well as manage the cooking and other household chores. Heaven forbids that they would inherit such duties! This was hard for Church Mouse to accept, especially since he and his two older siblings had assumed much heavier domestic responsibilities at an earlier age than did the younger set of kids.

This particular day was destined to end in a mother–son smackdown. Crazy Beulah patiently sat on the living room coach waiting for the infidel rodent to walk through the door. Sista Girl was in rare form that night. She was hell-bent on re-domesticating the perceived wayward child. Her focus was singular and monolithic: to ensure that her son did not turn out like the stereotypical Black males she saw in her home and in the media. Her single mission was to put her second son back into captivity. Church Mouse informed his mother earlier that morning of a school dance planning committee meeting he needed to attend right after wrestling practice. Beulah granted him permission but forgot that she did as the day wore on. When nightfall rolled around, she assumed that her son was out chasing skirts. Everyone knows that school activities are evil affairs. They cause boys to "look under girls' dresses and sniff the air for possibilities." Say what? Beulah's ideology was as amusing as it was perplexing.

The meeting at the front door was rapid and tense. Accusations and counteraccusations flew back and forth like prizefighters going at one another. Suddenly, Church Mouse mustered the nerve to be assertive. "Why won't you trust me?" he asked. "You're the one who always pushes me to achieve and be more than the average neighborhood kid," he reminded her.

"You just want to run the streets and chase women like your hoe daddy," Crazy Beulah shouted.

Wait a minute, folks. The writer apologizes once again, but there is no way he can continue without analyzing the mother's response. The concept of choir boys hooking up with hookers and hoes deserves a bit of investigation, don't you think? One might ask, "Isn't it true that ladies of the night cost money?" With what was the child supposed to pay the fabricated wenches? Food stamps? Fatback and greens? A block of government cheese? His free and reduced lunch ticket? Perhaps he could do their laundry and fold their underwear. In Beulah's distorted mind, male gigolos love sniffing the panties of bitch-ass hoes.

A series of exchanges like these flew back and forth as mother and son went up the front porch, down the concrete steps, back up, and then down again, until Beulah did the unthinkable: Employing heavy broomstick action to Church's head and body, she drove him out into the snow, with no shoes on his feet and no coat on his back! He had taken these items off at the front door when he first entered the house, and his mother would not let him back in the house to retrieve the all-important coverings despite ice and snow on the ground.

There at the door stood the Overlord of Nonsense. With her trusty weapon in hand, she proudly guarded her castle of craze. Church Mouse walked up and down the block believing his mother would soon cool off and come to her senses. No dice. Five minutes passed, but there was no change in Beulah's stance. Beulah's younger brother, Tree, came over to help resolve the crisis, but all to no avail. She ignored his plea to be reasonable. Ten minutes passed, fifteen, twenty; there was no change. Crazy Beulah did not get her nickname and reputation by backing down from anyone, much less some little suck-ass cockroach like Church Mouse.

A severe problem suddenly arose. Because of a freezing temperature and ice on the ground, the child's toes began to turn purple and hardened like small eggplants. Pain shot up the back of his legs into his hips as frostbite began to set in. Church Mouse attempted to slip through a crack his mother left in the doorway. "Whack, whack!" went the crazed lady's weapon. Church Mouse dived into the snow for cover. Back and forth he went. Wood and snow. Fire and ice. The victor and the vanquished. Caca and cream. Reality and dreams. Nightmares and nonsense.

Buck up, Church Mouse, and be a real man. Don't be such a cream puff all your life. You can weather this latest ordeal. Rumble, young man, rumble. [40] It is time for you to think rationally, even when the rest of the world chooses not to do so. Pretend that the snow drifting in your front yard will form a warm swimming pool that you can dive into from the top shelf. Transcendental meditation will persuade your mind that it really is not freezing outside; that your mother's broomstick is made of Styrofoam instead of wood. Rise above the fog, young man, even when you are surrounded by a cesspool of insanity. Stop looking for sympathy and pity. Children of all ethnic backgrounds experience similar trials and tribulations. They face just as much fire and ice as you do. And don't give us this unfortunate Black-child-from-the-ghetto rhetoric that you closeted liberals like to pull out of your asses. All races have the same-sized historical hole to dig out of. African Americans do not encounter any more problems than what poor White children encounter. So say the architects of American political spin.

Then a very unfortunate thing happened. Momentarily forsaking his conservative and religious convictions, Church Mouse exploded with a mighty burst of energy, rushed his mother, tore the broomstick from her hands, broke it over his knee, and punched her dead in the face with his fist. Uncle Tree's astonishment at his nephew's actions perched frozen upon his face. "That is so unlike you," he cried. Crazy Beulah sat on the floor stunned and dazed as her child ran out the door with his coat and shoes in hand.

Limping awkwardly down the street, the child resembled the Hunchback of Notre Dame chasing after a dinner mouse. A stream of jewels flowed from within. Tears turned into crystals as they traced his face. A few fell to the ground, creating miniature explosions. Loud cries for help burst onto the frozen concrete. The plea of a hurting child called out to any critically thinking adult who was willing to listen. It was all for naught. There was no rescue for the hurting child that night, nor was there ever one for the months that followed. There was only the sound of silence. The perfect ingredients for the birth of an American solo dancer.

It was this incident that ultimately pushed Church Mouse over the edge into another dimension. It was on this night that what little innocence he had left inside himself flickered and died. He never lost faith in himself, but the small amount of optimism he held inside for humankind evaporated on that day. It became clear in his mind that caring and sharing were not high priorities for those who misused love as an excuse for their abuse. He went to East High School and slipped into an open dock door. That night, he slept in a medium size janitor's closet located in the basement of the school. The next day he wore a thin under-jacket he had stored in his locker to help cover up the fact that he had the same clothing on. He got up early enough to wash up using school soap and his tee-shirt as a hand towel. [41] His eyes were red and reflected a hollow look. Classmates thought he was high on da chronic. They high-fived him all day because they now saw him as the shit. Cool daddy, sweet daddy, what it be like. You are now part of the in-crowd. Church Mouse was now a renegade of sorts, and his new lifelong goal became the task of crushing the skull of the fallen angel that hunted him and his people. It was not the healthiest of responses to adopt, but at least he did not choose crime, drugs, dropping out, or pimpology. Watch out, Lucifoot. Prepare to get your lip busted by the Vigilante Kid, beeyotch. [42]

Church Mouse striking his mother in the face was the incident that ultimately brought his absentee father, the King of Ghosts, back home from his nation-wide discovery tour. By the way, what exactly was his father searching for? Did he ever find it? Was it an attainable goal? Was it something he already possessed but just did not know how to dig down deep and pull it out of himself? (Again, apologies must go out to the reader. The writer obviously needs to go to literary school and learn how to write one book at a time.)

———————————————

A month after the broomstick and snowdrift episode, Church Mouse came home from wrestling practice to find a surprise waiting for him: his father seated at the kitchen table staring at him eyeball to eyeball. Mustache to peach fuzz. Neckbone to throat. Negligence to innocence. Pops had driven all the way from Jacksonville, Florida, to make one of his occasional visits, somehow hoping to rid himself of the guilt he carried around for not doing his share of raising his youngest son. The Road Runner himself often complained that his wife's behavior was over the top. He knew she could be irrational. He also claimed that too many of the kids were not his. Beulah had a big heart for taking in children that other people threw away, but sometimes she did so without her husband's consent. Her heart was in the right place, but at times, the father felt put upon. As the years progressed, each child came to endear themselves to the patriarch of the family in their own way, but during the early years, he saw the situation as one more excuse not to parent any of the children, including his lone remaining biological child.

Prospects looked rather grim for Church Mouse as he entered the house and came face-to-face with the man who had eyes of pickled flesh, hardened from the intake of too much alcohol and tobacco. The Ghost began to speak, his voice sounding as if it were filtered through an audio effects processor: "I heard you've been raisin' hell around here, little boy. All that changes tonight because Big Daddy is here to straighten yo little ass out," said the mysterious wanderer. Unlike the case with his older son, it had been twelve or thirteen years since the father had last used any form of physical punishment to discipline his younger progeny. There was really no need to, although Beulah and a few of his siblings might beg to differ.

The sight of his dad's return offered the young lad a mixed reaction. Initially, there was a burst of excitement. It had been almost three years since Church Mouse had last seen his father. *Daddy has come home to rescue me*, he thought. That feeling quickly faded when the son peered into his father's empty soul. Whoa! Give a brother a bit of a warning before you send him into an abyss. Church Mouse struggled to translate the sounds that emanated from the bowels of his mentor. "So, you think you're the big stuff now? You like to act macho and hit on women, huh? Well, I will have you know that nobody hits on my wife. She is my property. I am the only one who can do that!" the father shouted as he pounded on his chest in Neanderthal fashion. "Your ass is mine, boy, and I'm gonna put it to you really good," the Ghost growled.

The phrase "she's my property" ricocheted off two walls and the ceiling, landed on Church's left earlobe, and traveled down his audio canal with lightning speed, almost shattering his eardrum. Any thoughts of being rescued were destroyed in that one critical moment. *Daddy is out of the child-saving loop*, Church Mouse conceded. Unfortunately, both adults were out of several important parenting and reality loops.

Totally unfazed that she had just been disrespected as a female, Beulah waved her hand in the air as if she were in church receiving the Holy Ghost. Church Mouse was finally going to get a bona fide ass-whipping from the head male in charge. Glory Hallelujah, Beulah "done seed da lite!" Her whippings were starting not to have any long-term effect on the growing teen. His hide was toughening, and now during the broomstick and snowdrift episode, the child, unfortunately, struck back. Out of the corner of his eye, Church Mouse saw his mother do a little jig as she delighted at the thought of her estranged husband taking charge of the situation. Church Mouse is not 100% sure, but it looked like his mother did one of those "booty-pop" dancefloor moves made famous by hip-hop music fans of today. Whatever, girl.

So why didn't Church Mouse get a clue and react to the mis-parenting like most Black kids would have done? Why didn't he just become rebellious and start acting out? Sure, standing up for his rights could mean increased whippings and being grounded, but it also would have averted a sizable portion of the mental and emotional anguish he suffered throughout his life. But no. Instead, Mr. Oddball Extraordinaire wanted to utilize obedience and reasoning tactics. When that tactic failed, he went gangsta on his mother. Make it easy on yourself, Church Mouse, and just go negative like most troubled males from the ghetto do. Drop out of school. Smoke some funny cigarettes. Pimp a few hoes. Write and produce some trap music. Better have my money tonight, bitch! What is wrong with you, Church Mouse? Are you a glutton for punishment?

Again, the Ghost and his bride were not model parents by any stretch of the imagination. Perhaps they were too inebriated with wine and mental illness. They were consumed with their own set of problems. Chances are they, too, were at risk and still hurting from having to endure their own rough upbringing. Racism can negatively impact an entire community. In a sense, dysfunctionalism in Black families was kind of, well, do we dare use the word normal? Society is what we make it to be. Uncritically thinking White folk tend to judge what they themselves are the architects of. Americans are so good at throwing rocks at our own creations.

Hungry and exhausted, the Road Runner had little desire to dole out a physical punishment at 7:00 p.m. on the same day he arrived in town. He sent his son to bed with no dinner, with a promise of impending doom hovering over his head. The King wanted his son to think long and hard about what he had done. They say spankings hurt worse if you give a child extra time to visualize them.

A strange sense of purification began to overtake Church Mouse as he sat in his bedroom contemplating his fate. Suddenly, the fear he felt inside began to subside. Something new began taking shape in his troubled mind. "My God, I believe I actually want to be beaten," he softly whispered. He repeated the statement over and over, each time with more conviction. A whipping was the only thing that made sense of all the insanity that surrounded his family. "I finally get it," he said. "Children are to be seen, not heard. They are pack mules whose only function in life is to make adults comfortable. And skinny little trick-assed niggas who smart off and pop their mother in the mouth deserve to be permanently squashed," he reluctantly acquiesced. Sanctify my funk by throwing some extra butter and sugar on my grits!

Much to Beulah's dismay, Church Mouse never received the whipping his father promised. Her own brother intervened and spoke with the husband about the irrational behavior of his wife. He also talked about the father's extended periods of absenteeism and the negative effect it had on both the mother and child. Although the King was solid at sending money home, he provided little in the way of family leadership. This caused Beulah to be edgier than normal, although Beulah's definition of normal was an eternally elusive concept. Uncle Tree went on to explain to his brother-in-law that Church Mouse was a frightened child who needed his father. There might be wonderful things in store for the boy someday if his socialization were properly cultivated. On this day, Tree played the role of an intervening saint. But let us not go overboard with this blame-sharing thing. Truth is, Crazy Beulah, the queen of envelope pushers, was downright stubborn and archaic. Yes, the father was guilty of abandonment, but Mom was from an alien zip code, and deep down inside he knew his wife was tripped out.

In the end, the young lad did not get what he really needed: quality time with his father. The boy lacked that special flare his father so admired in his oldest son. The Ghost and June Bug were cast from the same mold: cavalier, unpredictable, and exciting. Church Mouse was too serious and religious for his father's taste. And yet, Dad had respect for his younger son. He was proud of Church Mouse's academic prowess. And so, the father began making a fragile connection with his son on that point. It was always a dream of the Runner that his youngest boy become the family's first college graduate. He had plans on sending him to the US Air Force Academy located down the road in Colorado Springs. He believed Church Mouse would make a good "pencil pusher" in the armed forces. "Leave the heavy lifting (i.e., infantry work) to the big boys with the muscles," he would often say. Whatever, dude.

When an absentee father fears emotional attachment to a child he barely knows, he begins to substitute real love with rituals and ceremonies of undoing. Richer parents use things such as an expensive iPhone or a new car as a bribe. For poorer families, you might have to substitute a rib or chicken dinner. Kentucky Fried Chicken and some orange drink will do just fine, Mr. Kline. Discussing school business and academic matters works particularly well if you have a gifted child. You should try it sometime. Spend a hot minute talking about career plans, but never utter the words "I love you" or "I'm proud of you." And throw in some spare change every now and then to help sweeten the pot. These practices will magically absolve you of parental omissions. There, you see—wasn't that easy?

Fragile unions easily unravel. Dreams turn to dust. Things fall apart.

———————————

Post-chapter mentoring tips for disengaged fathers: Men, please take your ass home and parent the kids that you brought into the world! If you find that you must leave your wife because she is wrong or there is a lack of understanding, fairness, or love do not make a half-spirited decision about it. Go all the way and make it a clean break. If you have a blended family and you are unhappy, what makes you think your biological children want to stay there when you have chosen to leave? Do not pawn your kids off on another person to raise, especially when the two parents are fighting each other. Think with your big head, not the little one. Set your drinking and skirt-chasing behaviors aside and go rescue your children. If you don't honestly know how to properly parent, then get some counseling or take some online courses.

Post-chapter survival tips for children who hurt: *A man should never hit a woman, even when she is dead wrong*. This is true for both young and older men. It is important for at-risk children to realize that two wrongs do not make a right. Violence only breeds more violence. Instead of striking his mother, Church Mouse should have found a telephone and called the police. Had he done so, he might have received the help he so desperately needed. Maybe he should have applied to be admitted to a residential setting such as Boystown. Today's children must use their mind and words to fight, not weapons or their fists. Despite obvious wrongs that have been done to you, it is still better to take the high road. Learn to let your higher power fight your battles. And be extra cautious of adopting a "righteous vigilante" posture in life. It never fails: Your haters will get away with starting a fight, while you are left holding the guilty bag for retaliating. In addition, do not wait for the world to be fair. If you do, you will set yourself up for a lot of pain and sorrow. Get your education, and *patiently bide your time until you can plot an intelligent escape away from people who do not know how to love you*. Truth be told, most of these folks don't even know how to love themselves.

CHAPTER 5:

WHEN THE DEVIL IS IN HIS MOON

B<small>EULAH WAS INFURIATED AT HER HUSBAND'S REFUSAL TO WHIP</small> C<small>HURCH</small> Mouse for striking her during the snow and stick incident. Not only did the teenager escape his mother's mousetrap but her own husband and brother appeared to have switched allegiances. The shoplifting episode that Church Mouse got himself into, however, was a different story. It angered the father of the home. Stealing was unpardonable to the retired Air Force sergeant. This time, there would be no bleeding-heart sentiment—no pardons to be granted by the traveling overseer. Beulah had the infidel rodent right where she wanted him: fresh from the grip of the law, straight into the hands of the wandering head of the house. She savored the ride home from the youth detention center as if she were sipping champagne. "I told you that you were going to grow up to be just like your criminal brother," she smirked.

Church Mouse wanted to explain that he was not a thief in the true sense of the word, but it was highly unlikely that either parent would believe that he actually paid back the stores that he "borrowed" from. When he mentioned the piece about being bullied by classmates for being a welfare child, Mom responded by saying, "You're the damn fool for going hungry just so you can please your asshole conservative friends." An ardent recipient of social welfare and food stamps, Beulah possessed the necessary mind-set to tell people who did not agree with her politics where to go. Beulah's perspective is not an indictment of all liberals. Many democrats have done a yeoman's job of fighting for the poor. Kudos to the brave! The fact that Beulah skillfully took advantage of the system, however, made her brand of ideology super potent.

Church Mouse lacked the psychological will to stand up to conservative peers when they teased him about receiving free school lunches. He felt it was wrong to defraud the government when both parents were able-bodied breadwinners, and yet he also understood the argument that many Blacks make about a right to receive historic restitution. The choice he made to shop-borrow plus throw God in the middle of his plan was NOT the way to go about it, however. Rather than get into arguments with classmates and parents about the pros and cons of reparations and other social engineering practices, Church Mouse simply chose to forgo eating lunch for the remainder of the school year. Needless to say, his academic performance and physical health suffered. Such is life in the fragile corners of this great nation of plenty.

The convenience store episode proved to be quite the embarrassment for Church Mouse. After having time to think about his twisted reasoning, he was willing to take his punishment like a man. Regardless, it was time for the conflicted child to be delivered over to a wandering spirit. For Beulah, it was a matter of putting the entire male gender on trial—a simple issue of the big no-good-nigga passing his defects on down to the little no-good-nigga in training. Left up to Beulah's discretion, she would light a stick of dynamite and blow up all Black men except for preachers. Even if he had wanted to, the father of the home could not wash his hands of this one. In his mind, there was no excuse for stealing. "This is going to hurt me more than it is going to hurt you," the inebriated one said. The King instructed his son to take off his shirt and lie across the bed. The boy eagerly complied. The bewildered father was not sure how to react to that.

Over the years, the Ghost came to view his second son as if he were a delicate China doll—a soft guy who needed to be handled with kids' gloves. He affectionately referred to him as "Tweety Bird," after the cute little Warner Bros. cartoon character. At one time, the boy was indeed soft and defenseless, but testosterone has a way of toughening up boys as they grow into their bodies. Throughout grade school, Church Mouse was denied participation in gym classes because of a slight heart murmur that was detected at birth. Even though the problem had worked itself out by the time he turned eight, his parents continued to deny him full athletic participation at school. Beulah even forced him to sit out of Junior High School physical education classes—an embarrassment for the young lad. She didn't realize that the boy had grown up to be as strong as an ox. But his classmates knew otherwise, often teasing him about being "cock strong." [43]

In the eighth grade, Church Mouse weighed a mere ninety pounds soaking wet. But he wasn't alone. His frail body type was all too prevalent among poor Black males who grew up in the Deep South: thin, sickly, and wiry looking. Younger brothers Slim Jenkins and the Marvelous One were textbook examples of the poverty physique. Church Mouse was not far behind those two. As he aged, growth factors such as a heavier protein diet, participation in sports, and the wonderful effects of male hormones helped to fill out his gaunt frame. And thank God for the family's northern migration. In two short years, a change in environment helped the boy to rapidly acquire forty pounds of muscle. Church Mouse might also want to thank Uncle Sam for the invention of food stamps. It is something conservative readers may not want to hear, but kids of poverty are thankful for whatever respite they can get.

Throughout Church Mouse's high school years, the father never attempted to watch his son compete in athletics. He never realized that the boy was a decent wrestler and an exceptional football player—talented enough to be a Division II all-conference defensive back and punt returner, if given a chance to prove his mettle. "Did you say you were the water boy for the wrestling team?" the father joked. "Why don't you stick to women and the books and let me and your older brother do the fighting and the heavy lifting in the family?" *I got your books right here*, thought Church Mouse as he mentally yanked on his male appendages.

Proud of his newfound masculinity, Church Mouse was not about to let his father rob him of the experience of facing up to the whipping like a soldier. The image of the helpless and fragile little cartoon bird was cute, but it didn't sit with the growing teenager. He wanted to be regarded as a stud, like his older brother. Dolomite was the word of the day and machismo was the flavor of the month. Church Mouse saw the beating as a rite of passage. Enter the dragon, young blood.

Crazy Beulah reveled in the fact that she had delivered her infidel son over to the ghostly one. Like a southern-fried sacrifice. Like his father and big brother; the master hoe and his juvenile first son. And now she could add the little rodent to the mix. Three losers in a row. Throw in the other two male children of the family—Slim Jenkins and the Marvelous One—and you've got yourself a blues quintet. Line 'em up and knock their heads together like the women characters in *The Three Stooges* movies do.

Today was judgment day for the sanctified child turned shoplifter. "Crack" went the King's belt as he warmed it up for duty by striking it against the bedpost. "This is going to hurt me more than it is going to hurt you," the ghostly one repeated. Tippy-tap, ratta-tat, dink went the belt to the backside of young Church Mouse. Huh? The King of Ghosts barely applied any pressure on his son's bare back. *What's all this pansy treatment about?* the child wondered. *My father still thinks I am Tweety Bird, the cream puff. For God's sake, man, strike me hard. Make me bleed. Make me fall in such a way that I cannot get back up. Hurt me so bad that it radiates into the bones of my African ancestors*, Church Mouse cried inside.

The father became angry when Church Mouse refused to cry. His older son never did that. June Bug would at least fake crying to curtail the whipping. But Church Mouse remained stoic and steadfast. Incensed, the King increased the level of pain with each lash. Crash. Thunder. Kaboom. By the fifteenth lash, the ordeal resembled the beating of a runaway slave at the hands of a psychopathic overseer. "Ah, now that feels more like it," Church Mouse softly whispered to himself. Not once did Church Mouse cry. An occasional flinch materialized here and there, but there were no tears, no retreat. No cream puff reaction. Eighteen lashes, twenty-five. The kid was cock strong, stubborn, and proud. At thirty, the Holy Spirit grabbed the King's hand and bent his fingers backward. "Augh!" cried the perplexed traveler.

Enough is enough. Darkness cannot prevail forever. The sun must bestow its light and warmth even when the moon chooses to act stubborn and not go to bed. God had seen enough, and he intervened to stop the madness. Church Mouse got up from the bed and calmly pulled his T-shirt over his scarred back. The son was finally vindicated. Perhaps now the King would stop conferring posh nicknames on him. Maybe now they could stand together as testosterone equals.

Opportunities quickly slip away. The King's parenting ego desired to be further stroked. Testosterone posturing was the flavor of the day and Dad craved another sip or two at flexing his muscles. He reached into his bag of tricks for one last shot at parental control. "Go get my hair clippers, boy. I am going to give you a military haircut. All you young punks walk around with these big Afros acting like revolutionaries. Well, we're about to get a little patriotic around here today," snarled the man who himself was more out of breath than his wounded progeny.

Timber, timber, all fall down. Before the father's latest edict, Church Mouse stood tall like a California redwood tree. And now he was reduced to a weathered cactus lying flat faced on the ground. The Signifying Monkey has left the building. [44] Church Mouse had just endured an old-fashioned grits-and-gravy, country-style beating, and not one drop of water fell from his eyes. Not one quiver entered his voice. And yet, the thought of his father cutting his Afro provoked salvos of snot bubbles and tears. "Please, Daddy, don't cut my hair," pleaded the boy. The King of Ghosts broke into a broad smile. "I gotcha now, you little pompous prick!"

Wait just a cotton-picking minute here: Is the writer missing something? Did someone mail the wrong script to the actors in this play? Did Church Mouse forget his lines? Were his cue cards placed upside down? Memoirs generally do not read like this. If you are going to cry, make sure it happens over something major—not something as trivial as a haircut! Real soul brothers pontificate like Shaft—that famous "I am a bad mutha-shut-your-mouth" R&B record and movie guy. But no, Church Mouse passed up his opportunity to respond on cue. Instead, he chose to cry about a haircut. What a little punk ass! Now, we might have to change the entire script. Who is going to foot the bill for the rewrites?

The answer to this outrageous scenario lies in a curious urban phenomenon known as "styling and profiling." During the 1960s and 1970s, hair was more than just a fashion statement. For young revolutionaries, it was the symbol of rebellion against the establishment. People wrote popular songs about hair. Let it flow, let it flow, way past your knees. For Whites, long hair signaled the advent of the post-modern liberal. All we are saying is give hair a chance. If I had a hammer, I'd smash all the hair clippers in the world. Puff, the magic dragon, accidentally caught his hair on fire with a bong. You know the songs; you know the era.

For Blacks, long hair was a sign of a new political consciousness. It was a way of telling White folks to take their white skin and their rules and shove it. Say it loud, I'm Black and I'm proud. We're a winner. Keep on pushing. To be young, gifted, and Black. [45] Hair was "all that and a bag of chips." [46] If your Afro was perfect, that meant that you were both the chip and the dip. Hair gave young people stylish points and political clout. Most Blacks wanted to emulate the hairdo of activist Angela Davis and songwriter Billy Preston. The Afro that Church Mouse sported was perfect like theirs. It was tight, and it was right.

Unfortunately, the Black Revolution did not mean the same thing for every African American who spoke about it. While most students embraced the true cultural symbolism of the movement, too many cheapened its meaning. The importance some Blacks gave to hair and other cultural symbols at times bordered on the absurd. For example, if a soul brother came to school all "fro'd out" (i.e., sporting a perfect afro), walking with a cool limp, acting jiggy, talking jive, and dangling a different girl on the end of his arm during passing periods, his reputation swelled to cultural iconic status. Never mind that his grades were suffering.

Take that same person, however, and transform him into a short-haired, moral, tender-loving individual with a passion for academics and family values, and curiously he became socially invisible. And if the young man decided to speak mainstream English—a sure sign of selling out—he would certainly be branded an "Uncle Tom." Sorry, democrat readers, despite the brilliance of the liberal 1970s era, it was also a time of escalated learned helplessness and excruciating nonsense. While it is true that many republicans are elitist and/or racist, the lack of ideological diversity and spiritual atonement for sin has always been a liberal democrat's Achilles' heel. Do Black Americans know how to spell eclectic balance? Their forgotten history?

Like so many young people, Church Mouse was a victim of unhealthy peer pressure. He made himself believe he needed the blessings and acceptance of his classmates to be considered worthy. But the desires of his peers did not always match your boy's conservative worldview. They say choir boys are boring. The fact that he refused to smoke da chronic was a sure sign that he was a sell-out. "What a waste," fickle Ebony foxes fumed. "The funk is no longer with the Church. Only a 'Snow Bunny' would ever want him now," some of them decried. [47] Soul sistas don sackcloth and ashes and mourn another brother that went astray. As crude and controversial as this description may be, it is an accurate portrayal of the fragile state of mind for many (though not all) young African Americans growing up in the '60s and '70s.

And now the King of Ghosts wanted to strip Church Mouse of his crowning glory. Piss on his royal highness. With snot bubbles popping and tears streaming down his face, Church Mouse bolted out the door like a man shot out of a cannon. The father, an accomplished track athlete in his day, later confessed to friends that he had never seen anyone cover so much ground that fast in all his recollections. For a micro-moment, the Runner entertained the idea that his son might be a gifted athlete. *Nah, he's too skinny*, the elder concluded. *His performance is a temporary anomaly. Adrenaline can make anybody briefly run fast*, the inebriated one convinced himself. Opportunities quickly slip away.

For nearly an hour, Church Mouse aimlessly wandered the city, searching for something—anything—that would serve as a life preserver. Tears flowed like an open faucet as he shuffled and sobbed. Kids in the neighborhood laughed as he deliriously talked to himself. A female student pointed her finger and whispered, "Isn't he the geek from school who tries to date girls who are above his league?" "I got your geek right here," Church muttered to himself. He was a tired soul. His body was that of a teenager, but his soul was ancient with sorrow. His gift of insight was beginning to turn inward, and he didn't want it anymore. What good is knowledge when all it brings you is sorrow and isolation? It is time to make a tough decision, my son.

Unfortunately, the problems that Church Mouse encountered extended far beyond his immediate family. While a dysfunctional home negatively impacted the child's mental and emotional health, it was just one part of a larger problem he faced. Had it been a simple case of child abuse only, he could have gutted it out for three more semesters, said his goodbyes, and then never looked back. If only it were that simple; but his problem was much bigger. Church Mouse was an oddball in the eyes of the world. There was no place in 1970s urban America for a book-reading, conservative, religious, skinny Black virgin. That kind of person stood out like a bunny rabbit at a bobcat reunion. Everywhere the young lad turned, it was like dinner time for predators. And there always seemed to be someone of a cellophane persuasion using guilt to either co-opt or exclude him. In addition, Church Mouse was one of those sensitive, eccentric type of kids that see the world through a different lens. He had that Michael Jackson type of sensitivity about him. He rarely went along with the crowd, and he was always searching for a deeper truth. Hood homies were irritated by this. They wanted him to be more like

Dolomite or Richard Pryor. Translation: Church Mouse did not fit in, and it was time to decide his fate.

As the angel of despair descended upon Church Mouse, he decided to make one last shop-borrowing attempt. He felt bad about the decision, knowing this time he would not be able to repay his debt. In that sense, it truly would be stealing. "Piss on it," he said. Charge it to the White man's debt to the country's under-citizenry. Chalk it up to some loose definition of reparations to Black folk. Consider it an affirmative action move. Better yet, let us just call your boy what he really was: a thief, a liar, and a loser. "This is my destiny," he whispered. The final solution is never a good one, but it is hard to understand that fact when you stand alone.

Astutely avoiding the mistakes of getting caught a second time, Church Mouse successfully slipped past the cashier with a thirty-count bottle of Sominex brand sleeping pills, and a twelve-ounce can of Coca-Cola. Deliriously staggering along the streets and mumbling to himself, he made his way to City Park, just east of downtown Denver. Unsure of how to proceed with securing his demise, he spotted a large industrial trash can with a hinged lid. Before climbing in, he took a stubby pencil from his pocket, and with a scrap piece of paper from the ground, he sat on a large rock and authored the following poem: [48]

QUIVER

Imagine rose petals
Falling amongst thorns and thistles,
Or a resilient floral arrangement
Bursting through the cracks of shattered glass and broken concrete.
Like the parched throats
Of dehydrated sons and daughters,
Like a thirsty Murphy's Child
Crying out for water.
They are seldom heard.

For they are symbiotic copies

Of our ambient pedigree,

Symbolic representations

Of things never meant to be.

Like "Indian" summers in November,

Or a parent you barely remember.

Like the almost bitter taste of sweet revenge,

Or a daunting specter that seldom ends.

It is a fantastic conclusion,

Almost as if my life was an optical illusion.

That I am predisposed in sin,

That only a few languish within.

Or at least they tell me so.

Never mind that I host your insanity.

Forever in time craves a strange recipe.

A sordid concoction of inebriated lies,

Wooden nickels, and dark secrecy.

There lies the rest of me.

Battered brains and tormented hearts,

Sometimes flow.

They flow like puddles of cool velvet blood,

Seemingly relentless upon children,

The most innocent of the guilty.

Cold

Dark

Deep

Silent

Brutal

Relentless.

Oh, would that I possess

But just one ounce of strength.

Maybe then I could roll back this blade

They call loneliness.
They say I am a loser.
It is a thought
That shakes the very foundation
Of why we live.

Is the writer missing something? The typical high school student does not speak like this. They talk about fast cars, sports, tennis shoes, and pretty girls. The naughty ones talk about getting laid. But this kind of speech usually leads to terrible events such as a mass shooting at a school—an event that can so easily be avoided by utilizing more love, positive mentoring, and caring. Wake the funk up and critically think for once, America!

The swollen child with the lacerated soul swallowed all thirty pills and washed them down with a stolen can of soda pop. The poison went down as if it were a mere afterthought. Why is it that life is so hard, and death is so inviting? As the compromised child pulled the lid of the trash can over himself, he gazed out onto the neon lights of the Mile High City and said his final goodbyes. With middle finger extended, he faintly whispered, "You have murdered me."

Be done with it, you sanctimonious prick. This is what you get for going against societal norms. For being an oddball. Wallow inside your poison and dream of a different world. Pray that your sleep will not be interrupted. Let your dream have an outcome of never awakening. Run from the pain that haunts you like lingering radiation from bad social engineering. Never mind that the bones in your body throb with waves of oceanic pain. Ignore the stone in your stomach, the tension in your clenched jaw, the furrowed brow that graces the eyes that see too much. Forget your desire to crush the skull of the predator that stalks you. Your muscles are too puny, and he's got his foot dead up your ass. The time has come to finish what they started in you. Fantasize about becoming a superhero—a planet jumper of sorts. Zap your parents with the lethal rays that protrude from your angelic eyes. And when you are finished doing them in, turn the dark power that exists within you onto yourself. Do it for our sagging economy—one less mouth to feed. Do it for the brain dead—liberals and conservatives alike.

No matter how old a person gets, a lacerated soul never fully heals. The hearts of hurting children never stop bleeding even as they grow older. They try to escape the residue of the poison that seeps into the marrow of their bones, but only spiritual healing can cure that kind of injury. Come, Heavenly Father. Come, Holy Spirit. For those of us who are scarred and broken within, admitting defeat, and giving up can be so inviting even well into our adult years.

When the devil is in his moon, he can exert a powerful influence over every-day people like you and me. Empty rhetoric and political pontification wilt in the presence of the mighty one, whose reign is thankfully only for a season. Traditional church attendance might not be enough. Sorry, religious readers, there is no diplomatic way to say it: The fallen angel is an impressive foe. Although he is much less than God, he is, nonetheless, more powerful than most of us. Truth be told, he possesses the power to kick our puny asses with one hand tied behind his back, while blindfolded and hopping on a peg leg. He merely coughs, and most of us pass out. Yes, God's Word is the antidote for Satan, but we often ignore an important truth. Too many of us do not know God from a hole in the wall, thus we abdicate our authority.

When the devil is in his groove, his power is greatly increased. As long as his minions are allowed to guard the chicken coup, he will never lack for sustenance. His success comes from an ability to drain the minds of uncritically thinking parents. The strategy is easy to understand once you study it close up: Keep adults high and believing that partisan bicker-ing is the way to go. Keep the Black race hooked on drugs, alcohol, style, emotional appeal, and half-assed problem-solving strategies. Keep White folk in denial about anything real. La-la is their land of OZ. Push parents to pursue individual rights at the expense of collective responsibilities—at the expense of their children's future. At the expense of their own sanity. Wicked. Effective. Ingenious.

It is rumored that the fallen angel is part male and part female. When he sheds his monthly issue of blood, his strength increases ten-fold. It gives him the power to go in for the kill—the task of devouring innocent children. He feasts on them as if they were a box of M&M candies. They melt in his mouth and in his hand. His drink is the urine of inebriated adults. Yes, it is true that one day Satan will get what's coming to him. But we must also admit that while on earth, he has proven himself to be a formidable foe. Ole Trick Ass (first cousin to Yo Trick Ask) is a heavyweight champion in his own right, for he is the prince of darkness. He is a genius—the Count of Trickery. Sorry for this inclusion, spiritual warriors, but the rule in "da hood" is that out of respect one must give a "G" his props, even if he is a wicked Sith. Even if his heart is made of dry ice. Satan's ass is grass, and the day of the lawn mower is coming soon.

───────────────────────

Post-chapter mentoring tips for adults and help-professionals willing to stand in the gap for hurting children: Children who contemplate suicide are not mentally ill. They are not freaks of nature. They are not crybabies seeking special attention. Most of them have tried sixty-nine different remedies to their problems, and none of those options seem to work. Giving up is not a personality defect, rather it is often a result of being genuinely exhausted and confused. Instead of judging these kids, try showing them some TLC. Mentor them for goodness sake! Spend time with them and get to know them as a person. You might be surprised to find that they are some of the saner people in the world. Most of them just want to be appreciated and respected for who and what they are.

Post chapter survival tips for children who battle with suicide ideation: Unfortunately, it is true: the world is full of semi-parents and pseudo-leaders who do not know their heads from their asses. No, not every person falls into that category, but there is enough bone-headedness and self-centeredness to go around to last a lifetime. Suicidal children must find appropriate outlets for blowing off steam. It may be music, art, poetry, sports, crafts, or some other healthy hobby. *Alcohol and drugs are NOT the answer, however. Neither is martyrdom, self-pity, and self-doubt.* In a strange way, these things, too, can become a drug of sorts. Do not put your faith in counterfeit cures such as material goods or fake personas that fade in the wind. Also, hurting kids must learn to adopt a service-to-others perspective. When you are feeling low, volunteer at the local Open Door Mission or a refugee resource shelter. Doing so will help balance your global worldview and give you a broader definition of disadvantaged. Lastly, learn to believe and trust in yourself. In this narcissistic, self-centered world if you don't believe in you, no one will.

CHAPTER 6:

ARMS TOO SHORT TO BOX WITH MY SHOES

DESPITE ALL THE POSTURING AND CHEST-THUMPING THE DARK ANGEL DID on that dreadful night, God was not impressed with the devil's weak attempt to flex his muscles. On the human dance floor of life, Satan might be "the shiz-nit," but in the eyes of the Almighty, the prince of lies is nothing more than a tricked-out gigolo with no pot to piss in, nor a window to throw it out of. [49] The Good Lord knew that Church Mouse was broken and not in his right mind, so He quickly dispatched a guardian angel to make an emergency intervention. The angel stuck her index finger down the boy's throat, causing him to gag. The top of the garbage can popped open like a pent-up cork from a shaken bottle of Boones Farms wine. A violent vomiting attack followed, emptying the contents of your boy's stomach. It was a brutal yet benevolent extraction.

Church Mouse continued to purge. Ready, set, hurl. Quickly catch your breath, C-Money, because here comes the entrée: Lima beans and rice spewed all over Church Mouse's Salvation Army pants. A little pig's feet over here and some collard greens over there. It is so uncanny how even in sorrow, soul food is an integral part of the African American storyline. Wheel about, and turnabout, and jump just so. Every time I churn inside, I chuck grits so. "I guess I really am a loser," the hurting child said. "I can't even succeed at killing myself."

A police officer stopped to inquire what was going on. "Are you alright?" the gentleman asked. "Where is your coat, young man? I'd be happy to give you a ride home." The policeman knew something was wrong but could only wait for Church Mouse to volunteer information. In the end, the officer was no match for the powers of a son of a ghost. "I've got it all under control, sir. Go home to your family—they need you," the boy telepathically communicated to the officer. Mysteriously, the officer complied. The King of Ghosts taught his progeny well. "Farewell, guardian of sanity and safety. May you find a silver bullet for the enemy that stalks our children. And when you find that trick, may you also find the courage to pull the trigger," whispered the beleaguered child.

Children of the world, open your mouths like a fire hydrant and spew forth the fruits of an urban experiment gone wrong. Purge the enemy from within. Do it before the sun goes down—before the window of opportunity quickly dissipates. Let the waters within you put out the flames of social unrest. Let it flow until it covers all the broken glass in your neighborhood. The empty bullet casings. Slip and fall if you must but get back up and douse the flames of absurdity with the tears emanating from your angelic windows.

As the confused child wandered the streets of the neighborhood, the angel bent his ear. "Who are you, child, and what is your destiny? What is the meaning of your name? What is your purpose in life? What are you searching for? What is your main deficit? Why do so many people dislike you? Whom can you trust? What are you willing to sacrifice in order to obtain the peace you search for? Do you know anything about the art of solo dancing? Do you know how to do the hucklebuck? What about the boogaloo?" Whatever you do, C-Money, make it old school. None of these new-school, "booty pop," gyrating your body parts dance moves, please.

The fact that Church Mouse failed in his suicide attempt made him more determined to succeed in a follow-up attempt. He began contemplating new ways he could exit this world. God correctly ascertained that the young lad needed divine intervention if he were to have any chance at survival. The child needed a miracle. Just then, the hungry and confused kid looked down and noticed a mysterious glow overtaking his shoes. As his feet began to brighten, a sudden urge to dance came over him. The shoes began to have a mind of their own. They began moving in the manner that R&B singer James Brown made famous. Feet don't fail me now.

Although this is a true story, the finer details of what actually took place that night are fuzzy at best. Whether or not Church Mouse's shoes took on magical powers is hard to say. What portion of the episode was real, and what was imagined? What parts were brought on by the effects of a drug overdose and his manic-depressive state of mind? Even as an adult, Church Mouse struggled to string together a coherent chain of events for that night. Chances are much of it was not real. Only in Harry Potter stories do shoes and other pieces of clothing speak. The delusional child even swears that his penny loafers smoked cigars and had faces that resembled Groucho and Chico Marx. And not only did Church Mouse speak to his shoes, but they also answered him back with wisecracks and jokes! He also thought he saw the angel who rescued him do a popular dance of the day known as the four corners. Do angels have big sexy eyes and the kind of thighs that can knock a strong man to his knees? Hmmm. More than likely, your boy was higher than a kite—a result of being in an exaggerated medicated condition.

Church Mouse had little desire to dance his way out of snowdrifts, but he could not help himself. His shoes had a mind of their own. A few of the neighborhood teenagers drove by and started pointing and snickering. "You ain't got no rhythm," one of them yelled. "I got your rhythm right here," Church Mouse snapped back as he yanked on his junk. No, his response was not the typical reply one gives when you are the subject of a major miracle. But then again, how often do a pair of shoes take on a life of their own and start giving out orders? And how often do heavenly beings dressed in hot pants stop by the ghetto to rescue a young, lacerated soul?

Dance, Church Mouse. Break out in a Jackie Wilson move and slide straight into Purgatory. Do the funky penguin when you come out of your spin. Now, do that herky-jerky thing that Pentecostal church folk do when they supposedly get the Holy Ghost. Break it down with a one-two step, but do not pop and lock. No disrespect intended toward today's younger generation but doing a "booty-pop" style of dancing while calling on the name of Jesus does not seem to go together. The writer could be wrong on this tip, but Jesus seems like He is more of a Jackson 5, goose-neck, and finger-point-to-the-sky kind of guy.

The more Church Mouse walked, the more his shoes took over. He was just a passenger going along for the ride. Each time Church Mouse attempted to rest his weary soul by sitting down on a curb, his shoes began to heat up and glow, thus prompting involuntary dancing to ensue. When he complained of being tired, his shoes looked up at him and said, "You need to shut the hell up and let us save your country ass!" Jiggy. Church Mouse almost responded to the snide comment, but deep down he knew it was said in love. Let it go. Let it flow, C-Money.

Each time Church Mouse attempted to stop, the dizziness became worse. Movement made him feel better, so he continued to walk. Occasionally, he would stop and bust a dance move not because he was feeling the beat, but because his shoes were bossy little buggers. All told, Church Mouse wandered in the snow for about an hour without a winter coat. As painful as it was, the experience of wandering in the elements saved his life. It afforded him a tenuous but palpable will to live. The cold, the adrenaline, the walking, the dancing, conversing with his penny loafers, and continued vomiting helped to dissipate the poison within. It was not what his heart wanted to do, but he knew his arms were too short to box with his shoes.

Reeking with the smell of puke, Church Mouse found himself knocking on the door of a classmate who lived two blocks from his house. She did not view him as boyfriend material. Few women are attracted to men that are broken and struggling with their identity. They prefer strong savior types. Still, she had genuine concern for her friend. She took one look at him and asked, "You need a place to stay tonight, don't you?" She had prior knowledge of her classmate's dilemma and genuinely wanted to help. Church Mouse nodded affirmatively and entered in. The girl's mother began asking questions, but the daughter quickly interrupted, saying, "I've got this under control, Mama. I'll explain it to you later." Turning to Church Mouse, she ordered your boy to go upstairs and take a shower. Yes, ma'am, I'll do anything a pretty girl asks. Not being in his right mind, Church Mouse danced his way up the stairs in Jackie Wilson style. Then he stopped to take notice of his classmate's physical attributes. Stay focused, C-Money! All honor and praises to alternative healing practices, but this is no time for you to take one of your patented bird walks.

The water rained down from the showerhead like manna from heaven. Each drop fell like the fruit of a sugar tit. Slowly, the boy sucked life back into his empty soul. Through the heater vents, Church Mouse caught a whiff of leftover food being warmed up in the oven. "It is important that you eat some vittles before you lie down to sleep," said a voice as clear as someone speaking over a public address system. Frightened, Church Mouse jumped back and turned off the water. He pulled back the shower curtain and searched the room for the source of the voice. It was not his shoes speaking because he had taken them off at the front door when he entered the house. The naked child looked under the sink and in the linen closet. There was no sign of an angel or a sneaky pair of slippers that made its way upstairs. Could it be the showerhead speaking?

"We gonna throw down on some serious grub tonight," the voice continued. "Lord, is that you?" Church Mouse asked with a quivering voice. "I know I haven't been all that I should be, but I was planning on going to church next week. And I am sorry about trying to take my life back at the park. I'll try to do better next time," Church Mouse said. He waited for a response. "Are you there, Lord? God, is that you? Do you want me to eat regular food or soul food? Will Mexican food satisfy your highness?" he asked. "Is anybody there?" There was no reply. No follow-up response. No Holy Ghost reaction. No revelation. No further voice. There was only the sound of an airball. The perplexed child toweled himself off, still not knowing what to think. He was not sure whether to be amused or confused. Was he imagining things? Were the sleeping pills still messing with his mind, or was he in the midst of a miracle continued? Some might argue that Church Mouse, himself, was the miracle.

Then he started laughing out loud. "Hey, wait a minute—I know what is going on here," the conflicted kid exclaimed. "Man, that ain't nothing but my stomach making hunger noises. Ain't nobody up in dis mo-fo but me, myself, and I," he quipped. [50] "I must be trippin' all up in dis dizzy bitch. Dem drugs I took be makin' me hear all kinds of ghosts and shit. Boo, hoo, hoo, hoo," Church Mouse cracked as he spoke in exaggerated street vernacular.

It is time for you to get some serious rest, little boy. Not only are you hungry and tired, but your internal compass is way off the mark. Most Black people wait until after they eat and drink before talking crazy. You haven't even sucked on a rib or smacked on some mac. Did you sneak around and sip on some yak? And to think they said you were a strait-laced choirboy with no carnal knowledge. But right now, you are flapping like a flag in the wind with a Carolina pole stuck up your country ass! Maybe it is time for you to stand down. The job of trying to change the world can wait another day. Let another sucker do that job. Rest your head on God's lap. Lay your burden down, my son. Press your heart unto the bosom of Jesus. Make the clouds your pillow, the moon your night light. The sky your blanket. Let the gentle winds rock you to sleep.

Gather your wits for the tedious journey that awaits you, Church Martyr. Embrace the quiet that precedes the storm that lies ahead. Save your strength for the marathon race that beseeches you. All that has happened tonight is just a prelude. The gentle wind you feel now precedes a fierce encounter yet to come. The day will come when you will be forced to summon every ounce of strength to defeat the enemy that continually stalks you. So, kick off your dancing shoes and rest for a while. You are safe for now. Hush, my child. The Holy Spirit has nullified the poison within you.

Now I lay me down to sleep. I pray the Lawd my soul to keep. If the earth should quake before I wake, I pray to God that my funk ain't fake. Amen.

———————————————

The choices facing Church Mouse were crystal clear: (a) go home and face continued unhappiness, or (b) drop out of school and become an emancipated young adult headed for the streets of San Francisco. If he was ever going to run away from home, now was the opportune time to pull that trigger. After walking the neighborhood for a bit, he decided on the former. Divided and indecisive, Church Mouse gingerly walked up to the front door of the place he called home. He contemplated whether to take a hardline approach with his parents, or a more diplomatic tone. Choices, choices, choices. What Church Mouse should have done was show up with a carton of cigarettes and a fifth of whiskey as a peace offering for his dad. A couple of free bingo passes would have worked wonders in dissipating Beulah's anger. His parents might recognize their child as a consummate broker, someone they could cut a deal with.

Because Church Mouse did not have his key, he knocked on the door and waited for someone to answer. Beulah did the honors. With teeth chattering like the characters in Stepin Fetchit, plantation era movies, the kid stood before his overseer, frightened out of his underdeveloped mind. [51] Beulah eyeballed him with a sassy, neck-rotating kind of look. "I guess I'll go for the honesty approach," the boy said to himself. "What have I got to lose? Everybody has a heart. No one is hardcore twenty-four-seven." Even the devil appreciates an occasional ice water break. Surely there must be at least one rainbow in hell. Just look at the multicolored hue in the glare of your mother's eyes, Church Mouse. It is residual proof that she is multifaceted and flexible. Straighten up and fly right, you closeted liberal.

"Where the hell you been all night?" Beulah barked. The quivering child marshaled enough nerve to speak. "Mama, I tried to commit suicide last night," Church Mouse sheepishly blurted out while hanging his head in shame. Immediately, Beulah retorted, "See there, I told you that you were no good. Only a no-good, little punk-ass child would try to take the life that the Good Lord has given them!" Whoa! Come again? Please rewind the tape and tell the writer that he misheard the words of the cantankerous woman. No. The Queen of Bravado had spoken, and Her Majesty sunk to a new low. Timber, timber, all fall down. And to think she threw the Lord's name into her convolution. (Sorry, readers, but the writer needs to take one more time-out.)

WTF! What is going on here? Is this some kind of media prank? Oh, wait a minute, I get it. This is all one big setup. Any minute now, some guy is going to jump out from behind a curtain and say the phrase "Smile, you're on *Candid Camera*," right? [52] In fact, the whole Church Mouse story is probably an April Fools' joke told in January. It might not even be a real story. Admit it. This is just a publicity stunt perpetrated by Church Mouse aimed at soliciting sympathy from emotional bleeding-heart liberals. This is his attempt to introduce to the world the concept of a Murphy's Child—kids who endure setback after setback and seldom catch a break. Stop faking the funk, Church Mouse. Tell the truth and admit that you are conducting research on at-risk kids and are embellishing the facts of the story, albeit for a noble cause.

"Okay, okay. Let me tuck my shirttail in my pants so I can look halfway presentable when the camerapersons appear," the writer requested. "Alright, I think I'm ready. You can start rolling film now. Where is the TV guy?" asked the writer. He waited with eager anticipation. Church Mouse could only muster a distant gaze. He was swollen with a wry face. A tear rolled down his face, leaving behind a crevice. There was nothing Church Mouse could say. There was only the sound of silence. Like a basketball shot that was launched, but it never hit the rim. Nor did it touch the ground. There was only the sound of air. At that moment, the writer finally realized the truth, and then he, too, trenched his face. Hello, darkness, my old friend.

What is it about this script that keeps it from following a logical and caring path? Why is everything so dismal when describing the life of a Murphy's Child? Could it be that *Leave It to Beaver* type families only exist on TV? [53] Are they only real for White folks who live in rural areas and in the suburbs? Do inner city children need floodlights to help them find a way out of their abyss? Is there a wormhole in the void between hell and the ghetto that children can escape through? Is there really something behind door number one, or is someone trying to slip readers the "green weenie"? Is Church Mouse fabricating the whole story? Is the writer embellishing the facts in hopes of increasing book sales? Are there really rainbows in hell? Trace it.

Face it. There is a slight possibility that Beulah might have been using reverse psychology. An inconsiderable chance, yet possible. In her distorted view of reality, this might have been her way of making her son toughen up— preparing him for the harsh world he was about to inherit. If you tell young boys over and over that they are wannabe criminals and worthless, maybe they will become angry enough and go full-tilt the opposite direction just to prove naysayers wrong. Yes, that has got to be the answer; the way to make a Black man strong is to constantly tell him that he is weak—just like how the system treated Young Malcolm X! If this is what Beulah had in mind, then we might have to conclude that sista girl is a guru—a transcendent being of mental superiority. Maybe, just maybe, Beulah wasn't crazy after all. She might be a psychological genius. A riverboat gambler. Please say it is so, even if you must fake it.

Shake it. The response Crazy Beulah gave her son reverberated in Church Mouse's eardrum like an earthquake registering 10.0 on his Richter scale. About this time, most kids would have folded, and young Church Mouse, too, was on his way down. But just then his shoes began to glow again. God may not come when you want Him to, but He's always there right on time. The shoes made Church Mouse jump up and do the camel walk. Beulah was mystified by the boy's behavior. Then the tide suddenly turned. "It's my turn to play. Enough of this ignorant, sin-ridden, poverty mess," the Almighty snarled. One wave of God's hand, and up from the ashes of Beulah's thermonuclear babbling sprung a new creation. Like singer Michael Jackson, a new child came up from the floor all shiny and renewed. Miraculously, the boy was transformed from a loser into a conqueror—glimmering in the inner-city tradition but separated and hardened by the fires of absurdity.

Like a brick upside the head, the truth about child abuse and social ambivalence caught Church Mouse squarely between his eyes. Wait a minute. Now I get it! he said to himself. "I finally understand what is going on here. I am not crazy after all. In fact, I might be one of the saner people around. The people running this house are the ones who are crazy! And the folks at school may not have all it together either. Come to think of it, the people who run this country appear to be loosely wrapped. And all this time I thought I was the problem," exclaimed the rejuvenated child. Suddenly, the pieces of the puzzle began flying into place. *Sometimes when people are not what they ought to be, they overcompensate by making you believe that you are the one who is lacking.* Mercy, Lord.

Church Mouse began dancing as if there was no tomorrow. James Brown would have been proud of his superbad protégé. Beulah gazed at the mysterious behavior and asked, "Are you on drugs or suh-in? Do you need to see a shrink?" she asked. "No, I don't need a doctor. All I need is a beat. Hit me on the one, Baby Girl!" the teenager cried out loud. Beulah was baffled to say the least. It was one of the few times in life she was speechless.

This incident marked a seminal day in the development of the man we have come to know as Church Mouse. It was in this moment that he evolved from being a loser into a change agent. At last, he discovered his true calling in life, but the celebration was bittersweet because daylight immediately began to French-kiss darkness and they shared tongue. This is the day that Church Mouse nobly entered the human relations twilight zone. Here is a toast to your new awareness but be assured problems will not suddenly sprout legs and run away. But for now, get up on your feet and P-A-R-T-Y like it is Independence Day, C-Money. Shoes don't fail me now!

The boy's father ordered him to his room. Church Mouse took a Gene Kelly [54] leap up three stairs, turned around, and did a Chuck Berry [55] gooseneck move. Then he let out a Little Richard "Shut up" and winked his eye to accentuate his point. [56] The King of Ghosts cut his eyes toward the blasphemous child. "Boy, are you mocking me?" he asked. The King then took off his belt and headed upstairs to take care of business.

There on the bed lay Church Mouse kicking his feet in bicycle motion and deliriously laughing. Momentarily baffled and frightened, the father stood mystified by the odd behavior. "Are you sick, son?" the ghostly one inquired. "Tah hee-hee," the sanctified one responded. "Speak to me with real words, boy. Are you mental? Maybe we should take you to see a psychiatrist," responded the concerned king of runners. Church Mouse continued to bounce and giggle. "It's okay, Daddy," he replied. "Everything is fine. Now that I've found the beat, I'm going to bust a move and make you proud. I will be a good boy from this point on. I now understand what I need to do. I know how to be happy now. Everything is copacetic. You and Mamma will have no more trouble out of me," Church Mouse assured his father.

The dumbfounded parent paused to catch his composure. "Well, okay, Baby Brother. Just as long as you don't flip out and go crazy on us. And you better not cause any more trouble around here," he snapped. Remembering the reason Church Mouse ran away from home in the first place, the King turned his attention to a task left undone. "Now, go get my hair clippers. I'm still gonna cut that Afro and make you look more Air Force presentable," he snarled. Church Mouse bounced up, and eagerly complied. The Ghost scratched his head. Beulah did an unholy ghost dance as the boy's hair hit the floor. She swept up the remains and discarded it with honor.

When you live in the Twilight Zone, something like a botched suicide attempt can have a long-range positive impact if you are good at turning lemons into a refreshing drink. But you must be part Houdini to pull it off. As Church looked inward, both healthy and unhealthy habits began to develop. In one sense, he began to heal and grow inside. For the first time he looked in the mirror and liked what he saw. And yet at the same time, he became melancholier and more distant than ever before. It is an easy predicament to fall into if you've been raised to be an island adrift. Why try to understand a world that is turned upside down? Why breathe when you can exhale? But how can a person experience spiritual growth and emotional disintegration at the same time? How does one acquiesce, and yet still win? How can you have daylight and darkness at the same time? In Crazy Beulah's zip code, any and every result is possible.

Shhh! Can you hear your own words, Church Mouse? Do you believe in the messages captured in the many songs that you have composed over the years? What about the ones titled *No Man is an Island, Do You Care for Me,* and *Solo Dancing*? Can you feel the rush that comes from a perfect dance routine performed in isolation? Do you applaud yourself, or do you maintain silence when you come out of your James Brown spin? Do you experience love, or do you hear crickets? Can you get with the naked groove of a dirty little secret? And if they knock you to the ground, you know where to find your freedom. You know where to find your peace.

So low? Solo!

———————————————

Out of respect for the new toughness the King of Ghosts saw in his second son, he decided to no longer call him soft names like Tweety Bird and Spankie Dankie. From that day forward, Dad referred to his second son as "Baby Brother." The new moniker made young Church Mouse feel strong and vindicated. Finally, he could stand on equal ground with his older brother June Bug. Big favors sometimes come in small packages. But the die had been cast, and there was no turning back. From the eleventh grade on, Church Mouse embarked on a strange quest of pursuing philosophical opposites—one that embraced tremendous insight and spiritual growth on one hand, and yet physical and emotional turmoil on the other hand. His evaporated baby face was replaced by a question mark. It was then that he first acquired the scowl on his brow that became his signature adult look.

Some people call Church Mouse's response to child abuse, racism, and learned helplessness a form of self-imposed martyrdom. Hood homies call it stupidity. "Why waste time trying to change a world that doesn't want to be changed?" asked one skeptic. "Wouldn't it be simpler to just go along for the ride and have as much fun as you can during your younger years? You can always get religion when you grow older. For now, you could smoke da chronic, sip on some yak, slap a few booties, and party your ass off! That way you get the best of both worlds. Have fun now, and plan for a life with Jesus later when your testosterone levels fade," one of his homies posited. Perhaps there is merit to that philosophy for some people, but when a person becomes the property of God, such options are summarily squashed. For Church Mouse, they did not exist, even if he had wanted them to. Every time he contemplated taking the half-assed or selfish route, his guardian angel would show up and knock him to his knees.

Thankfully, the teenager never made a second attempt on his life. He contemplated it several times as an adult but was able to snap out of it each time the fallen angel descended upon him. Had it not been for a pair of magic shoes and an intense dislike for Lucifoot's voodoo, Church Mouse would have easily become another ghetto statistic. He used as a new coping mechanism the idea of becoming a social and political activist. Earlier, Church Mouse would have never hung out with a radical crowd. After the failed suicide attempt, radical dissentient students nurtured and befriended him. For the first time, it felt like he had found a true family. He joined a controversial music group that patterned itself after the popular underground political rap group known as the Last Poets. [57] Their music urged Blacks to keep your eye on Whitey's trick ass. It was a temporary growth stage that did not represent Church Mouse's true politics, but he had to experience it as part of his overall American socialization process.

Church Mouse was the group's percussionist and a background singer. He and his venom-spewing cohorts emulated every word of The Last Poets' style, from stage mannerisms to harsh language that referred to majority group members as "dogs" and "White devils." The group also had words for boneheaded Blacks who were overly motivated by sex, wine, and partying at the expense of the Black Revolution. They were viewed as sell-outs. Narcissistic types who unconcerned about social justice from all races and ethnic groups were also on trial. Curse words and inflammatory rhetoric were an integral part of the musical genre. Surprisingly, the administration allowed the group to give performances during school assemblies. The group successfully invoked their First Amendment right of political speech as their defense.

Interestingly enough, Church Mouse's reputation amongst his peers took a sudden and dramatic upward turn. Like a shooting star bursting onto the Mile High City skyline, Church Mouse went from school nerd to political superstar overnight. High school students of all colors were ready to reject conservative and suburban values that were not yielding results for People of Color. People at the local level began to embrace the revolutionary thought expressed at the national level. White male students were in awe of the group because of their honesty and bravado. It probably also had a little to do with the fear of a rising Black planet. Cool Black students who normally did not spend time talking to Church Mouse would now walk up and give Church Mouse an exotic homeboy handshake. What it be like, bro-ham. Popular ebony foxes who would not have given him the time of day were suddenly interested in his new swag. An adoring group of White girls even started buying things for him. Because Church Mouse had a cross-cultural reputation, he was viewed as the safer member of the group to be interviewed. It is amazing what a few "kiss my ass Richard Nixon" comments and "Whitey better hide tonight" statements can do for a soul brother who is low on popularity and self-esteem.

The message emanating from the group was decidedly angry and separatist. It pleased the Black student body at East High School but concerned faculty members. Teachers were alarmed by the sudden transformation of the student they once considered the perfect role model. In their eyes, he was one of the "good Blacks," and they had plans for his life, but now they were not so sure. His grades began to suffer, and for the first time in all his schooling, he received grades of D and C on his report card. And of course, the low grades were in math and science classes. In a span of one month, Church Mouse metamorphosed into a person with a split personality. On one hand, he was a venom-spewing radical, yet on the other hand, he became intrigued with another experimental fancy: White fundamental religion. Go figure. It was a predictable response to the mixed messages given to youth during the 1970s.

Church Mouse became adept at living in two worlds: daylight and darkness. Praise the Lord and pass the gun. Pray for world peace, but also keep that White devil in check! To his credit, not once did he ever commit an act of violence. He was a disciple of Martin Luther King Jr., and that fact helped to preclude him from pursuing a darker path. He was, however, captivated by the philosophies of Malcolm X, Huey P. Newton, and other radical Black leaders. Zealously studying their words, he discovered the intellectual side of the Black Revolution.

It was also during this era that Church Mouse acquired an affinity for the music of Marvin Gaye, Curtis Mayfield, and Sly Stone. Gaye's award-winning album *What's Going On?* was the perfect medicine for at-risk teens asking critical social justice questions. It came at an ideal time. Too bad no one ever answered Mayfield's question as to why Freddie from *Superfly* had to die. That question still lingers today. The lyrics of Sly Stone provided Church Mouse with the keys to survival. Sly's music was steeped in the topic of how to overcome haters and frauds. Repeatedly, sometimes as much as twenty times in succession, he played the two anthems that provided him hope: "Stand" and "Everyday People." Upon the shoestrings of a few protest songs, a newfound love for writing poetry, a curiosity to know God in a deeper way, and the power of a mystical pair of shoes—on these few factors hung the youngster's fragile will to live.

At home, Church Mouse did all his chores and obeyed every rule—even the unreasonable ones. To keep the peace, he played the game, but it was all a smoke screen. He was singularly focused on the most important task of his life: the day he would leave home and gain independence. The circle was now complete. Like his father, young Church Mouse had finally evolved into a full-fledged ghost—a disengaged person who was ready to run at the drop of a hat. The only difference between the father and the son was that the younger was a friendly ghost seeking someday to become a change agent. The elder was a wandering spirit.

———————————————

The best part of this story was not that your boy's shoes danced him to salvation, but what took place the following day after his suicide attempt. The female friend who took Church Mouse in for the night had enough wisdom to go into her counselor's office and report the incident. Because Church Mouse was admired by school faculty and because they secretly knew that he lived in a dysfunctional home, several of them got together and decided to stand in the gap and become surrogate parents to the hurting child. Even with his experimentation with political radicalism, concerned educators understood what was really going on behind the scenes. They understood that some homes are not places of love and nurturance. They knew Church Mouse would implode unless he received specialized attention.

While prayer works wonders for at-risk children, hands-on mentoring and love can perform miracles of greater value. It was a blessing when teachers went the extra mile and did things like slipping the kid a couple of bucks for lunch. Because Church Mouse chose not to use his free and reduced lunch ticket for the remainder of his junior year, the monetary help he received from teachers was greatly appreciated. Educators also built up his self-esteem by getting him involved in extracurricular events and encouraging him to run for student senate, which he successfully won for the next year. Church Mouse was especially proud when he was picked as one of two students to attend the Colorado Boys State student government conference. The attention he received from his mentors felt like salve to a festering wound. Who would have ever thought that love and a little TLC would have more healing power than a pair of magical shoes?

We have all heard about kids that like school so much they refuse to go home at night. If allowed, they would stay there forever. This can be both a bad and a good sign. If the reader takes nothing else from this manuscript—if most of the lessons in this book are ignored—there is one message that must pierce your heart before you lay this work down and move on with your life. And, that message is: When a child is forsaken by their parents and siblings, by friends, by poverty, by racism, by the government, by religion, and by his/her own racial group—when the entire world has turned its back on them—hurting children can still be saved if just one caring adult mentor engages them. *Oftentimes, it is an educator at school who becomes the primary difference maker in deciding whether a Murphy's Child succeeds in life or falls through the cracks of society*. One caring adult can make a world of difference to a hurting child in need. Of all the post-Biblical miracles known to humankind, this one is the greatest.

———————————

Banana Babe shook her husband until he agreed to wake up and stand to his feet. "What is wrong with you today?" she asked. "Tell me the truth. Have you been drinking? Are you sick? Do you need me to drive you to the hospital? You have not been acting your normal self lately, and I'm beginning to worry," said the concerned wife. Church Mouse knew he had to think fast to conceal his heavy intake of medication. Understanding that he needed to deflect suspicion away from himself, Church Mouse responded with a snappy "Hit me on da one, yu sexy thang. Now, come ova here and bust me a slob, Baby Girl. [58] And while you at it, let me get a taste of sum-a-dem yams, so's I can gets my sexy on." [59]

Banana Babe covered the ears of her youngest daughter and rushed her out of the bedroom. After closing the door, she placed her left hand on her hips in sassy soul sista fashion and broke out in a broad smile. "So, is that's what's wrong with you? You just need a little bit of me to help you feel better," she said. "Girl, just laying eyes on you would make a blind man talk about wanting to see again," Church Mouse cleverly responded. "Boy, yu so crazy," Banana Babe replied as she tried to hold back the fear that there was a deeper issue left unrevealed. "You get a little frisky when you're tired, don't you? Go back to bed with your silly self before you make me to turn you out all up in this mug," she replied.

Bingo! Banana Babe had just been served a dish of smooth psychology, and it came with a side order of chicken-fried truth and red Kool-Aid to boot. Do fries come wit dat sanctified cover up? Because Church Mouse was able to think fast on his feet, the incredible scar that he harbored within was kept sheltered. His dirty little secret remained protected. Through sleight of hand, the funk was successfully faked.

The circle was now complete. All power and praises to his father, the King of Ghosts. He may not have been the best role model to his son, but his ability to teach his progeny the art of illusion was nothing short of legendary. There is a good chance that the father, too, was not properly raised and mentored by his parents and elders.

Post-chapter mentoring tips for parents, educators, and counselors: It bears repeating over and over. Of all the lessons the reader can garner from this book, there is one that towers far above all others. When traditional institutions like family, schools, social services, police, government, and even churches fail our children, *the involvement of one caring and engaged adult into the life of a hurting child can make all the difference.* Yes, healing and remediation should start in the home, but it cannot end there. Sometimes it takes a village to raise a child. A loving and caring (related or non-related) mentor can change the lives of children who are on the verge of exiting this life. Educators must become more aware of students who are bullied at school. They are easy to spot because they tend to sit by themselves in the lunchroom or on the playground. Please do not let them drift by themselves. Get them engaged in meaningful activities. Please keep in mind that there is an official curriculum and an unofficial one. The latter is more important than you think. Teachers must do more than just impart academic knowledge and skills. They must also empower students to self-actualize and thrive despite adversity. And always remember the axiom that says ALL OF THE STUDENTS IN THE SCHOOL BUILDING ARE YOUR KIDS. Not just the ones assigned to your classroom.

Post-chapter survival tips for children who battle with depression and suicide ideation: In an ideal world, an adult mentor should swoop into your life and rescue you when trouble shows up. Unfortunately, for some Murphy's Kids, that scenario will never happen. Sometimes the only person you will be able to count on is YOU. This is a sad statement, but it is true. It is also important for you to realize you may not be the main problem at all. Sometimes it is a situation where you might be one of the few sane people left in an insane world! Stand for what is right, even if you are hurting and discover that you will have to stand alone. Learn to adopt a stubborn refuse-to-lose mentality. Sometimes you must take the rope provided to you, tie a big knot at the end of it and hang on. The Bible says, "Weeping may endure for a night, but joy cometh in the morning," [**Psalm 30:5**]. There is a guardian angel assigned to watch over each one of us. Always remember even though certain people may abandon you, *you are loved and you are not alone.*

CHAPTER 7:

ARE YOU SURE YOU WANT SUM-A-DIS?

STUMBLING INTO THE LIVING ROOM, THE KING OF GHOSTS ASKED HIS SON to go get him a pack of smokes (i.e., cigarettes) from the nearest liquor store. Digging into his pockets, he realized he had less money than he had first thought. "Hey, Baby Brother, can you spare a brother fiddy-cents?" the inebriated one asked his teenage son. "Yes, Daddy," said Church Mouse as he reached out to brace the fall of his staggering father. It was Church's last bit of change he had secured from cashing in empty pop bottles, but he didn't mind.

"What is a nigga 'pose to do," the King lamented. "I met this one dame at the club last night, and I paid her good money, thinking she was going to give me some nice action. Man, I got gypped! I wasted my money on that girl. I was hoping for some juicy pussy, but all I got was some old soggy shit. I would have been better off buying a month's supply of smokes. You know what I mean, Bubba Bean?" asked the wavering King. "Gimmie five, Baby Brother," the inebriated father urged his son. The Ghost swung wildly in the air, attempting to prove that the alcohol in his system had not affected his coordination. He missed the point of contact by a mile.

The family had moved from the single-family home they occupied at 18th and Vine streets into the housing projects in the poorer Five Points section of town. It was a downward move financially, and one that put Church Mouse further away from East High School. If he were not given a ride or bus fare, he would have to walk about thirty-five blocks each way to and from school compared to the three block trek he was formerly used to. He made the decision to stay enrolled at East High instead of transferring to nearby Manual High School for his senior year. He was elected to student council at East and wanted to serve out his term. He had one summer to figure out his transportation issues.

Meanwhile, fulfilling the King's request was easy. The Five Points section of Denver had a glutton of outlets selling many brands of social dysfunction. Cognitive dissonance and cultural poison ruled the day. Social dysfunction was normalized in Denver's ghetto. That area of town is now gentrified, but back in the 1970s liquor and cigarettes stores were on every corner. The father's habit of heavy drinking, combined with chain-smoking and hoe chasing, was a set of behaviors viewed as acceptable by the many burnt-out male souls who called Five Points their home. The debate between conservative pundits who say the location of social problems is in the person versus liberal thinkers who highlight faulty systems is a false polemic. *If reform does not happen simultaneously at both levels,* failure will be inevitable.

The child's disorientation was not from being thrown off by his father's admission of infidelity to his wife, nor was Church Mouse surprised that his father was stone drunk. Over the years, he had grown to suspect the former and expect the latter. At the age of seventeen, Church Mouse—although still a virgin—had grown accustomed to the locker room talk of his male peers. Conversations about sexual prowess did not throw him for a loop as they did when he was younger. In fact, the topic was beginning to pique his curiosity. What challenged the boy on that day was that his dad rarely spent quality time talking to him about intimate or personal topics the way he did with his older son. The younger son yearned to learn more about his father's hopes and dreams. Sometimes, the King would convey bits and pieces when he was drunk, but it mostly came out as gibberish. When the King was sober, he did little more than nod his head and say, "Wuz up, Baby Brother?" An occasional "Are you still hitting the books?" would proceed from his mouth, but little meaningful conversation followed.

The closest Baby Brother ever got to his father was during the times the elder needed a back rub. The King voiced approval of his son with pleasurable grunts and groans, but rarely did those syllables turn into meaningful sentences. Sometimes, the King followed up by giving Church Mouse a dollar, but seldom did he spend quality time conversing with his son. In fact, the father rarely looked his son in the eyes. Perhaps the boy reminded him too much of what he was not—of what he could have become. Instead, he would give his son a quick pat on the back, then rush out the door to the local bar. As the man of the house climbed into his carriage, his wife would yell out the front door, "Tell all dem hoes I got my eye on them and you." These were creative conversations and colorful times.

Today was supposed to be different, however. It was supposed to be a day of redemption—a chance for lost souls to share a moment of communion. A time when father and son would swap boy talk with one another. It did not have to be a deep conversation. A moment of meaningless dialogue about any subject would do—the weather, the Denver Nuggets basketball team, the Denver Broncos football team, Batman, Muhammad Ali, Jesse Jackson, Jackie "Moms" Mabley, or even a conversation about poontang if the King happened to be hard-up for a topic to speak on. Daddy had yet to deliver the traditional father–son talk about sex, so this was as good a time as any to learn the remaining aspects of the birds and the bees that Church had not already learned from the streets. The scene was set, and the mood was right.

The fact that the son became privy to disreputable information he knew would rightfully send his mother off the deep end was not what bothered the young lad. The real underlying problem was more tragic: Church Mouse returned from the store with great anticipation, only to find his father sprawled over the bed dead asleep. In short, there would be no moment of meaningful nor superficial father–son communication. No guy connection. No testosterone talk. No sports flexing. No male grunts and exotic hand-shakes. No sex education. No scandalous talk. Not even the sound of a brick hitting against the rim of life. There was only the sound of silence. As a result, the father and son who barely knew each other continued their drift apart.

A few cockroaches ran across the King's left shoulder. The crusty creatures mistakenly made themselves believe they had special privileges in Beulah's various homes. They thought they had home-girl status with her. Church Mouse gently pried the girly magazine from his father's hand and began fanning the critters away with it. He covered his dad with a blanket made of holes, and then went to his room and began looking at college catalogs.

The next morning brought a new round of hope. Although the King was not completely sober—it usually took him a couple of days to completely dry out—he at least was not semi-comatose as he had been the day before. In fact, he could be quite a delightful and entertaining guy when he was only half-drunk. "Come on down and talk to me about college," Dad called upstairs to his son. The boy's heart quickened. He was anxious to discuss his ticket out of town.

For a brief time, the King caught a clue and began spending quality time with his son doing such things as planning for college and teaching him how to drive a car. They say that each storm brings with it a chance for a rainbow. On this day, the King informed his son of a secret stash of money of which his wife had no knowledge. It was retirement money that was set aside for a deserving child's college tuition. The King spoke of good grades, obe-dience, responsibility, and staying out of trouble as the criteria he would use to determine which child received the award. Because young Church Mouse was the child that best fulfilled those requirements, the King announced that the scholarship money was tabbed for him. The father's desire was to enroll his son in the US Air Force Academy, located just a couple hours down the road in Colorado Springs. Dad's professional contacts as a career serviceman, along with his son's cumulative GPA, seemed enough to clear any entrance hurdles that might arise. All that was needed was to get good grades and work out admission details. "Praise the Lord. I can almost taste my freedom," Church Mouse whispered. Suddenly, life began looking rosy for the hard-luck child. It always does when it is viewed through wine-colored glasses.

Most of the King's promises had a way of vanishing into thin air. This was one of the criticisms that his first and second wives leveled against him. He was a good man, but his follow-through was shaky even on a good day. Enter the disappearing rabbit trick for a Murphy's Child. Church Mouse was crushed when he discovered a new truth about his father: The college nest egg was nothing more than a fabrication. Before the promise had a chance to materialize, it evaporated into thin air. The father may have believed that someday his ship would come in. Maybe he drank up the college fund. Or perhaps he fudged on the truth believing educational financing would materialize after he had discussions with the right people. Maybe the King had a special racehorse or a greyhound race dog that was going to do him right. Someday. One day. Never mind. Wooden nickels can't even buy bubble gum smokes.

Church Mouse was too naïve to understand that inebriated promises are no match for big dreams. He was too young to understand that by street standards, good guys finish last. Punk-assed nerds who get good grades and recite the pledge of allegiance have few inheritance rights according to 1960s and 1970s inner-city rules. Organizations such as the NAACP and the Urban League certainly do not honor that view of life, but the perspective in the streets do not always line up with forward-thinking Blacks and time-honored institutions. It did not take Church Mouse long to figure out the devastating effects of alcoholism and what it can do to even the stateliest of men. A few insignificant words here and some fragile promises there never hurt any-one, right? A year later when it came time for college, there were zero funds available. It was all a mirage. If the King had just said nothing at all, there never would have been any letdown.

A porcupine can never be passed off as a bunny rabbit. Caca only flows in one direction. Lipstick kisses beseech the Ides of March. Inner-city children crash and burn. Things fall apart.

Denver nights are known to get rather cool, even in the dead of summer. Sometimes the wind whips down from the Rocky Mountains, sending a chilling reminder that cuts to the bone. Just like a hawk descending on baby chicks, stormy weather can come in a variety of forms in a Rocky Mountain minute. On one particular night during the summer of 1971, there was an unusual amount of activity descending from the mountaintop. It was only a temporary inconvenience for Church Mouse, who was feeling a mile high. Flirting with pretty women and making the right moves on the dance floor made your boy feel like he was on top of the world. The sensation of sipping Boone's Farm wine and floating on air can mitigate one's perception of what is real and what is not. And, if your favorite girl happens to be out on the dance floor throwing everything she's got at you, the night becomes that much more enchanting.

All the hype and fanfare of a neighborhood house party was not enough to keep destiny from tugging at your boy's heart. Something was missing, but Church Mouse could not put his finger on it. All the right variables were securely in place. The room was jumpin' and the girls were bumpin.' Sly Stone was thankin' and his Family was thumpin' all across the open sky. The smell of sweet perfume and Mad Dog 20/20 wine permeated the room, a place that was filled with fine honeys. Fellas in the house bark if you know anything about that. Church Mouse was dressed to the nines with a fro that was kickin.' Ebony foxes in skin-tight jeans with big eyes and luscious thighs were laced along the walls. Lord, have mercy. Give a brother some smelling sauce. Slap him before he becomes comatose!

And don't forget about that special girl on the other side of the room who had that inviting look in her eyes. "Can I interest you in something? Would you like to sample sum-a-dis?" her eyes kept asking Church Mouse. "Here, kitty, kitty, kitty. Please drop that lame excuse of a man you've been hanging with all night and come on over here with C-Money. Throw in a pump and a bump when you brush up against me, girl. Pow, pow, pow! Ah, yeah, baby. I bet I know who that dance move was meant for. Say what? You want to teach me how to do the four corners the proper way? Now that's what I'm talkin' 'bout!" Church Mouse imagined saying in his mind. He may have been a virgin, but he was seventeen and jacked up on testosterone. Even a blind man would have smacked his lips over the delicious morsel that was beckoning him!

Despite pretty girls, raging hormones, and lots of great music, there still was something not right about the night. None of what usually transpires at your typical teenage house party seemed to hold Baby Brother's attention. Something mysterious kept pulling at him. He could not put his finger on it, but it felt like a seismic shift was about to happen in his life. Thinking it must be a temporary condition, he continued to fake the night away. Tell your magic shoes that it is time to funky up, C-Money. But why were they so quiet? Did his penny loafers have something against the new brand of funk music that hit the early 1970s scene? Perhaps the popping of bass guitar strings was too radical. A stank attitude, those two sometimes had.

Little did our star child realize that when he came out of his David Ruffin spin his life would take a sudden and drastic turn. Rubbing his eyes and shaking his head in disbelief, he noticed that the people dancing and whirling all around him suddenly looked different. It scared the living daylights out of your boy. The scene grew progressively worse each time he strained to refocus. At first, the people on the floor looked like trees dancing. Eventually, they took on the form of Munchkin-like characters from the Wizard of Oz. He rubbed his eyes again only to find that the kitty cat lady he was dancing with now appeared to be a hungry lioness! "Are you sure you can handle this?" her eyes growled. Whoa!

Do not even bother to rub your eyes anymore, Church Mouse. It is time to split this joint. Who knows, maybe this party is not the right place for you to be. Maybe Denver is the wrong city for you. This planet may not be the right place for you to be either. Perhaps you just don't belong. All night long you have felt out of place. Maybe God is trying to tell you something. Besides, it is getting late, and you have an appointment back at the crib with your kinfolk Uncle Government Cheese and Auntie Powdered Milk. Those two were a godsend for poverty kids; still, he gave Church Mouse constipation while she gave him the runs. Hanging his head, Baby Brother set out to begin the long trek to his new home across town in Five Points.

"Hey, sweet thang, don't leave yet. I've got a little surprise for you," called the kitty cat so deliciously described by Church Mouse that it almost made the writer want to put down his pen and dive into the pages of the manuscript. Focus, please. But Church Mouse did not hear the beauty's call. He has a habit of turning inward when heaven beckons. God had plans for Church, and losing his virginity that night was not one of them. Sometimes God saves us by taking away the sweet taste of temptation and leaving behind a saltine cracker desire. Repeatedly, the Almighty stepped in and guided him during times he could not even find an obvious nut laying on the ground. Will somebody, please reach over and slap some sense into your boy? This was the type of girl that he had wished for but she had always escaped his reach. He is going to kick himself Monday when the fellas start teasing him about blowing her off. Never mind, it is too late. Selah, selah. Your boy has gone inside himself, and it will be a while before he returns.

As the music faded in the distant milieu, the transformation emerged completed. Like his father, he had a ghostly characteristic about him—albeit the friendly kind. That desolate feeling that preceded his failed suicide attempt six months earlier jumped on his back again that night. Like stink stuck on poop, it was thick and saturating. Searing. Silent. Compelling. Familiar. Familial. Unspoken tears flowed from within as Church Mouse walked and mumbled to himself, "Who am I? What am I? Where am I going? If I succeed in getting there, what will it all mean?"

The young lad purposely took the long way home by turning the forty-five-block trek home into sixty-five blocks. He needed the extra time to think. Besides, he was not that eager to go home and greet the family roaches. All things being equal, disrespect must be delivered decently and in order. It is outlined that way in the book of blue funk. Yes, the party was not satisfying, but neither was anything at the place he called home. For Church Mouse to stretch the limits of his curfew, he would have to walk around in circles, covering the same ground over and over. Does this sound familiar to anyone?

Enter psychological bravado as a cure for what ails a broken child. Church Mouse yanked on his junk and yelled out into the night sky, "I don't need none of you bitches. All y'all can kiss my country ass!" "Funk you," an older White lady yelled back at him from her front porch rocking chair. He quickly apologized, and then saluted her. She was grooving on a song by a new group called Earth, Wind, and Fire. It was tight. But what's up with all this street bravado and isolationist talk? Aren't we taught that everybody needs somebody? Church Mouse rubbed his eyes again when he thought he heard the sexy kitty cat calling his name from a nearby bush. It was just a stray coon. "Oh, I get it" the weary child said. "Ole Trick Ass must be up to his ploys again. Will somebody please slip that mother function a mickey. Make him swallow a pill so big that it will make him study war no more," Church Mouse demanded. Say what? Lucifoot is really a go-go-boot-wearing female in disguise? It is time for bed, Church Mouse. Your objectivity is seriously compromised. You cannot continue to walk in circles all night. You have been retracing too many of your previous steps, and it is beginning to affect your sensibilities.

Roll on up to the crib, C-Money, and hear a familiar sound piercing the night air: "Don't touch me, you two-timing hoe," a female voice screamed. "Don't make me come over there and snatch yo crazy ass up," replied a male voice. "I promise you I will cut a mutha-fucka if eee eva lay a hand on me," said the woman. "Are you sure you want a piece of me? Are you sure you want sum-a-dis?" responded the male voice. Church Mouse paused momentarily, then quickly came to his senses. "Oh, it's just Mom and Dad immersed in another one of their ongoing 'negotiations.' I wish those two bobbleheads would get it together," mumbled the young lad as he climbed the stairs to his bedroom.

Do not even stop to acknowledge one ounce of the foolishness you hear coming from your parents, C-Money. Keep your eyes on the ultimate prize—the day you can bust out of this joint. Keep your mind focused on the saner things in life. Walk right past your parents and go straight to your room. Put on your jammies, say your prayers, and call it a day.

"Baby Brother, I want you to come in here right now," an irritated father yelled out to his son. "Your mom and I have something important to ask you." Church Mouse's heart quickened. His magic shoes looked up at him and shouted, "What are you waiting on, dude? Take your boonkey into the room and see what's percolating in the family coffee pot!" [60] "Look us both in the eye and tell us which one has been the better parent to you," scowled the King of Inebriation. "Don't be afraid. Go ahead and spit it out!" the King insisted. The stunned and confused child did not know how to respond. At first glance, there was no advantage in the boy answering the question at all. An injudicious response would make him that much more the loser. The most truthful answer could have easily gone something like "It's a coin toss as to which one of you is worse. One of you has a heart made of stone, and the other is often disengaged and intoxicated. Sometimes I feel like am the parent and you guys are the children." That answer would have been accurate, but it would have incurred the wrath of both parents, so scratch that option.

If Church Mouse stated that Beulah was the better role model, he would disappoint Dad, who was fighting on his behalf. On the other hand, if he said the King was better, it would crush his mother's fragile ego and make it appear that she bore the sole blame for all the dysfunction in the home. The son took all of a millisecond to peer into his father's eyes. It is astounding what one can find on the way to the heart of an empty soul. Battered brains and tormented hearts sometimes flow like puddles of Kool nicotine residue and Jack Daniel's waterfalls. Life-snatching fluids relentlessly flowing inside the chief of players. Cold. Dark. Silent. Relentless. Echoes of social commentary gushed forth until Baby Brother finally pinpointed what he was looking for. And there it was—that ole familiar look in his father's eyes. The teenager suddenly saw an opportunity about to slip away. *Daddy is about to leave town for yet another one of his extended vacations*, Church Mouse surmised. *This time, I plan on leaving with him*, he thought.

The teenager nervously turned to his mother and said, "I choose Daddy. You have not been a good mother to me." Boom, boom, boom! Like a Joe Frazier uppercut to the jaw, the son's confession knocked the mother flat on her keister. Never in her wildest dreams did she conceive this day would happen. Older son June Bug? Most definitely he might choose to take the conversation there. But little kiss-ass Church Mouse? Never in a lifetime did she think that scenario would happen, for he was Beulah's most obedient and compliant child. Not in her most turbulent fantasy had she ever envisioned that the family's flunky would turn his back on her. To this day, Church Mouse remembers every nuance of the monumental hurt in her eyes. The image continues to sadden him; still, he would not change his decision.

What was Beulah thinking in her head? Did she really believe her bullying tactics would sit well with a child who aspired of one day becoming a US Senator? Sure, it is possible that Church Mouse might never climb that high. He might have to struggle just winning student council president of his high school. But to dream, a child must be free from anxiety and fear. Free to swing for the fence. Children need to be cultivated and caressed, mentored and directed. Fourteen years of extension cord and broomstick whippings, unnecessary threats, house arrests, and fear overload do not qualify as appropriate leadership training. How can children become all they can be if they spend all their energy dodging projectiles launched from ignorance and the culture of poverty? Beulah had convinced herself that her son's skin was elephant thick, that the sting from her lethal tongue would not penetrate to the bone. That it would not leave a scar. Beulah had a bad case of missing the obvious. And the King of Ghosts? He was inebriated, and he was about to exit the scene again.

Mom and Dad continued to fight for most of the night. The next morning came in a blink of an eye. The King of Ghosts had made up his mind. He was going to take his son and his mother back to Omaha, Nebraska. Younger sister Sunshine looked her brother squarely in the eye and asked, "Are you really going to leave us?" Without looking back, Church Mouse replied, "It's something I just got to do. One day you'll understand." She called him a traitor and stormed out of the room. Younger brother Slim Jenkins wanted to tag along, but he had overheard the King say earlier that it was not his duty to take care of Ricky's boy. Ouch! How about a little diplomacy, dude? Jenkins did not ask to be a part of this family. Rather, Beulah "appropriated" him. At the very least, he was thrown away by his biological parents. To this very day, Slim Jenkins continues to search for a true home—for a loving and safe place to be.

Conflicted was too young to understand what was going on. The twins, Temperament and Silhouette, were too numb from dealing with their own case of child abuse. The Marvelous One clung to his older brother's side. The special needs child had grown to view his older brother as a father figure. Church Mouse was the most adept family member at helping the child deal with his speech and learning disability. He spent extra time building up his brother's self-esteem by teaching him how to perform in talent shows. He spent hard-earned money outfitting his little brother with up-to-date clothing. All these benefits were abruptly coming to an end. Unwilling to face the guilt of abandoning his siblings, Church Mouse quickly loaded up his belongings and stayed outside until the King of Ghosts escorted his mother to the car. Beulah stood from a distance and viewed all that transpired. Stunned, she had little to say to anyone that morning.

Together, the three weary souls pulled off in a vehicle that was headed for Omaha, Nebraska. Church Mouse never looked back to wave goodbye. He was headed back to his ideological roots. Back to the people who understood him best. No, they were not as refined as his Denver friends. Many of them were downright ghetto, but they were more down-to-earth and authentic, and Church Mouse felt a real kinship with them. Church Mouse needed to get away from the uppity mindset of middle-class Blacks. He was going back to a place that was curiously devoid of a well-rounded historical and socioeconomic perspective. Be careful what you ask for, C-Money. So long, Mile High City, but please keep the backdoor open if it doesn't work out.

Weaving and wobbling all over the highway, the King of Ghosts continued to press on for the first twenty minutes. Having drank quite heavily the night before, his father was in no condition to complete the task he had started. Church Mouse began to fear they would have to turn around and go back. Once the threesome reached the outskirts of town, however, the King pulled over to the shoulder of the interstate and got out of the car and said, "Okay, Baby Brother. It's all yours. Take us into Omaha!" A stunned Church Mouse perked up. The kid possessed only a learner's permit and had never driven the highway. The extent of his driving experience encompassed about a three-square-block area that surrounded his house. "I've got confidence in you, son; it's just like riding a bicycle. Once you climb into the saddle, it is like taking candy from a baby," replied the delirious dude.

As Church Mouse nervously buckled his seat belt, he noticed Ma Dear opening her door to vomit onto the ground. She was terribly ill and probably should have stayed home with Beulah or been taken to a hospital. "I'll be okay after I take my medicine," she faintly pleaded. "Well then, it's time for the Three Musketeers to go out and conquer Interstates 76 and 80," reveled the drunk Runner. After fifteen minutes of slowly advancing the car, Church Mouse found a way to turn a little luck and sheer will into success. He taught himself to drive on the fly. It was time to become an adult. Nothing was going to keep him from realizing his life's goal: the pursuit of freedom, sanity, and virtue. Going back to Beulah's crazy castle was not an option.

Church Mouse tensed his body all the way to Omaha. Stiff as a board, he became. From that day forth, the familiar posture helped to bring a measure of order to his chaotic life. Whether driving down the interstate with no prior experience, taking a test in school, dating a girl, running for public office, or navigating normal details of daily living, the way Church managed most of life's challenges was by stiffening his body like a slab of concrete and donning a stern, serious demeanor. Way into adulthood, he managed most pressure situations that way. Question: How long can one push the body like that before it fights back? Before it gives out?

Church Mouse grew tired after two hours of driving, so he decided to pull over. Besides, it was a suitable time to gas up and use the restroom. The King was passed out in the back seat. He mumbled something about smokes, then rolled over and dozed off again. His wallet fell out of his pocket onto the floor. Picking it up, Baby Brother noticed enough cash in it to make it to Omaha. "I better hang onto this for safekeeping," he told himself. After Ma Dear returned from the restroom, Church Mouse offered her some ginger ale to soothe her upset stomach. The Alzheimer's patient was in no condition for conversation. She obediently swallowed some over-the-counter flu medicine her grandson purchased for her. Within minutes of getting back on the road, she, too, was out cold and did not awaken until the threesome arrived in Omaha seven hours later. For all intents and purposes, the drive to Omaha was a solo ride.

Attempting to stay awake became an arduous undertaking for Church Mouse. Interstate driving is a scenic pleasure in most parts of the country, but no one warned him about western and central Nebraska. The repetition of cornfields and flat landscape can tire a driver emotionally more than the drive itself. The exhausted teen went up and down the radio dial looking for a station that would hold his interest. Mostly he found offerings of country music, talk-show formats, and news stations. All three options kept him engaged for a while, but he needed something more dynamic to keep his juices flowing. Songs about your favorite pickup truck can only take you so far before you doze off. Searching through his father's music collection, he hoped to find some Temptations, the Supremes, or some Ray Charles. He only found an 8-track of Little Richard hits. While it is true that Richard is a founding father of rock and roll music, most 1970s teens could only listen to so much of "Tutti Frutti" and "Good Golly, Miss Molly" before their heads imploded. James Brown had introduced funk to the music scene, and now

Dyke and the Blazers were taking it higher. There was also a new group called Funkadelic that was causing a big stir. The delirious King seriously needed to update his music catalog.

Then it suddenly hit him: the way to conquer dozing off at the wheel was not by ingesting loud music or coffee. No. Church Mouse needed something more potent. All he needed to stay awake was a simple remedy—a miracle drug called adrenaline. Accentuated with frustration and liquid sugar, the potency of adrenaline increased his odds of safely making it into Omaha. Church Mouse was adept at summoning demons from his past, but he had always done so in small bite-sized pieces. Never before did he open the floodgates of his past to face the full depth of the hurt that was repressed inside. That journey would take him all the way back to his early days living in Algeria, Turkey, Southern California, Texas, Ohio, South Carolina, Japan, and Nebraska. To accomplish the task of successfully staying awake, the young lad had to awaken demons that were long put to sleep. They provided him the strength and stamina to push through and gut it out. Venturing into emotionally charged territory was scary, but he had no other choice. Liquid sugar was not enough. "Are you sure you want sum-a-dis? Are you strong enough to handle the uncut funk?" whispered Ole Trick Ass in your boy's ear. And where does a broken heart begin its nostalgic journey of sorrow? Try starting at the beginning.

For eight hours straight, Baby Brother swayed back and forth between depressive and manic states of mind. Seventeen years of old video clips that had been safely tucked away in a remote corner of his mind began to play back to back in rapid succession. Some of the memories were distant and faint, while others were as clear as a recent automobile accident. Most of the time the tapes played back at hyper speed, but occasionally they ran in slow motion. Church Mouse stiffened his back, clenched his jaw, furrowed his brow, glared his eyes, drank his Mountain Dew, and pressed his feet to the floor. The experience was likened to that of an adrenaline baptism. Sensory overload, ladies and gentlemen. Sorry, folks, once a nostalgia flick starts, it is hard to turn it off. When the lights go down in the theater of life and the feature presentation begins, there are no potty breaks—not even for members of the management team. The only scheduled pause that is allowed is if the film breaks in the middle of the showing.

The initial high one gets from Valium might be a rush, but the side effects of an overdose are a bitch. Church Mouse slowly turned over in bed to see what time it was. It was early Monday morning. Like every other adult in the world, it was time to get up and go to work. But he was in no condition to stumble and bumble his way through a workday at the job. Why risk gaining a reputation for being a pothead or an emotional wreck when all he wanted to do was make sense out of nonsense? Sometimes you have to disguise your funk.

After being disengaged with his wife and kids the entire weekend, he now faced the possibility of having to skip work. Looking at his bloodshot eyes in the bathroom mirror, Church Mouse could see that him showing up on the job would benefit no one. Even if he went in, he would be nothing more than a walking zombie. But it is important to be clear on one important fact: His absence from work had little to do with routine sickness or with conjuring up a fake excuse to stay home. Emotionally, Church Mouse was not a well man by any stretch of the imagination. He needed more than just a day off. He really needed a year-long sabbatical. And he certainly did not need Valium and other potent medications as a long-term solution.

The experience he encountered with the failed graduate entrance exam, having to exert extra energy to keep his friend Pookie Johnson out of jail, the overdose of medication, and now memories of past mistreatment coming at him like a flash flood were no accident. God works in mysterious ways, and flashback therapy was part of the antidote The Good Lord wanted for our boy. Alas, the exhausted hero who took the art of healing others to legendary heights finally understood that he, too, needed to be reconciled. The past beckoned the young man like a game of craps. Be careful not to throw snake eyes, Church Mouse. Face it. Place it. Case it. Trace it.

Speaking loudly enough so that his wife could easily eavesdrop, Church Mouse called his boss to say that he was ill with the traditional flu. Rather than admit the truth that he was having a nervous breakdown, he informed his supervisor that he had a bug that might take several days to recover from. Sanctified liar. Holy son. Child of the road less traveled. You have chosen physician-assisted sleep and solo dancing as your vehicle of choice to complete an incredible journey. It's not a terrible choice but be careful. Both can become highly addictive if they are abused. Lay your head unto the bosom of Jesus, dear child. Pray that your sleep is regenerative. And may you awaken renewed and healed once the roll of the dice bounces off the wall of life.

Post-chapter mentoring tips for parents, educators, counselors, and other service providers: Mental illness does not favor one race more than the others. It can impact people of all backgrounds. If a person who suffers from depression does not find a way to release the pressure they are under, they will either explode or implode. Unfortunately, our main character waited too late in life to seek professional help. It negatively impacted his physical, mental, and spiritual health. Still, late is better than never. Minority persons must fight against the stigma of seeking professional help. Contrary to popular myth, therapy is not just for White folk and rich people. People of Color can benefit from counseling too.

Post-chapter survival tips for children who hurt: It is important to realize that an addict is still an addict. Abusing prescription and over-the-counter drugs does not make you any better than those who take street drugs. Controlled substances cannot address the roots of your problems. *Rather, focus on what is real in your life and discard those things that are fake.* Drown out the foolishness others try to dump in your lap. Let unrealistic expectations and criticism roll off your back. *Learn the art of searching for the positives you can garner from a negative situation you have little control over.* This is one of the prime survival factors garnered from the resiliency research. This task is not easy, but it can be done. Also, find a hobby or a pastime that brings you pleasure and gives your life meaning. Thicken your skin and learn to become more forbearing. Patiently bide your time. When an opportunity for freedom comes open, make your move decisively and do not look back. Lastly, when it is all said and done and you look back on all the pain, *fight the urge to exact revenge.* Set yourself free by taking the high road.

THE INCREDIBLE SCAR WITHIN

YOUNG CHURCH MOUSE QUIETLY SLIPPED INTO A SEMI-COMATOSE STATE OF euphoria. His tiny, underdeveloped frame could only fight so long before succumbing to the evil that vexed him. The closer a child approaches their demise the more death seems to don an angelic face. What once was feared now becomes inviting. Like bees to the honeycomb or flies to feces. Like a televangelist suddenly stricken by the lure of a lady of the night. Like a democrat's itch to spend the public's money, or a republican's desire to roll back civil rights legislation. It was the kind of attraction that is toxic and euphoric. It was familiar and familial. Death held a fatal attraction for the child. The year was 1956, and for whatever reason, God saw fit two years prior to deliver the child in a home with parents who were distracted by the trappings and problems of contemporary society. But there was no strategic plan or operating manual provided in the delivered package.

Hearing a faint scream for help, Miss Figlia, the family's Turkish housemaid, flew into the room and pushed June Bug off his perch. He was seated on top of his younger brother attempting to suffocate him with a pillow! Figlia quickly removed the weapon from the toddler's face and sat him upright to catch his breath. The boy struggled as he gasped for oxygen. Euphoria in reverse can be quite a harrowing experience. Some say it can be as taxing as death in full drive. Young Church Mouse stumbled to his feet and then quickly scampered into the bathroom. The small brown-turned-purple child closed the door and then hid himself in a space between the toilet stool and the wall. Shivering and shaking, his eyes grew large with raindrops. With teeth chattering and knees drawn into his chest, the little child cried, "I sorry, I sorry."

Sorry, folks, but enough is enough. The writer has held his tongue for far too long. Up until now, he has been fairly good about giving people the benefit of the doubt, but there comes a time in life when a person must push the nice-guy stuff to the side and speak the truth. There is no other way to put it, folks. The attempt on young Church Mouse's life is a classic example of grade-A, punk-assed, poverty bullshit. Forgive me, religious readers and conservative friends. The writer genuinely wants to clean up his speech, but he cannot in this case. Books are books, balloons are balloons, bananas are bananas, and caca stinks no matter what a person's ethnicity or socio-economic status is. A quick scan of the grocery shelves reveals that there are no air fresheners to mask the scent of symbolic feces. The Mr. Clean brand might be able to produce a special disinfectant product, but as of right now, the rancid stench of sin is carried far and wide in the winds of ambivalence. The child abuse version of sin is especially suffocating.

Pause for a moment and think about this scenario, folks: What did the small child do to deserve such treatment? Did he spill food on his clothes or soil his training pants? Did he forget to put away his toys? Did he eat one too many treats that should have been saved for his older brother? Was he "acting White" by watching too much educational TV? Perhaps he squealed on June Bug for something the elder sibling did wrong. Yeah, that is it—the toddler was getting the normal payback that most stool pigeons receive. Snitches get stitches, even baby ones.

At the age of two and a half years old, the little guy was not mature enough to be a sinner. This is not rocket science, folks. Stinking thinking seldom makes sense. And if any of the reasons offered above are true, they would at least solve a difficult problem—the task of making sense out of the spiritual side of culture of poverty. While the justifications provided are flimsy, they at least offer a small semblance of reality—some explanation for why doves sometimes cry. In June Bug's eyes, the attack happened because young Church Mouse was at fault. His little bitch ass must have deserved it. It was his fault that Mom and Dad decided to have another child. Maybe Church Mouse was hogging all the spotlight and shading his older brother's shine.

In today's society, most people cannot manage unfiltered truth. They prefer a form of reality that is first passed through a PC strainer. They want to pick begonias and sing happy songs. They want to feel warm and see the sun rise and set with regularity. But no, Church Mouse persists in digging up events that most people choose to bury in an unmarked grave. Why does he keep pushing to expose things no one else wants to talk about? Play by the rules, Church Bitch. Family secrets are meant to be locked away in a vault forever. Sprinkle some powdered sugar on your funk, C. A little *Mary Poppins* will do, thank yee. You say you want the naked truth? *So much for mega book sales and large profits*, the writer thought to himself.

Over the years, the true essence of June Bug's character has remained elusive. Was he a demon child or a visionary genius? A protector or a Sith? Was it the usual case of sibling jealousy? Did June Bug hate his little brother? Maybe, but probably not. During his adult years, June Bug became a role model to young people and a leader via his work with community radio. He grew to be one of the better people Church Mouse associated himself with. During their younger years, however, June Bug behaved like he was a member of a terrorist organization. How does a young boy who comes out of his mother's womb unprogrammed and guiltless learn such cruel behavior? I mean, most five-year-old children play pretend karate chop and shoot-'em-up, not this real-life homicidal bullshit. Still, a demon-child explanation does not add up either. Something else must have entered the equation when June Bug was younger. The mere contemplation of killing his younger brother reflected something drastically askew in the family. Was it possible that he was acting out a script that was given to him by someone else?

Rainy Eyes. Not the watery ones that graced the face of a toddler totally scared out of his wits, but the familial ones of the woman who birthed the two boys. The confessions of a teary-eyed mother many moons into her elderly years shed light on a motive that young June Bug may have had—a morsel of truth that might explain the older son's behavior. It goes like this: While living in Ankara, Turkey, Rainy Eyes gave birth to a third baby—an innocent child nicknamed Dubious—and the King was not the biological father. Rainy Eyes had conceived a child by another man while living in Omaha during a time her husband was away on TDY (temporary duty). Female infidelity was very unsettling to men during a time when apple pie, baseball, the Bible, and US Senator Joseph McCarthy ruled the day. In the 1950s, a woman who did this sort of thing was viewed as the ultimate lowlife, even if the men they married were guilty of the same infraction. Today, infidelity is not as big of a deal although it is still shunned. Life in the 1950s, however, was simpler and more predictable. Yes, London Bridges do fall down, but in today's society they are rebuilt within a matter of days, my fair lady.

Two versions of the story behind the infidelity exist. The King alleged that his wife was a promiscuous two-timer who lacked the willingness to be faithful. Rainy Eyes vehemently disputed that charge, protesting that she was raped by an associate friend who suddenly changed his colors and turned against her. Rumor has it that the perpetrator was a thug member of the local Omaha police force. The King responded to his wife's assertion with "If she wasn't such a flirt in the first place, the door for that kind of thing to happen would never have been opened." Rainy Eyes countered by saying, "Any man who doesn't romance his new bride on their wedding night and leaves her for extended periods of time without demonstrating proper affection and family leadership is just as much part of the problem." Like honey-roasted chicken churning on a rotisserie, the omissions of both parents rotated round-n-round on the open fires of life. Their stories glisten in the night and fill the sky with a bittersweet aroma.

Don't be fooled—being enlisted in the armed forces does not automatically make a man pristine and innocent. On the contrary, women are drawn to a man in uniform and tend to throw themselves at servicemen. Men got away with relationship double standards as if these were a rite of passage. During the 1950s era, infidelity was pretty much an expected requirement for initiation into most male fraternities. Chances are slim to none that the King honored his marriage vows during times he spent away from his wife on active duty. The fact that he tipped out on his second wife means he probably did the same with his first wife. There is no way of definitively proving that point, but Church Mouse had a hunch that the frisky sergeant had an active libido and probably "knocked a few boots" himself. [61] Then again, there is a small chance Church Mouse could be wrong about the King's early marital behavior. Just because a person is born male does not automatically make him guilty of infidelity. Maybe it was the actions of his first wife that pushed the father to become more of a playboy during his second marriage. Slim chances can prevail, even in the face of overwhelming odds.

Whore. There, the writer finally wrote it. Hoe, if you prefer the Ebonics version of the word. Church Mouse was never totally convinced that a portrayal of his mother as an openly promiscuous woman was an accurate one, but his father preferred to classify it that way. Chances are Mom's problems stemmed more from being naive regarding worldly matters on one hand and being poorly mentored by her parents on the other hand. Church Mouse always felt that his mother's family was a bit detached and secretive. The older her siblings became the more they came around, but in their early days they, too, seemed disengaged. Let him without sin cast the first stone, however. Navigating White America during the 1920-1965 period was no walk in the park, as Blacks were forced to contend with incredible mixed signals. Yes, Rainy Eyes had issues, but it never occurred to the King that he, too, would don the "whore" label once he married his second wife.

No one will ever know which version of the story represents the full truth. Perhaps there is a tinge of accuracy in both accounts, but it is also quite possible that Rainy Eyes' story is far more complex than a few street words can articulate. Nevertheless, the King was faced with the embarrassing predicament of fathering a child that was not his own. He was livid, and he was hurt. Friends snickered and talked behind his back. "How could any man contemplate raising another man's child? You must be pussy whipped," they unfairly cracked. The solution? Don't get mad; get even! The King purposely set out to make his wife's life as miserable as possible. He abused her emotionally and told her she was ugly when everyone else knew she was pretty. He told her she was not worthy and called her Jezebel. What is that you say—suffer the adulterer's baby? Whoa, wait a minute! Could it be that the King went there?

Sin begets absurdity, and evil recruits more stupidity. According to a very sketchy account provided by Rainy Eyes, her husband lost his sensibilities and responded in an irrational way: He instructed his oldest son, June Bug, to cover the face of the newborn child with a pillow and make it continuously gasp for air. Please say it is not true. If the explanation is valid, it was a sinister plot born from the heart of a broken man. It is not clear whether June Bug was the sole assailant, if the father joined in too, or if any parts of the explanation is real. If it is true, the plan most likely was not to kill young Dubious, but only to make him suffer. And what about the suffering child, you ask? Was he permanently damaged by the mischief? This conclusion remained one brick short of speculative. One got the impression that Dubious fought a bevy of emotional, health, and behavioral problems up until his premature death in 2003.

For the father to have concluded that his oldest son had the wherewithal to rightly discern between roughing up a target versus killing it was utterly insane. Maybe The King was inebriated when he gave his son the directive. Hopefully, June Bug understood the difference. Believing his father had given him the green light to make the newborn suffer, June Bug might have deduced that if one part of his competition could be nullified, why not go for an exacta? Jealousy had already been firmly entrenched in June Bug's young mind once his parents demonstrated the audacity to bring a second child into the world. And now, there was a third one to boot? Make it a clean sweep, JB. Take out both intruders, Dubious and Church Mouse, for the price of one. Mail in the stats when you are done. If this explanation is accurate, the idea of a murderous coup became easier to contemplate now that the father of the home sanctioned the use of gangster tactics against the newborn. If the explanation is true, then mercy Lord.

In the game of elimination, certain intruders are slated to be killed, others to be roughed up, and still others only to be shoved to the ground. Dubious was offered up as a target for one of these choices, but June Bug apparently did not get the memo on the treatment of young Church Mouse. Perhaps the five-year-old was too young to rightly delineate the rules of the gangster game. Chances are the King of Ghosts never realized that June Bug was also attacking his second son. "And what about Mother?" the reader might ask. Did she call the police? She was just being herself: incredibly disengaged, depressed, and playing the role of the victim.

Ah yes, the Culture of Poverty and his first cousin Stinking Thinking. Together, these two knuckleheads flex and then splatter innocent kids like diarrhea hitting a high-speed fan. The stench of children sacrificed on the altars of human indifference spreads far and wide. The after-smell reeks in the nostrils of God. Man-made perfumes are not potent enough to cover up the odor. Sorry, folks. The writer admits the irreverent nature of this description, but do readers truly understand life on the shaded side of the American underbelly? Do they realize that Murphy's Kids from tough environments usually do not grow up to be normal? Do these kids buy guns then shoot up their school? Do we then sentence certain groups to damnation by insisting that they are lazy and need to "just pull themselves up by their own bootstraps"? Please, tell us it isn't so.

The writer begs to differ. This is not a story about revenge. It is not a tale about whining and crying, nor is it a "please have pity on me" saga. Rather, this is a warning. A warning to parents that Hell is real, and that mistreatment of children is one sure way of securing permanent residence there. It says so in the Good Book (Matthew 18:6). While this account tells of one family's problems, it is, unfortunately, a typical American story for children of all races who quietly reside in the shadows apart from our conscious awareness. The writer abhors child abuse like he hates the smell of chitterlings boiling in Beulah's kitchen. Some of our children get caught up in societal predicaments only to be spit out like used chewing tobacco. Most Murphy's Kids are forgotten within a blink of an eye. Some of them rob and steal to survive. Some of them die. Some of them kill others before they die. It is our responsibility to help these children heal.

From November of 1955 to February of 1957, the King's family was temporarily stationed first in Libya for a few months, and then in Turkey for the remainder of the time. The city of Ankara provided a perfect place for the King to serve his country while licking his wounds. It was also the birthplace of Dubious, as well as the place where mis-parenting established a strong foothold in the family. The dramatic impact of a foreign culture on the family was difficult enough, but at least life outside of the States offered a temporary haven for the King's bride to hide and deal with the embarrassment. She did not believe in abortion, and so she had the baby. The King used the time to think about his options, discover what he was really made of, and decide whether to stay married to his wife or divorce her. Rainy Eyes hoped that she could reestablish her love and commitment to her husband apart from the discouraging views and comments of disgruntled relatives and friends from both sides of the family.

Fortunately, both Dubious and Church Mouse survived the attacks on their lives and made it back safely to the mainland. Well, at least physically they did. Flip a coin, however, on the psychological development of the two. Young Church Mouse quickly learned how to scream and run at the first sign of his brother making sudden and harsh advances toward him. He also learned how to stay out of June Bug's way. The way not to get hit by an incoming fist was simply to not be there when the punch arrived. A little

Muhammad Ali action will do, thank you. Had it not been for the Turkish maid's awareness, however, odds are there would be no Church Mouse for us to interview and write about. Thirty seconds more and the child would have been a statistic.

Young Church Mouse cowered between the cold ceramic bowl and the wall, shivering, and shaking. The frightened child's mind raced back and forth, contemplating several ways he could become a better little brother. Even as a young tot, he wanted to please those who were unhappy with him. Little did he realize that this course of action—an insatiable desire to make others like him—would later become his greatest undoing. The physical attacks on his life coupled with rejection formed an internal wound that scarred Church Mouse until he reached his late sixties. In the end, the many problems that he navigated were mitigated through counseling and prayer. What was born of human ignorance was blunted by God. Come Holy Spirit. Dubious, however, may not have been as fortunate with his healing process.

And what about Dubious, you ask? What became of the innocent child who was cast into the role of the family scapegoat? He survived to age forty-eight before his health went bad. Still, it must be said that if the scar Church Mouse carried within his soul was legendary, the one Dubious bore must have been epic. No matter how much pain Church Mouse encountered in his life, it paled in the presence of that which was endured by Dubious. Limitations of time and space prevent us from doing justice to his full story. Another time and another project, perhaps. May God bless you, young man, and may you grow to make wise decisions as you circumvent the treacherous waters others have forced you to navigate.

It would be wrong to conclude that the attacks on Church Mouse were a necessary evil that helped him prepare for proper manhood training. Blood is thicker than water, but with relatives like these, who needs enemies? But then again, the King and June Bug may not have been monsters. Perhaps they were just human, and young Church Mouse was a little "Uncle Tom snitch bitch" who needed to be properly dealt with. You can tell that by the color of one's piss. If a person chooses not to "smack and smoke" like most cool dudes do, then he might not be a true soul brother. The rule in the hood is that a real man must show his alpha male side. Is it true even for toddlers? Alas, there is slight chance that the Rainy Eyes account of a vindictive father teaching his older son how to be a young assassin might not be accurate. That conclusion ends up being one person's word against another. Once you get to really know the father of the home, a profile of him teaching gangster moves to his oldest son does not seem to fit his nature. Once you introduce alcohol and mental illness into a Twilight Zone equation, however, anything can happen, especially in connection to the poverty ridden section of North Omaha.

Readers are free to consider the possibility that June Bug may not have been a demon child at all. In fact, he, too, may have become a family scapegoat. Maybe he was set up to be the family fall guy. Or maybe he truly was a bully. It is also not a stretch to say that Rainy Eyes' memory and recall capabilities were suspect. The story of the two younger boys being attacked by June Bug might be overstated, for the crime does not fit his adult profile. But then again it might be dead on. And a broken heart can have a devastating effect on a spouse. Although the King of Ghosts was a gentle soul, he also had an addictive side to his personality. And he, too, had to deal with mis-parenting when he was a child. Could it be that June Bug was a victim of bad role modeling from his mentor who was himself at-risk? There is no glory in demonizing a young boy who may have been set up. And there is no victory in pounding a broken man's heart into the ground.

Whether or not a two-year old is old enough to accurately remember the antecedents and details of a bogus attack is debatable. One thing for sure is that young Church Mouse did not fabricate the day he almost lost his life. The end result of multiple attacks and rejection from June Bug and Crazy Beulah over many years ended up affecting Church Mouse for life. As he grew older, he suffered from reoccurring bad dreams. During two marriages, his wives often had to awaken Church Mouse from bad nightmares of someone trying to kill him. He also wrestled with a terrible case of claustrophobia. It played itself out worst when doctors attempted to have Church Mouse enter an MRI machine. He did not conquer that fear until the age of sixty-eight.

Maybe Church Mouse and Dubious were expendable. End of sentence. Move on. And maybe Rainy Eyes truly was victimized by a rogue policeman. Just because a woman chooses to be disengaged as a parent does not necessarily make her a whore. A woman's word didn't carry much weight in the 1950s. Her perpetrator probably was a crooked cop and a rapist. And what about the stuck-up stork who delivered Church Mouse to the wrong family? Why does your boy continue to deliver babies to Twilight Zone zip codes in the ghetto? Surely, he could drop Black and Brown boys and girls off in a suburban neighborhood every now and then. I mean, if he refuses to do his job in a satisfactory manner, maybe he should receive a pink slip, right?

Good help is so hard to find these days.

Once the family returned Stateside from their stay overseas, the idea of staying married to a cheating wife and raising a child that was not his own was something the King just could not bring himself to do. The three boys were at their maternal grandmother's house the day the father made a life-changing decision. Utilizing a false pretense, he gave his mother-in-law the excuse that he was picking up his two boys to take them to a movie. Naturally, the invitation was not extended to young Dubious. Immediately, the father hit the highway and drove all the way from Nebraska to California, while making brief stops in Dallas and Las Vegas. Before leaving Nebraska, however, he hunted down the rogue policeman during his off-duty hours and kicked the stuffing out of that turkey. The beatdown was thorough and complete. Rumor has it that the North Omaha precinct captain purposely looked the other way because he knew his guy was guilty, and the community looked upon the King as a local favorite. Back in those days you had two sets of rules: the written law and the brotherhood code. The latter ruled the streets. There are certain things that a man just didn't do. Messing with another man's wife was one of them.

Shortly thereafter, the King divorced his wife on grounds of infidelity. She fought for her two boys, but the court awarded full custody to the father—an unusual occurrence for the 1950s. The pain that Rainy Eyes felt from losing her first two children was unimaginable. It would be a long time before she was allowed to come back into their lives in a meaningful way. By then, Church Mouse had become wrongfully propagandized in his view about her. The incident marked the end of one era and the beginning of another. So long, Omaha's cobblestone streets. Hello, Southern California palm trees, beaches, and a tasty new fruit called dates.

Somewhere along Route 66, young Church Mouse, June Bug, and their father became a tight-knit family. Granted, it was a fragile arrangement held together by a spider's thread, but at least, it was a true family. Father and sons—footloose and fancy-free they were, rolling down the highway singing songs and having fun like playful kids. It was also the first time the King gave equal time to both boys. Up to that point, he had concentrated mostly on his oldest son. It felt good for Church Mouse to be bounced on his father's knee and be equally recognized, even if it was short lived. The child liked the idea of being called Tweety Bird as a nickname. "I tawt I taw a putty tat," the King playfully said as he mocked the cartoon character and tickled his baby. The baby lit up like a Christmas tree whenever his father did his Warner Bros. routine. Even June Bug forced a smile when he heard the little guy giggle. Mail in the stats, ladies and gentlemen.

US highways in the 1950s had a few more dangerous intersections and sharp curves compared to today's typical road designs. Early highway driving required motorists to remain super alert. One day, the boys were asleep—June Bug in the front passenger seat and young Church Mouse in the back. Earlier, their singing and laughter helped the King stay awake, but the boys eventually punked out on him. They did not have the stuff to hang with the Jack Daniels and tobacco king. But he, too, was growing exhausted and began to nod at the wheel. Suddenly, a sharp curve in the road appeared, requiring him to take drastic corrective measures to regain control of the swerving car. Just then, the back seat passenger-side door flew open, and young Church Mouse, asleep on top of an army footlocker, began sliding out the door headfirst. The child's eyes popped open as he came face-to-face with the sight of concrete and grass and the sound of screeching tires. It seemed as if death had a fatal attraction for the kid. Again, God had other plans. He immediately dispatched an angel to block destruction's score.

Keenly aware of the imminent danger unfolding, the King skillfully steered the car with his left hand while reaching back and grabbing his son's foot with his right hand just before the child went out the door. The situation required two simultaneous moves, and the coordinated King was more than up to the challenge. Like an old pro, he saved both the car and the life of his two children. Giving attention to only one of the tasks would have been disastrous. Again, this recollection is from a three-year old child who may not have remembered the incident with exact accuracy. Church Mouse does remember, however, that his father was greatly shaken by a near automobile accident of some kind and needed a moment to recover.

Dad pulled the car into a truck stop to calm his nerves over a cigarette and a cup of coffee. Young Church Mouse remembers sitting in his father's lap and receiving a long hug from his idol. "I almost lost you to the bad putty tat," the concerned father told his baby. "I'll hit that bad putty tat on his big head," replied the little boy. Amused, the father and the older brother broke into spontaneous laughter. The boy looked at his two mentors and bounced up and down with joy. The incident made the child believe that his father and brother would always be there to rescue him from danger. The family unit felt warm and unbreakable. Unfortunately, after this incident, acts of rescue from either source became scarce as hen's teeth. Both men meant well, but they lacked the focus to be consistent. The father provided two more instances of significant rescue for the child, and the older brother provided one. After that, the idea of child protection for Church Mouse dried up like a desert.

He would have to make the thread of safety he received early in life stretch forward into the future like a rubber band. Please don't pop on a brother.

Perhaps God might genetically engineer the spider to spin a thread made of titanium.

———————————————————

As time progressed, both boys began to accept the fact that their biological mother was no longer in their lives. The impact on June Bug was greater because he spent the most active time with her. June Bug was her favorite, and he wanted the old days to return. Rainy Eyes remained a foggy memory for Church Mouse, however. Being so young plus the fact that she was not around contributed to Church Mouse not remembering much about her. He had more memories of her mother, Kiawatonka. She cared for the boys during Rainy Eyes' frequent absences. For Church Mouse, it was as if his biological mother never existed.

It was during the time spent in Southern California that the King met and married his second wife, Beulah—a Gullah woman from Mt. Pleasant, SC. Beulah was a jovial soul who had a life-of-the-party personality. She did not mind taking on a ready-made family. She did not have the physical beauty or the flashy sex appeal of Rainy Eyes, but she was a good person who was fun to be around. From the very beginning, the boys could tell that Beulah had a few personality quirks, however. She had a used-car salesperson persona about her. She was good at hiding her idiosyncrasies. Yet, she was far from being the bipolar woman she later evolved into. On the whole, she was a solid fit for the family—well, at least during the early days she was. Her presence in the home was just the settling factor the father and his boys needed. Family success had a promising outlook. One might even conclude that mailing in the stats was a slam dunk.

Problems began to materialize early in the marriage, however. Beulah found out that her husband was a player's player—a lady's man. In addition, there is a chance that the King never completely got over his love for his first wife. In her day, Rainy Eyes was one of the great catches of North Omaha. The King was the toast of the town for snagging one of its beauties. His feelings for Beulah were real and sincere, but he also had a thing for popular, flashy women. Beulah could easily sense that she was not number one in the eyes of her husband.

It is true that the King married his second wife partially out of a need to have a steady parent figure take over the chore of raising his boys. Chances are Beulah used that as a hook to reel him in. She was a champion when it came to smooth talk and co-opting abilities. It was not a smart move on the part of either parent, however. A marriage of convenience involving kids usually ends up backfiring, and the children end up suffering the most. The King did not fully understand or appreciate his second bride. She was an old-school, ride-or-die southern woman whom you do not cross. The popular phrase "Hell hath no fury than a woman scorned" was coined on Beulah's behalf. The King of Ghosts did not see the storm coming. It was also during this time that he transitioned from being a social drinker into a full-blown alcoholic.

The new family arrangement provided a mixed blessing. Even though daily life had stabilized, the boys also sensed the possibility of a bright future about to evaporate. It took some time before they felt comfortable enough to call the new woman in their life "mama." Granted, she was a stabling force for the boys, but they resented becoming indoctrinated by Beulah's strict set of southern rules and regulations for raising children. Still, the new family arrangement was not so bad once the boys got used to it.

Church Mouse dealt with the stress of family structural change by throwing himself into his play. His tricycle and new scooter were his favorite toys. June Bug was given the job of making sure his little brother stayed within safe boundaries when he went outside to play. But June Bug had his own play agenda, and he could not keep an eye on his little brother every minute. With only a momentary blink, Tweety Bird was easily prone to flying beyond the established boundaries. So far out of bounds young Church Mouse went on one occasion that he ended up squarely in the middle of a nearby highway with a semi-truck barreling down on him. As the driver locked his breaks and honked the horn, the truck began to buckle and swerve. The just-turned four-year-old child was frozen as he sat mesmerized by the mass of metal plunging toward him. Run, little boy! Do not just sit there and witness your own demise!

Out of nowhere June Bug came to the rescue. In one swift move, he guided the tricycle, with his brother seated atop, safely across the road to the other side. The relieved driver of the vehicle tipped his hat to the hero of the day, and then proceeded down the road with caution. "I thought I almost lost you to the bad putty tat," June Bug said, mocking his father's comedic routine. Stunned, young Church Mouse gingerly smiled and said, "Thank you, Big Brother!" Church Mouse will always be indebted to his older brother for the rescue he provided that day. Without June Bug's intervention, he would have become a statistic.

Throughout the years, this scene has caused much cognitive dissonance for Church Mouse; for it was only three months after this incident that June Bug slammed him to the kitchen floor, hit his head with a hammer, and burnt the front of his hair with matches. June Bug threatened to beat him up really bad if he snitched on him. Scared out of his wits, the younger brother complied. He lied to his parents and said that he fell off a chair and hit the front burner of the stove while trying to get some cookies from the cabinet above. Unfortunately, Dad bought the excuse hook, line, and-sinker. Mom thought that the explanation was suspicious, however. The reasoning for such abuse by June Bug appears to have a similar connection to the pillow attack that took place earlier in Turkey. Apparently, Church Mouse was becoming too popular, and jealousy sent his older brother into frequent fits of rage. When the boys grew into their adult-aged years, his older brother became one of the better people Church Mouse knew. His behavior as a young child and teenager, however, remains one of the more perplexing things about this story. It did not help that Beulah often raved about how good her second son's behavior was compared to the older son. That fact may have added to June Bug's feelings of sibling jealousy.

It was during this time that daylight began flirting with the idea of having intercourse with the family's darker side. If you howl at the moon long enough, you might transform into a ghost. If you shoot the moon, maybe the resulting spray might help cover up a few family warts.

———————————————————

Cross-country automobile rides tend to wear out both adults and children. The drive from Riverside, California, to Omaha, Nebraska, and then to Columbus, Ohio, was long and arduous for the four-year-old preschooler. Even quick stops to pick up his favorite food, ice cream, were not enough to settle down the confused child. The year was 1958, and June Bug, too, was taken aback by the swift turn of events. The sudden change was made even more traumatic when the father accidentally backed the car onto the boys' new puppy dog during a rest stop. It was instantly killed, and the boys remained somber for several hundred miles afterwards.

The King and his new bride were uprooting the family to a new location. It was part of the mobility routine most military families grow accustomed to. The day the family departed, they swung by a friend's house and picked up a young lad by the name of Slim Jenkins. Slim had previously visited the boys' home as a new play partner. They immediately noticed that Jenkins was a troubled child who had behavior and social adjustment issues. Little is known about this child other than the King would sometimes refer to him as "Ricky's boy." Information regarding the time and place of his birth and biological parents are sketchy at best. Many years later in 2010, Jenkins met a man from North Carolina who had the same name and look as he, but his name was not Ricky. He was a "bishop" in the Pentecostal Church, but he never denied or confirmed that he was the biological father. Other relatives also introduced themselves, but Slim was never able to get much detail about his life before Beulah. Neither was he able to secure a birth certificate from California, South Carolina, North Carolina, or any other state. Thus, Slim never secured a driver's license. Even as a senior citizen, he traveled the streets of greater Charleston, SC, on a bicycle. Yes, it is true. While Church Mouse had legitimate battles with child abuse and mis-parenting, he was not the most negatively impacted. There were other siblings from both the South Carolina and Nebraska families who were worse off than Church.

Beulah's initial thought was that her mother, Queen, would raise the abandoned child in her ancestral home of Mt. Pleasant, SC. Grandma Queen took him in. It would be the last time Slim would see the folks who birthed and initially raised him. Welcome to your new family, troubled son. Hope your stay is a meaningful one. One that was carefully thought through.

The two adults and three children crammed themselves with all their belongings into a 1953 Pontiac as they set out to explore a brave new world. The city of Columbus, Ohio was their final destination, but first there was a temporary stopover in Omaha, Nebraska. The visit allowed the family a chance to look in on the King's mother, Ma Dear. Church's recollection of this brief interlude is fuzzy, but there were three things about that visit that stood out. The first had to do with walking to the local Hinky Dinky supermarket with brother June Bug to buy some d-Con brand mouse poison. Ma Dear, an Alzheimer's patient who had a fierce dislike of rodents, went to almost comical lengths to rid her house of rodents. If she saw a mouse in the house, she would stand on a kitchen chair, scream, and rustle her hair as if the mouse had jumped into it. Most mice cannot jump that high. Her obsession, both real and perceived, was a chuckle all the kids shared.

The second memory Church Mouse had of their brief Omaha visit was that of a dog named Chico. The beautiful creature had one major flaw: He was a large dog that was not housebroken. Somehow, Chico managed to catch on to the part about doing his number two on the newspapers on the back porch, but for one reason or another, he never mastered control of his bladder. Go figure. You would think most animals would get a clue and connect the dots. One form of housetraining should jump-start other forms. But no, all around the house—on walls, carpet, linoleum, and especially furniture—Chico would cock his leg high in the air and "let her rip." There is a slight possibility that he was in fact looking out for his mother's best interests. Perhaps the animal was attempting to put out the fires of absurdity brought on by the culture of poverty. In that sense, he was using his body part as a fire hose. This interpretation is somewhat of a stretch. Nevertheless, Chico was smart enough never to do his business in the presence of his master. And although the house reeked of urine, the aging Ma Dear never realized the problem because of her failing sensory abilities.

Utilizing contemporary hip-hop vernacular, one might easily conclude that Chico was a "player hater." [62] The boys tried to intercept the creature when he was about to whiz on the furniture, but he would have none of that. On one occasion, the mutt snapped at Slim Jenkins and ripped a small portion of his shirt sleeve. Jenkins jumped back to avoid the dog's full wrath. Just before Chico cocked his leg to urinate, he looked at the boys and rumbled in a low growl, as if to say, "You little spooks better recognize. Gank me on my own turf, and I will roll up on you three bitches. Don't make me spray you niggas wit dis jungle juice!" [63] I guess even pet dogs want to be comedians these days. Hey, chill out Cujo. [64] The boys don't mean any harm. They just stopped by to let you know that your way of doing things is how pandemics get started. But no. You prefer to "jump on front street" like a bully. You want to hit Ma Dear's furniture on the one before you take her to the bridge. Yes, Chico was a funky brother, but unlike James Brown, he never got on the good foot. Where did he get his funk from—a Cracker Jack box?

A third memory—one that was less entertaining—involved the boys nervously sitting on the living room sofa across from an attractive lady that Church Mouse had no recollection of ever meeting. Her brother accompanied her. Why did the kids have to get dressed up? And where was the boy's father? June Bug knew what was going on and remained calm. Slim Jenkins, the curious child, went up to the lady and tried to befriend her. Irritated, Beulah warned, "Don't let me have to come over there and snatch you up." Jenkins returned to the sofa but kept chattering, which was his nature. Confused, Church Mouse was quiet and curious, which was his nature.

Church Mouse sensed there was a reason for the meeting, but he had no idea what it was. You know what they say about gifted children: sometimes you must give them a thump on the head before they comprehend the commonsense stuff. Beulah was successful in indoctrinating the boys with the code of the Deep South: Let the adults do the talking while the children do the listening. After a quick ten-minute visit, Beulah ordered the boys upstairs to take a nap. It was only 3:00 p.m. As they climbed the stairs, young Church Mouse looked back over his shoulders at the visitor and telepathically asked, "Who are you, and what do you want?" The woman acted as if she wanted to say something, but her words never materialized. Church Mouse was not about to encourage her. Although Beulah was not yet fully unwrapped at this point in time, the young child knew all too well the consequences of rubbing his stepmother the wrong way.

The mysterious woman did not have the type of visit she had hoped for. She probably went home and cried her eyes out. Chances are her tears left behind a crevice so deep that her hopes and dreams sailed into oblivion. After the boys climbed into bed, June Bug softly whispered to his younger brother, "That lady is our real mother, and the man is her brother." Stunned, young Church Mouse did not know how to respond to the news. He went over to the window and stared out, trying to understand the meaning of all that had transpired. Church Mouse would not meet the woman again until the summer of 1968 when Beulah co-opted him to perform a dastardly deed against her. The next meeting after that took place in the summer of 1972, when she unexpectedly bailed him out of jail due to an altercation he had with a local thug.

"Y'all better get in the bed right now! If I hear any feet walking around up there, I'm gonna climb these stairs and whip all y'all's little asses. Don't even talk to the mice and the roaches, 'cause I'll come up there and whip they little asses too," Beulah yelled up the stairs. Crude yet entertaining. Church Mouse was probably hallucinating, but he could swear he saw a mouse flip Beulah the bird. The young lad was speechless. Somehow over the past two years, he had made himself believe that Beulah was actually sane and that she was his biological mother.

Maybe it had something to do with how young he was when he was taken from his mother. Or perhaps the brainwashing process that the King and his curious bride instituted worked to perfection. Or could it be that Rainy Eyes failed to make a lasting impression on her second son? If the answer to the latter is yes, then it is partially her fault. Who knows?

Maybe Chico knows. Please tell him to say it, don't spray it.

Post-chapter challenges to wayward parents: Newsflash—it is not always about you. It's about family. It's about your kids. It's about your collective community. It is about the safety of those who are vulnerable. How far have we strayed from our traditional African cultural values? Did slavery and Jim Crow strip us of our memory—of our culture and soul? It is also not about your politics and personal beliefs. Rather, it is about building a nation where we can forge a critical middle. Please concentrate on things that matter. Stop prioritizing creature comforts over family and community responsibilities. It is not always about the local club, the car you drive, the clothes you wear, or diamonds and pearls you sport. Adults of America, come back from the various bird walks you've been on. It's OK to have fun, but please do your "fricken" job. Reach back and help the children in need. Please reprioritize your goals and save our nation one child at a time!

Post-chapter survival tips for children who hurt: Newsflash—As incredible as it sounds, the people who hurt you do not always fully realize what they are doing. Some of it is because of selfishness, but a part of it is because our society promotes an inward instead of an outward focus. Yes, this statement sounds preachy, but it is nevertheless true. Some people don't know their heads from their asses. Some clueless folks will even con themselves into believing that it is your fault—that you made them hurt you! It is enough to make your head swivel on a pole. If you can, learn to concentrate and focus amid your pain and sorrow. Sometimes you have to be the catalyst for change. If YOU do not do it, it may not get done. Take the high road and find creative ways to stay in the game. At the right moment, pivot and then make that all-important three-point shot as the game clock of life is about to expire. We need you here with us by our side. With you in the game of life, you make us collectively better! The world is an emptier place without you, even if others do not bother to tell you so.

CHAPTER 9:

THE WINDS OF CHANGE

The time spent in Omaha, Nebraska, was only meant to be temporary. The King's new military assignment was Lockbourne Air Force Base in Columbus, Ohio. [65] He preferred an assignment at Offutt Air Force Base in Omaha, but that assignment was not an option at that time. The days spent in California were a time of joy and intrigue for the boys and their new mother. Riverside was a comfortable home that the boys hated to leave. The brief stopover in Omaha was a time for the King to introduce his mother and friends to his new wife and attend to a few business matters. There were more questions than answers related to the family's Omaha layover. Life in Ohio, however, was mostly laced with happy times and healthy memories. As far as Church Mouse was concerned, those days were too few. It was there in Ohio that the King and his new bride had the best opportunity to jell as a legitimate blended family.

Still, there were moments of pause. One example was that Church Mouse had mixed feelings about attending kindergarten class in the morning, and then coming home as a latchkey child in the afternoon. Both parents worked so he spent afternoons alone. Unfortunately, Beulah made it his daily chore to watch the daily soap operas for her. The boy despised having to report to his mother about adult shows. It is somewhat of a stretch to conclude that a five-year-old boy could adequately report on people jumping in and out of each other's beds. He was not old enough to comprehend the maneuverings of shady women and their cheating men. The character known as Ericka from ABC's *All My Children* daytime drama was a hard one to nail down for the boy. Was she a heroine or a pill? A blessing or a trick? How does a kindergarten kid describe her to his new mom? Did the father know about his son's domiciliary duty? Did young Church Mouse understand what females meant when they warned their flirtatious men about "keeping it in their pants?" *What was the "it" that the women were talking about?* the lad wondered.

The King's two boys were at that age when life's growing-up lessons were upon them. Like most young children, his sons began to have legitimate questions about the differences between boys and girls. This was truer for June Bug, but Church Mouse also heard gossip from neighborhood kids regarding the topic of sex. A quick look at the literature suggests that younger children (ages four to eight) should be taught general knowledge about body parts, body functions, and proper etiquette between the sexes. A conversation about the difference between a penis and a vagina, as well as breastfeeding newborn babies, would be appropriate for that age group. Older young children (ages nine to thirteen) should begin to have conversations about how babies are made and the importance of proper sexual etiquette and behavior. By the time children reach their high school years, they need a full debriefing on STDs, contraception choices, the dangers of growing up too fast, natural consequences, and the responsibilities of adulthood when making wrong decisions.

It was in Ohio that young Church Mouse first saw a woman's breasts up close and personal. Dacia, a new family friend, brought over several bras for Beulah to try on her day off. It was not unusual for women with larger cup sizes to mail-order their product needs, or at least scout out rare specialty stores around town to get properly fitted. Young Church Mouse saw the bedroom door cracked, so he entered in to announce to his mother that her favorite TV soap opera was about to start. He walked in on what seemed to him to be "alien body parts from another planet." Although Beulah was a short woman, her upper body was well-endowed. Her bosom was triple the size like that of singer Dolly Pardon. To the naïve child, those breasts had the appearance of galactic basketballs. *And what was up with the small dark circles?* the child wondered. It looked as if space titties were invading buckeye territory. Run for cover, little boy!

Shocked, the child turned to leave. But just then Dacia invited him back into the room for an anatomy lesson. She joked that her friend's breasts were like superheroes, and that when he was a baby, he sucked milk out of them. The comment made Church Mouse gasp and cover his mouth. *No way*, he thought. The child had no recollection of ever performing such a task. The two women snickered. Dacia even invited him over to "juggle" his mother's breast. He declined the offer. Dacia did not deliver her lesson in a way that child psychologists would have endorsed. Still, her desire to educate and demystify sex education was well-intended. Very few parents had these kinds of conversations with their children. It was also deemed taboo for 1960s schools and churches to broach the topic. Sadly, most children learned their sex education from the streets and through personal experimentation. The episode ended when Beulah turned to Church Mouse and said, "Don't tell your daddy what you saw today," before dismissing him. She knew that her youngest son was super compliant and easy to manipulate.

Church Mouse was first introduced to sexuality beyond the veil of childhood innocence by way of his big brother, June Bug. He was sweet on a young girl who lived in the housing projects located across from their apartment. The two kids would play "house" like grownups do, and part of their routine included sitting under a blanket while touching each other's private parts. June Bug wanted his younger brother to feel the sensation of eroticism, so a date under the blanket with the girl who was two years older than little brother was arranged. She was happy to oblige. Because Church was nerdy and awkward with the experience, the girl never offered the opportunity to him again. He was shy and too young to appreciate it. Once again, the chance for Church Mouse to join the "keep it funky" club with his hip older brother was thwarted.

The attractive neighbor girl, however, did take Church to her house once to view her parents engaging in a midday summer rendezvous. There was a dime-sized hole in the bedroom door that allowed kids to spy in. The opening was never repaired because the parents did not think their children would be clever enough to stand on a nearby chair and peek in. When Church saw his friend's parents engaged in missionary-style sex, he was both appalled and titillated at the same time. He wondered why the mother seemed to be especially happy with her legs in the air. "Hallelujah," the daughter whispered in the boy's ear. On that day, something was awoken in Church Mouse that never died. There was a whole new frontier opened to the young lad that both frightened and intrigued him. His conservative demeanor made him quickly leave, however, as he ran home to watch afternoon cartoons. For the first time, he was able to identify with the cartoon wolf character that bulged his eyes, flapped his arms, and howled at the moon whenever he saw a pretty girl. Prior to the experience, he simply thought the cartoon wolf was special.

The days spent in Ohio were not all spicey. Most of it was a time of joy and innocence. One of Beulah's favorite stories to tell was when she sent the five-year-old to the store to purchase an item. It was a ten-block trip each way that included navigating a four-lane commercial street with stop lights. Beulah felt her son was ready. He successfully made the purchase, but on the way back he noticed a sprinkler system watering the grass of a business that had closed early for the day. He set the product down in a manner that avoided getting it wet, and then commenced to playing in the water by running through it and attempting to dodge the water drops. The experience was so enjoyable that the young lad lost track of time. Fearing that the child was lost, Beulah set out in her car to search for him. The clerk in the store vouched for the fact that the boy had left his establishment safely, but he was not sure which direction he went. Beulah experienced a mild panic episode as she began to contemplate the possible abduction of her child. There was solace when she caught her son out the corner of her eye playing in the sprinkler system. She was much too relieved to be angry at him. Up to the day she passed away, Beulah told the story to her friends about how cute and innocent her child was performing his very first errand for Mommy. When first hearing the story, June Bug just rolled his eyes.

As far as Church Mouse was concerned, the days spent in Ohio were too few. Some of his better childhood memories took place there. The boys really enjoyed it when the family moved out of the projects into a single-family home that was on an acre of land. The back yard had several apple and pear trees that they loved to climb and use their adventurous imagination during playtime. Eating the fruit was an added benefit. Then there was the time when the boys' father dressed himself up as a woman on Halloween night. Boy, did he ever look funny!

Beulah's oldest child, Nefertiti, came up from South Carolina to join the new family for a summer school break. She was classier and more refined than her mother. Nefertiti was Ming Dynasty supreme. [66] She was a welcomed addition to the King's expanding family. Beulah's younger sister Efficiency joined her niece for the much-needed summer break. She was a wise and stately woman. Her twin brother, J-Bird, also made the trip. He was a barrel of laughs. One fond memory Church Mouse has was how Uncle J-Bird would change the lyrics of popular songs on the radio. For example, in Gary U.S. Bonds' 1961 hit song *Dear Lady Twist*, the original refrain stated, "Get up from your chair." J-Bird altered the lyrics to say, "Get up offa yo boonkey." When Church Mouse asked him what a "boonkey" was, he poked out his rear end and said, "I'll teach you more about that when you come down to the mother land." It was a funny saying, but the young lad still didn't know the full meaning of his uncle's cry to "Put your booty up and poke out your behind!" Ah yes, for the good times.

Beulah and the King appeared to be in love. Even June Bug took a sabbatical from his budding career as a Tasmanian Devil. For a brief moment in time, he was civil. Dare to dream, Church Mouse. Dare to exhale and smile. Mail in the stats. They say all good things must come to an end. If so, somebody better catch the mailman before he gets too far down the road. We may have to revise those stats before they go public. Sometimes, fate attaches a rubber band to the dreams of ghetto children and snaps them back like a cruel April Fools' joke.

Renege. That is what Murphy does best. He consistently goes back on his word. The King was suddenly deployed to a new air force base located near Macon, Georgia, and for whatever reason, the family's economic fate took a dramatic turn toward poverty, hard luck, and despair. Prior to the move, the family's socioeconomic standing hovered around the lower rungs of middle-class status, with a real shot at improving to a higher level someday. Shortly after relocating to Beulah's hometown in rural South Carolina, the family's economic status tumbled to the lowest rungs of poverty. It was during this time that Beulah buckled under the weight of her disappointment of not reaching her goal of upward social and economic mobility. The idea of Beulah realizing her middle-class dream began to fade like a basketball shot that never touched the net nor the ground.

Post-chapter mentoring tips for parents and educators: There are certain topics such as sex education that cannot be left to strangers and the streets to instruct our children. The ideal school level to introduce the topic is still up for debate, but parents who do not engage with their children at all on the subject will end up having to settle for what they get. It is better to take control of the situation and do not allow important things such as sex education and self-identity issues to be left up to chance.

Post-chapter survival tips for children who hurt: Everything that is good to you is not always good for you. Find your inner compass and follow it to success. Learn to trust your gut feelings and your conscious regarding decisions in your life that define manhood and womanhood. It would be nice if there is a critically thinking adult available to guide you, but don't hold your breath. Some Murphy's Kids can't even get a pot to piss in. Their tears never touch their cheeks because they immediately evaporate. They dissipate into thin air. Learn to block out all the disappointment and the static interference that comes your way. One way to block out the noise is by dancing to some good funk music. Feet don't fail me now. Alas, don't rush adulthood. Enjoy being a child while you can.

CHAPTER 10:

HEY TOTO, I DON'T THINK DADDY TOOK THE RIGHT INTERSTATE EXIT

B ECAUSE B EULAH'S MOTHER LIVED FAR FROM WHERE THE K ING WAS STA-tioned at Warner Robbins Air Force base near Macon, Georgia, the decision was made to have the family live with Grandma Queen in a rural town called Four Mile just outside of Mount Pleasant, South Carolina. Four Mile and Macon were about a four-hour drive from one another. It was not the best decision the King could have made, but he must have had his reasons. Perhaps the marriage was going sour, and he desired some distance away from his bride. Or maybe Queen needed her daughter's immediate help around the house. The rationale surrounding the father dropping his two boys off in a time-warped community while living in a different town remains sketchy even to this day.

There are multiple ways life in South Carolina during the 1950s and 1960s can be described. Church Mouse decided to synthesize and adopt four competing, yet symbiotic, versions of his experience living in the Deep South. That synthesis includes: (a) a researcher's unveiling of factual evidence that clearly reveals problems with poverty, racism, White privilege, and little if any advancement of the Black community; (b) a curious yet amazing view among local religious Black citizens that poverty was "nothing but a chicken wing" [i.e., a small thing mediated by the grace of God], and that race relations between South Carolina Blacks and Whites were not all that bad; (c) cultural and economic shock that led to hunger, physical underdevelopment, and mental depression for young Church Mouse and some (though not all) of his peers; and (d) a view adopted by Church Mouse the college professor that says some of his northern peers were deprived of experiencing true Black culture in its fullest form. In the mind's eye of an older and wiser Church Mouse, a synthesis of all these viewpoints is simultaneously viable and accurate. The following is a further breakdown of each of these interpretations.

An Historical Perspective:

The Carolina colony was settled in 1670 and named for King Charles I. The region was split into north and south provinces in 1710. Because of agricultural needs, South Carolina relied heavily on slave labor to work rice and indigo plantations. Its first capital city, Charleston, was the largest slave port in the United States. The majority of enslaved Africans in America passed through the port of Charleston. In comparison, New Orleans was the next busiest slave port, followed by Richmond, Virginia, and Jacksonville, Florida. By 1720, Blacks made up most of South Carolina's population. In 1860, South Carolina became the first state to secede from the union when President Lincoln (R) called for the abolishment of slavery and suggested changes in free trade practices. The first battle of the Civil War was fought at Fort Sumter right outside Charleston. For a brief period after the war, General Tecumseh Sherman's Special Field Order #15 allowed "Forty Acres and a Mule" styled reparations for freed Black slaves. Sadly, Andrew Johnson (D), perhaps America's most racist president, outlawed the concept that would have drastically changed the history and the trajectory of Black people in America.

Although the race relations record of South Carolina is not as brazen compared to that of Mississippi (which had 538 documented cases of lynching African Americans between the years 1882 and 1968), the palmetto state perpetrated the eighth highest cases with 156 incidences. [67] The term "lynching" is believed to have originated in South Carolina at Lynches Creek in 1868, when a group of White men instituted vigilantism as a form of frontier justice against Blacks and progressive political types. [68] Other examples of White mob violence include the lynching of twelve Black men from Union County during rampant Ku Klux Klan (KKK) terrorism in 1871. Research conducted by the Equal Justice Initiative reveal that in 1871 there were eleven lynching incidences and more than six hundred brutal beatings of Black South Carolinians by the Ku Klux Klan from York County. [69] In July of 1876, a White mob lynched six Black men and injured many others in the city of Hamburg when citizens chose to support Black and progressive White republican candidates for public office. Frazier Baker was gunned down in 1898 because the town of Lake City did not want a Black postmaster—a job bestowed on him by President William McKinley (R). There were twelve lynching incidences in 1889 alone, and another fourteen in 1898. [70] The number of overall Black killings in South Carolina is higher if one accounts for undocumented cases of lynching and deaths by gunfire and beatings.

A contemporary example of horrific hatred towards Black people in South Carolina happened on June 17, 2015, when White supremacist Dylan Roof (R) killed nine Black parishioners of Emmanuel A.M.E. church in Charleston while attending a Bible study. Roof stated in his blogs that he hated Blacks, Jews, Hispanics, and East Asians and wanted to avenge the so-called multicultural dishonoring of White people.

At all levels, South Carolina elected more Black officials (316) during the Reconstruction era compared to the other former confederate states. Despite this fact, heavy resistance to emancipation and Black freedom still existed in South Carolina. Even though citizens elected five Black Reconstruction candidates to the U.S. Congress—Republicans Joseph Rainy in 1870, Robert Brown Elliot in 1871, Robert DeLarge in 1871, Alonzo Ransier in 1873, and Robert Smalls in 1875—racist South Carolinians could not stomach the idea of Black or White elected officials advocating for the Civil Rights Act of 1875 and other early social justice legislations. When federal troops were withdrawn from South Carolina in 1877, Black politicians at all levels were forced out of office and threatened never to run again. The early progressive example set by republicans suddenly evaporated all over the South in the face of new Jim Crow laws and special economic deals cut with southern democrats. The rise of the KKK, sponsored by southern democrats, sealed the fate of Blacks who had gotten just a brief taste of freedom. It would take another eighty years before a reinvigorated Democratic Party along with a few remaining progressive republicans championed the second round of Black civil rights of the 1960s era.

Education attainment across race has not been and still is not equal in the state of South Carolina. Statistics from The Education Trust demonstrate that the Black/White achievement gap continues to be a problem in most states across the nation. [71] One study shows that public schools in South Carolina have the distinction of being rated in the top ten worse among states over the last fifty-year period. Another report found that South Carolina had the third largest White–Black and White–Native American K-12 achievement gap in the nation. [72] Although all students are improving as a whole, the gap between groups has remained relatively the same over the years. Most sociologists attribute the difference not solely to racial factors but also because of poverty. *U.S. News & World Report* states that South Carolina has the tenth highest poverty rate in the nation with the median household income being $10,000 below the national average. [73]

With a few exceptions, South Carolina has always been a conservative state that promotes business, elitist, and pro-Dixie policies over interests of Blacks and other disadvantaged groups. Blacks and poorer Whites have been mostly left out. Racism is real in South Carolina. Contrary to popular myth, however, it has not always existed in the name of the Republican Party. The institution of slavery and South Carolina's initial foray into Jim Crow segregation were propagated by White Southern Democrats. They boldly followed the example set by President Andrew Johnson and other racist democrats of the day. Inspired by Barry Goldwater during the presidential election of 1964, it took the flipping of party allegiances by US Senator Strom Thurmond to convince South Carolina Dixiecrats to leave the Democratic Party and join the republican ranks. Today the state remains republican dominated, but South Carolina is now conservative-red compared to its former and curious conservative-blue history.

For many decades, African Americans had little meaningful representation from either political party. Between 1880 and 1960, Blacks were likened to a motherless child dangling in the winds of brazen racial hatred and deafening political ambivalence. In honor of Abraham Lincoln, Blacks remained loyal to the Republican Party, but they were not provided meaningful reprieve from racial hatred by White domestic terrorists, most of which was democrat initiated. The Kennedy and Johnson administrations made an indelible impact on immediate civil rights legislation in the 1960s. Since then, democrats have championed civil rights, but the jury is still out regarding the long term, 360-degree plan of the party for long-term self-empowerment of Black, Brown, and Red peoples. Some political observers argue that a few crumbs and an entitlement mentality does not equate to true political and economic freedom. Since the 1960s, however, it has been mostly far-right wing republicans who have pushed the envelope on racist and elitist rhetoric and practice. Curiously, the Republican Party has ignored its own social justice creation. Sadly, some contemporary republicans even speak out against it.

In the twenty-first century, Tim Scott, a Black Republican, was elected to the House of Representatives for South Carolina in 2011. He was then appointed to an open Senate seat in 2014 and officially elected to that position in 2016. There is a place in politics today for Black republicans *if they would choose to promote the civil rights and social justice platforms of their 1870s predecessors.* The greater issue is whether today's Black conservatives will represent the progressive platform of yesteryear's Reconstruction-era Republicans, as opposed to modern-day Tea Party–styled politicians. Republicans who ignore and/or minimize civil rights are useless.

In contemporary society, a false polemic is preferred. Many Blacks love to refer to Black republicans as an Uncle Tom or an Aunt Jemimah without getting to know them personally or studying their platform. Yes, some Black conservatives deserve the ridicule, but many of them do not. Black history started long before the 1960s revolution. For example, the first Christian church was Black not White. [74] Africa and the Mideast had universities and medical doctors long before Europe did. [75] Blacks have a rich history of con-servative. liberal, and moderate perspectives. We are the original eclectic thinkers of the world. Don't let them put you in a box. We must learn to fight our war simultaneously on multiple fronts. All other American races except Blacks seem to understand this principle. The KKK has taught Blacks well how to fight one another and remain divided. It is a wicked and ingenious plan that has worked to perfection.

Gentrification of formerly Black-owned lands has clearly been a recent problem in Mt. Pleasant. Historic "heirs lands" (i.e., communal areas that were guaranteed to stay in the hands of the descendants of slaves) are now being gobbled up by beachfront condominium and resort developers. Slick business tycoons are taking advantage of loopholes in the law. Too many undereducated Blacks are selling properties for far below market value without honoring neighborhood covenant rules and consulting their elders. Question: Are elected officials fighting on their behalf, or are they rolling over? Because the heir's program was designed to be a shared covenant arrangement should a proposed sale of land take place, it has caused much consternation when individuals go off on their own and make deals with developers. The sum total is that communal lands are quickly dwindling and large areas that were formerly 80% Black-owned are now being rapidly replaced by popular vacation spots for mostly rich White folk, further erod-ing historic Gullah Geechee culture and the traditional customs of the area.

While the pursuit of civil rights, diversity, and economic equity is not totally absent in South Carolina's history, social justice issues have historically not been on the state's top five priority list. For a brief time during Reconstruction, it was a top priority, and one could make an argument that South Carolina was among one of the more progressive states by 1870s southern standards. Once Reconstruction passed, however, other priorities such as agricultural exports, industrial development, the expansion of technology, the promotion of tourism, fighting the forces of liberalism, protecting the status quo, and the preservation of old Dixie culture took center stage. For example, South Carolina was one of the last states to remove the flying of the Confederate flag at the capitol building. Today, there are at least 112 spaces with Confederate monuments remaining in the state. There are boundless examples of civil rights and social justice potential in the state of South Carolina. There is also much that remains to improve on, however.

Through the Eyes of a Transplanted Northern Black Child:

Life in the Four Mile section of a sleepy rural town called Mt. Pleasant, South Carolina, in the early 1960s—WTF (once again folks, what the James Brown funk)? This was the boys' first contact with poverty, unbridled disadvantage, and blatant racism. What they encountered was complete economic and cultural shock. What had been a life of relative ease and comfort was suddenly transformed into a nightmare of want and despair. Had the boys never known prosperity, adjusting to the unfamiliar environment would have been a manageable transition. But the father had given his two boys the same lower middle-class upbringing that he had received from his parents. When they arrived in South Carolina, the economic bottom fell out for the family. At least Slim Jenkins had a head start on his stepbrothers. Beulah immediately sent him to live with her mother prior to the Ohio move. Whatever economic and cultural dissonance the two boys encountered Slim Jenkins already received the full Monty of that experience.

Growing up outside of the Deep South, June Bug and Church Mouse had never seen the level of poverty and racism they were about to experience.

Welcome to country living southern style, young city boys. Kick off your urban and put on your hayseed. Take off your shoes and stay awhile. Wait a few weeks before you put them back on again. Roll in the bushes with a wild boar or take a swing at mosquitoes the size of hummingbirds. From the California brick house to the Carolina outhouse. In Queen's immediate neighborhood, running water and indoor toilets were mostly nonexistent in the early 1960s. Church Mouse feared the outhouse—a foul abyss carved into the ground. A rancid hole covered by a flimsy outer shell about to topple over. Thousands of fly maggots swarmed inside years of deposited feces. They say a little caca is good for the local crop. But why does country stink smell so different than its city counterpart? During tough financial times, June Bug and young Church Mouse discovered that newspaper, a Sears catalog, or even gray moss hanging from trees sometimes had to be substituted for toilet paper. Sorry for the raw details, folks, but this is what real poverty looks like. "Where fa yu daddy go (where is your father)?" a neighborhood kid asked Church Mouse. "I want to go back to Ohio where they have inside toilets and people who speak regular English," the young boy murmured.

Being a woman of honor, Queen was happy to help Beulah's family by taking them into her crowded abode and sharing what little she had. Though the boys were happy to lay down their weary heads after a long and tiresome trip, they were apprehensive about the strangeness of the new place. The language of the Gullah culture did not sound American. "Da Lawd be a mighty fine God to bless me wit dees new grand chillen," said Beulah's wise and gracious mother. One day, young Church Mouse went outside with Slim Jenkins to play. The boys started a friendly contest to see who could throw rocks the farthest distance. Queen came to the back door to chastise the boys. "Yu bet stop chuckin' dem rocks ova yonder fo yu juck eee bruva winda. Make me ramble ma mout 'bout dees tings, and I'll baux tree de'il out yu boonkey. Yu ya me, boys?" Queen yelled out. [76] Not fully understanding the ramifications of his action, young Church Mouse responded to his newly acquired kin with a hearty and sassy "You talk funny." She walked over to him and laid a fist sandwich right on his kisser. To the ground, the little guy crumbled. The Queen of Wisdom might have been a saintly woman, but she was not a person to allow disrespect from a little pissant. Her cousin, Bubba, began to laugh and shake his head. "Yu fancy northern niggas gots plenny to learn 'bout dees muthas in da South. We 'specs da women in dees parts, 'cause dey is da backbone of dis munity," the giggling cousin replied. "Now up wit ya boonkey from da ground. Cum hang wit me so I can teach y'all how to catch a cotton mout." Yeah, just what Church Mouse always wanted to do—learn how to catch snakes.

Urban Ohio, where have you gone? Southern California, why have you forsaken the King's kids? Palm trees and paved alleyways, where are you hiding? Even the cobblestone streets of Omaha seemed like a welcomed alternative to the winding dirt roads lined with potholes so deep that local children were rumored to have disappeared in them. Four Mile was a place hidden from the rest of the world. Small dirt roads led into thickets of dense trees and green foliage. Strange animals jumped out of the brush, said the N-word, told one-liner jokes, and then jumped back into the bushes. "Why did the colored man cross the road?" asked the fluffy bunny. "To make you a part of his evening dinner?" replied the coon. "Whatever, dude," said the irritated rabbit. Spicy yet colorful conversation, to say the least.

The people of Four Mile constituted a civilization lost in a time warp. Satellites and GPS technology were not around to help locate tucked-away communities like these. You had to pull out an old-fashioned paper map to find it. To a transplanted northern urban dweller, the outskirt areas of Mt. Pleasant was no pleasant place to live. Today it is, but not in 1960. Four Mile was a sleepy community one could easily find in a Reconstruction-era movie. Church Mouse never realized that he would meet people who could pass for a Stepin Fetchit relative. Southern racism had a way of dumbing down the collective achievement level and aspirations of Black citizens who lived in poverty. Small rusty tin-roofed houses sat high on cement blocks to avoid flooding. Some of these homes looked as if they could easily be toppled over by a stiff wind. Most of them desperately needed paint and repair.

Mutant-sized roaches and other strange-looking insects climbed the walls of most Four Mile homes.

If you visit Four Mile and its neighboring communities today, it would not be recognizable to the average 1950s Gullah citizen. Commercialization and gentrification have drastically changed the sleepy, poverty-ridden collection of villages into one of the most sought-after American vacation spots located along the eastern seaboard. The township that was once graced with families who earned $5,000-per-year incomes is now littered with millionaires. Even the sacred Gullah culture is evaporating right before our eyes. In five decades, Charleston's neighbor went from a caterpillar into a beautiful butterfly with stock options on the side.

Ah, yes, the majestic city of nearby Charleston—a storied fixture in southern history. As previously mentioned, she was the largest and busiest port city that took part in the American trade of Black slaves. Today, the greater Charleston area is a tourist destination, but back in the 1950s and 1960s, it was a redneck's paradise. The Old South was alive and well when Church Mouse and June Bug met their new family. Poverty was very evident and stark. Black people fought over the crumbs that fell from the White man's table. Young Church Mouse was shocked to witness an elderly Black man shuffling down a sidewalk step off the cement so that a White couple could pass uninterrupted. "Good morning, ma'am and sir," the old man said as he tipped his hat then remounted the trail to continue his journey. Mr. Charlie (White males) was godlike and omnipresent. He owned and censored everything—even the sweat off a fieldhand's balls.

Although the historic Supreme Court decision of *Brown v. Board of Education of Topeka* had been handed down several years earlier, schools and other public spaces in the Deep South were still segregated. Southern governors and mayors often told the federal government and northern politicians where to stick their civil rights laws. Old plantation mansions swayed majestically in the wind. An original slave auction block is still on display in downtown Charleston for tourists to muse over. Rumors of Klan rallies were commonplace. It was common to witness an elderly Black person board a bus and go all the way to the back, passing several empty seats up front, despite recent court decisions. All around swirled remnants of manufactured ignorance. Stark reminders of the underbelly of this otherwise great nation.

Mt. Pleasant, Charleston's stepsister located across two rivers, was home to the most African of American citizens. The Four Mile section of town was so named because the community was located four miles from the Cooper River bridge. The residents there were a transcontinental people. Pure African many of them were, some without a drop of White or Indian blood in their genetic makeup. American in citizenship, but Bantu and Niger-Congo in heart, body, soul, and spirit. Living among the Gullah people took some getting used to for the boys. Slim Jenkins adjusted most quickly, followed by June Bug. Church Mouse struggled like an immigrant trying to learn a new culture, however.

Gullah was both the culture and the language of the local citizenry. Many a tale has been written about the people from West Africa who were forced to settle along the S.E. coast from Jacksonville, North Carolina, to Jacksonville, Florida, a 450-mile stretch. Purposely isolated and kept away from more boisterous and freedom-seeking Blacks who had lived on the mainland for a longer period, Gullah people preserved traditional African culture, only slightly altered since their original days of capture. The separation of Gullah people from other southern Blacks had an unintended blessing in that it allowed tribal groups to adapt to Western culture slower and on their own terms, unlike the more brutal assimilation of original Black slaves in other parts of the Deep South. The exploration of the Gullah people and their culture is a fascinating study. [77]

Racism had a special impact on the citizens of the Deep South. It turned many Whites into bullies without their knowledge or consent. It contributed to a sense of second-classness among Black adults and fostered low self-esteem and a low achievement orientation among Black children. The vestiges of self-hatred were poisonous. Petty jealousies ran rampant in the

Deep South. For example, the King's boys were stunned by the importance skin color held in the minds of Four Mile citizens. To the lighter skinned African Americans, the shorter, coarser haired, and dark-skinned African Americans were called "Black Ju-Jus," jungle bunnies, and tar babies. Darker skinned Blacks, in turn, called lighter skinned Blacks "red," "piss color," or wannabe White folk. The latter were considered to have "good" hair. The residual effects of the White Man's systematic effort to disenfranchise Blacks were caustic and successful. Many Blacks were totally enthralled with the idea of assimilating into the dominant culture. They were unable to see that they were being taught to hate their history and culture.

In South Carolina, poverty radiated all the way to the bone. The sight of hungry children running around with snotty noses and no shoes was commonplace. High school dropout rates were among the highest in the nation. Academic achievement was among the lowest. More significantly, a high percentage of Black males grew up with little direction and few goals in life. Whatever few scraps Mr. Charlie let fall from his table reluctantly went to the Black female. Black women who were just keeping the family from unraveling ruled whatever small vestiges of power Mr. Charlie would allow Black people to have. Conversely, zombie-like grown men aimlessly wandered their communities gambling and drinking away their paychecks. The phrase "no-good-nigga" became popular. It was as if the breakup of the Black family had been carefully orchestrated. If you are truly "woke," the rest of this equation is easy to fill in.

Gullah beliefs, customs, habits, food, and language were non-mainstream, to say the least. One almost got the feeling of living in a foreign land; the poorest areas of the Caribbean easily come to mind. It was the first time the boys had been introduced to new foods such as benne seeds and hog maw. Pig feet were sold over the counter in country stores. Several hoofs swam in large jars that used mysterious thick yellowish-brown liquid to keep them preserved. It looked and felt like glue. The concept of eating cow tongue was gross to the average bougee northerner. The thought of taking a steak knife and slicing a tongue while using hot sauce to give it extra flavor was enough to make an urbane connoisseur gag. Rotate and then modulate. Beulah lost her mind when she tried to make her kids eat cow brains. She served it as if it were corned beef, but the kids knew that something bogus was afoot. She then tried to trick the kids by mixing it into scrambled eggs. Can you say trick ask? And then came the dreaded conversations about chitterlings, aka the intestinal tract of the pig. When Beulah cooked them, the whole house had an interesting smell for hours upon end.

The most ridiculous meal came one day when Beulah tried to make her children eat chicken feet! Can you imagine cereal-bacon-eggs-and-toast-eating California kids being forced to eat a plate of chicken pods? The visual of that moment is enough to make a person cluck three times. June Bug fed his portion of chicken feet to the dog hiding under the table. Crunch, crunch, crunch went the creature's canine teeth. Slim Jenkins ate his chicken feet, but he first made them dance in James Brown fashion before he devoured them. He was an innovative soul. Church Mouse snuck his serving into his pants pockets and then threw them into the bushes when he got outside. Four Mile had beaucoup bush areas people could easily hide stuff in.

As Church Mouse became an adult and learned that the exotic foods were part of a strategy Black folk utilized to survive hunger, he grew to understand that Beulah was not completely out of her mind. Greedy southern Whites took all the good parts of the pig, the cow, and the chicken and left the scraps for Black folk to eat. The ingenuity of the Black woman was to take the throwaway goods and turn them into a delicacy. It was a brilliant strategy, albeit strange for first-time migrants from the urban North. Church Mouse was slow to catch the rhythm of the Gullah cultural stroke. That is why they referred to him as a White Boy.

Grandma Queen and her mother, Ethnography, navigated the trans-continental language, customs, and culture fluidly. Ethnography was a stately and humble woman. She made a living by working in the homes of the descendants of former slaveholders. Up to the day of her passing, Beulah made the claim that her grandmother was emancipated from slavery at the age of twelve, making her 112 years old when she died in 1965. The 1930 census does not support this claim, however. It shows Ethnography's birth date to be abt (about) June 25, 1875, making her ninety years old when she passed. Beulah counters with the argument that racist Reconstruction-era Whites arbitrarily miss-assigned government statistics to Black folk. Beulah remained confident in her assertion and her story is compelling, but for the purposes of this document, it is safer to go with county records. Regardless of Ethnography's age, she was a walking encyclopedia, with much information to share. Church Mouse, a grade school student, was far too young to realize the wealth of information he could have gleaned from her. He was fortunate to inherit her Bible, but no family member attempted to write down, tape, or video-record her thoughts before she passed. From an education point of view, that omission was very unfortunate.

Grandma Queen and her mother, Ethnography, frightened Church Mouse when he first met them. In his mind, he thought them to be foreign visitors from Africa or Jamaica. Their skin color was much darker than what he had seen up north. Both ladies had silver hair that looked like a royal bonnet. Their high cheekbones jumped out at you as if to shake your hand and ask, "Want some grits and butts' meat, honey chile?" The teeth in their mouths appeared to come forward at a twenty-five-degree angle. Both women had sheepherder's legs, like stilts. Both were physically stronger than the average female, even though their frames were slight. Queen and Ethnography were ethnically gorgeous. Africa was majestically distributed throughout their bodies. During his early years, however, Church Mouse was propagandized by dominant group norms to believe that their culture and physical attributes were something to be ashamed of.

Through the Eyes of a Traditional Gullah Citizen:

Not all friends and family members agree with Church Mouse's account of living in Four Mile. And not everyone agrees with the historical perspective offered in this account that South Carolina was (and still is) a struggling southern society that Black people are forced to navigate. Although the schools in Nebraska are rated higher and Blacks are generally not subjected to the abject level of poverty still found in certain rural pockets of South Carolina, African Americans from the Northeast, West, and Midwest often lack the wider historical and cultural perspective that citizens from the Deep South possess. Everything is not always about money and creature comforts. Southern living has a few advantages. Down south, schoolteachers are revered, and students bring treats from home to show their appreciation. Up north, too many parents look for ways to get a big payday by suing their children's teachers. In Four Mile, Black children still say "yes, ma'am" and "yes, sir" to their elders and teachers. In Omaha they say "aight" (alright) and throw up duces (a peace sign). Teenagers in both places sag their pants, but at least the rural ones still put on a suit and a tie when they go for a job interview. They correctly understand that there is a bicultural switch that must be controlled and toggled throughout the week.

South Carolina has more Black people (27%) compared to Nebraska (6%). [78] Both places lack a large homegrown Black middle class like Atlanta has, but Nebraska is really behind. From outward appearances, there seems to be a greater percentage of black businesses in the Charleston area as opposed to Omaha. Both have their versions of juke joints, hair salons, and small BBQ eateries, but at least the ones in South Carolina stay open for more than ten years. In North Omaha, Black businesses tend to close after a two—year stint. A few shut down only after several months because of problems related to rowdy crowds and/or gang violence. Black land ownership in Nebraska is nowhere close to that of South Carolina. There are people in Four Mile who don't have large savings accounts, but they own land. Many residents of North Omaha don't have a savings account at all, and they barely make rent on a 125-year-old house located on a small plot of land infested with lead. Black churches down south are mostly full and have a healthy membership of young people and men. Black churches up north are mostly female driven with dwindling teenager and male participation. The comparisons can go on and on.

One criticism of the Black citizenry in South Carolina is that they are not revolutionary minded enough. They are viewed as too forgiving and "we shall overcome" oriented. This long-held view resurfaced when the members of Emmanuel A.M.E. Church publicly forgave Dylan Roof for the June 17, 2015, racist killing spree of nine Black citizens. One local leader bemoaned that Charleston Blacks were displaying a "plantation mentality" by forgiving Roof. Critics believe that legitimate anger and protest were being muted in exchange for the social acceptance and friendship of White folk. From the outside looking in, it did appear that some Blacks skipped over the initial stages of the grieving process and went directly to the fifth stage of forgiveness. Racist Whites saw that as racial weakness. Revolutionary Blacks view it as Uncle Tom, boot-licking behavior. Local Gullah citizens equated it to spiritual maturity. Pick your poison.

First impressions are sometimes lacking in understanding the full truth of a situation. It is true that an outsider can ask an older Black resident about the condition of race relations in South Carolina, and the answer they get might go something like: "We do not have a race problem here. Black and White people know how to live with each other in peace." Conversely, there are twenty-first-century Black women from the Deep South who still work in the generational kitchens of families that at one time owned slaves or fostered a Jim Crow mindset. A few of the women in Ethnography's family did that kind of work. There are Black men who happily shine shoes like they did in the olden days. Plantation tours are an everyday occurrence. All of this happens while vacationers can visit an authentic slave auction block while taking a Gullah commercial tour. Not all Charleston residents view a connection to the sordid past as something to be ashamed of. Some of it does bother Church Mouse, however.

It is a reality that shocks many northerner visitors, but there is a deeper level to understanding the local mindset. Sometimes the Black response has little to do with kissing up to White folk and more to do with two important philosophies: (a) A sincere belief in the power of divine providence. A conviction that God is in control, and that in the end the first shall be last and the last shall be first, and (b) A slick, reverse-psychology method of letting Whites believe that their feces do not stink. This is purposely done to discourage Whites from poking around in Black matters. Interestingly, not all Blacks are on board with so-called progressive legislation. One example is that some Blacks from the Deep South do not believe integration has been good for the race. Many believe that all-Black schools do a better job of educating and raising children compared to integrated schools. While most southern Blacks do not believe in "separate and unequal," there are a few who see value in a "separate AND EQUAL" paradigm for schools.

While it is true that a few Black southerners need to advocate more and do less accommodating, many have perfected the art of reverse psychology. They put more energies in keeping what they already possess, while also guarding against the unintended consequences and inevitabilities that assimilation and gentrification bring. Translation: Sometimes it is good to tell fragile White people that they are special so they will go sit down somewhere and leave Black folk alone. The stance incorporates the belief that in the end God will sort it all out. I have never seen the righteous forsaken, nor witnessed His seed begging for bread (Psalm 37:25), many Gullah people quote from the Bible. Some people view this as a strength and not a weakness.

It is also true that many Black South Carolinians don't have a college degree, but they feed their families the best way they know how. Sometimes it takes more bravery and courage to take that approach than to burn down a building or throw a rock at a cop. Black elders hold a special place in certain communities of the Deep South. Most professors at historically Black universities teach their students to honor the values and worldviews of their Black elders by not speaking out against them. These brave individuals have paid a heavy price so that younger generations can succeed. Black professors teach that whether liberal, moderate, or conservative, Black students should not criticize the very shoulders they stand on. Amen, light bulbs. [79]

Through the Eyes of a Critical Thinker:

Yes, it is true—not everything about South Carolina is sad and bad. Despite the poverty and the presence of both blatant and institutionalized forms of racism, the experience of living in the Deep South made Church Mouse a far better man than had he not done so. As a child, he hated the move to Mt. Pleasant with a passion. However, social intangibles such as good manners, hospitality, humility, a splendid work ethic, learning to be content with little material possessions, and keeping the MLK Jr. version of the civil rights struggle alive are inbred into southern Black children from the minute they are conceived. Many southerners stand firm in the belief that lessons gained from living in the Deep South can never be equaled by the physical comforts sometimes found in the urban Northeast, West, and Midwest.

Lessons learned from living in Dixie helped transform Tweety Bird from a cream puff into a strong Black man. The experience of growing up in the Deep South revealed a piece of history that is often left out of most school textbooks. When the family finally moved back to Nebraska, Church Mouse and June Bug held an advantage over their peers, who had only partial (though still legitimate) experience with poverty and racism. Omaha teachers were impressed when they turned in top-notch essays about Black history and social justice issues. That topic was a natural part of the school curriculum and southern upbringing. The people of Mt. Pleasant also instilled in Church Mouse a lasting spirituality that taught him valuable lessons about perseverance and overcoming obstacles. Black citizens of South Carolina showed him that brilliance exists only if it is wedded to service to others. Growing up in the Deep South taught Church Mouse how to serve with humility and grace.

The intrinsic lessons that the Gullah Nation taught the King's crew were priceless. A Rock of Gibraltar, Grandma Queen possessed a sixth sense about life that separated her from her peers. She was a citizen everyone in the community respected, and her word alone carried untold weight. It was from this noble woman that young Church Mouse first learned the principles of virtue and honor. She also introduced him to the Christian faith via the house of worship she attended, Olive Branch A.M.E. Church. The time spent in the Deep South also gave Church Mouse character traits he would not have received growing up in any other part of America. Just when Church Mouse was about to disown the whole southern experience, the Good Lord revealed to him a higher purpose.

Despite all that may be wrong with the Deep South, it introduced Church Mouse to what it really meant to be a true citizen of the world. Many northerners never get the chance to experience the raw education that southern living provides. They make a claim of being "woke," but in many ways they are sleepwalking and deprived. Yes, creature comforts, material gain, and civil rights acquisition are at the top of the list, but we must not overlook the importance of character building and value education. The experience of living in the Four Mile community of South Carolina introduced Church Mouse to the Gullah Nation and all their wisdom. It shaped him to be a Renaissance man and a 360-degree, eclectic thinker. It also introduced him to a wise woman of extraordinary faith. Grandma Queen fashioned in him an unshakable belief in the need for integrity and honor. She instilled in her grandson a willingness to answer the call to virtue. Her influence guided Church Mouse away from self-centeredness toward Kingdom principles and the embracement of perseverance as a survival tool. Queen helped her grandson to not be just another American consumer. Her lessons about trusting God saved his life. Without her early intervention, Church Mouse would not have become an overcomer and a resilient warrior. Long live the Gullah Queen and her legacy!

Post-chapter suggestions for elected officials and political pundits: We must take a 360-degree approach to solving our problems. All parties must be on board with a bi-partisan commitment to set politics aside and do what is best for our children. Too many conservatives simply ignore the problem, or they operate within a "kumbaya" paradigm that gives citizens a warm fuzzy, but there is little of substance that can be utilized to help solve complex problems at the street level. On the other hand, too many liberals adopt a "sacred cow" mentality that protect expensive programs that simply don't work. Located somewhere between these two positions are children who fall through the cracks of society. Most Murphy's Kids are not as resilient (or as lucky) as young Church Mouse. Instead, they grow sour and turn to alcohol, drugs, crime, abuse, and future abandonment of their own children. When a fault is assigned, rarely are system factors discussed. Rather, the guilt is placed squarely on the person or their family's shoulders. This is the conservative reaction to poverty. Conversely, liberals continue to shun personal responsibility, lower the cultural bar, and blindly throw money at problems that can only be solved at the spiritual and self-sufficiency levels. They are surprised when the desired results don't manifest themselves. As previously stated, Americans are good at throwing rocks at their own creations.

Post-chapter survival tips for minority and other disadvantaged children: Sometimes parents, social service agencies, and governing bodies will buffer in a circular round on the flat screens of life and not provide you with the tools you need to survive. They mean well, but they are ineffective, nonetheless. You may have to become your own salvation. Beware of those who preach that the way to go is to latch onto one philosophy—one perspective only—and run with it like a crazed evangelist. The way of a true critical thinker is to take in all sides, all knowledge, all information, and then "eat the meat and spit out the bone." Very few scenarios in life are black/white, devil/angel, and democrat/republican, or binary defined. Free yourself from the smoke and the mirrors of pleasing the crowd and kissing up to interest groups. Challenge the big lie that says all Blacks must buy into group think in order to be counted as authentic. While it is important to uplift and support your race, the lie that says all African Americans must act, think, and vote alike comes straight from the pit of hell. No other racial group does that, so why do Black leaders promote it? Become an eclectic and critical thinking leader, not a follower of popular dogma. Caution: adopting this independent stance will probably lead to social isolation and rejection, but always remember the axiom (and the song lyric) that says, "You have you to complete, and there is no deal." [80]

CHAPTER 11:

HOTTER THAN FISH GREASE

T HE FIRST SECTION OF THIS CHAPTER MIGHT BE A DIFFICULT READ FOR MANY readers. It involves talking about a taboo subject matter that is typically saved for Neo-Freudian mental health journals or private conversations you might have with your homies. The topic is: Black love and the problem of Black single-parent homes and high divorce rates. The discussion is born out of centuries of Black people having to navigate slavery and Jim Crow racism, as well as managing physical poverty and the culture of poverty. Despite its controversial nature, it is an inconvenient truth that cannot be avoided. Sensitive insider cultural conversations are never an easy topic to broach.

Prior to the 1960s Black cultural and political revolution, male–female relationships were an explosive topic of discussion in the African American community. That discussion was true all over our nation, but it had special significance in the Deep South during the time right before great leaders such as Martin Luther King Jr. and Malcolm X emerged on the scene. The reputation of Black men within the circles of some (though not all) Black women was at an all-time low. The Black family was unraveling as it was purposely targeted to be destroyed through the various undermining tactics of White racists, both conservative and liberal. The number one tool to accomplish that goal was to create single-parent households, while also paying Black workers less than a living wage. It was a wicked and effective design. It was proved to be more than successful. The high number of Black families headed by women was something Church Mouse noticed immediately upon his arrival to South Carolina. When he attended services at Olive Branch A.M.E. church, he noticed that aside from ministers, women were the dominate force in the sanctuary as well as society in general. Outside of the preacher and a few of his close male associates, Black women wielded much power and ran the community.

During the 1960s, Black males in Four Mile were resigned to a life of hard labor during the week, and then very hard partying and drinking on weekends. It was as if they were suffering from acute depression. Yes, there are theories floating around that blame food stamps and government assistance programs as the main reason why Black men systemically left their homes. Church Mouse only partially buys that theory. He remembers a period before assistance programs came into existence when men were at home, taking care of business. Females ran the show, but their men remained steady up until they lost faith in the early 1960s. Church Mouse is willing to be corrected, but he is one of those who believes that White people and too many (though not most) Black women have historically run good Black men into the ground. At times, it felt like an orchestrated conspiracy. Church Mouse also admits that Black men can at times be their own worst enemy. Too many chose to be abusive and unfaithful. It is a controversial and complicated "chicken versus egg" discussion that has many different layers.

Too often Black love was (and still is) unnecessarily toxic. This was especially true when the topic of Black men dating White women came up. Black men who cross-pollinate were called race traitors. Conversely, White women who sought out Black athletes and wealthier Black men were viewed as gold diggers. Church Mouse never got into the weeds of that discussion because his focus remained on the unity of all Americans. Interracial dating is commonplace and generally accepted today. Still, many Black women felt cheated. There are certain things she faced that most White women never had to deal with. The suppression of civil rights in America alone was suffocating enough without having to deal with extra distractors. Racial injustice in Dixieland was especially toxic. And now the Black family and community were crumbling from within. Most things in the Deep South come biggie sized. Roaches are gigantic. Coons are larger. Mosquito bites are marble sized. Rats are like little dogs. Economic setbacks were like mountains. And now Black divorce rates and broken family were growing like runaway inflation. Even matters of the heart and the art of love are augmented times five in the Deep South. The love of a Black woman to her man is sweeter than sassafras moonshine. Her scorn for being jilted is hotter than the devil's spit.

Beulah utilized soul music to describe her feelings about love. When she was head over heels in love with her husband, she would float around the house singing Otis Redding's "For Your Precious Love." But when he disrespected her, she would put on Sam Cooke's version of the "Frankie and Johnny" song and pretend to pop off in her husband's rear end with an imaginary shotgun. Beulah was daylight and darkness personified all in one neat bundle. She often bragged about women she personally knew who got away with shooting their men in nonfatal places like the leg or the buttocks because of infidelity. Prejudice in the Deep South was so thick, it was not unusual for biased White cops to not arrest Black women because "the wife was just defending herself against the aggressive Black male." The real racist ones would say, "Let coons oversee their own nigger business." Many Whites secretly wanted Black people to eliminate each other anyway. Real or perceived, fair, or unfair, it was during the late 1950s that the whole concept of the angry Black woman got its strongest foothold.

Contrary to popular myth, an unfaithful male is not the only cause of divorce in the Black family. Black females must also accept their part, even if they do not bear the lion's share of the blame. During the 1960s, being bashed by females was a ritual that southern Black boys had to endure as a normal part of growing up. Young boys had to pay the sins of the older men in their community. Living in poverty and having to hold down the fort all by herself was a heavy burden most Black women had to shoulder. The pressure turned some of them from angels to grouches. Still, many Black women need to be softer. No man, regardless of color or ethnicity, wants to hang around an angry, complaining female. It is not sexy, and 90% of the time the man will end up leaving. Some will say that is a sexist attitude, but it is real, and it won't change in this lifetime. Try a little tenderness—a little honey and sugar—instead of dragon fire.

Black men need a partner to help them heal from the collective boot that the system has planted dead in their ass. It says here that Black, Brown, and Red males have been racially and socially targeted the most. This statement does not take away from the exceptional circumstances that women of color have to endure. Navigating a racist society for both genders is harder than landing a B-52 airplane in the fog. But the plan was to destroy minority races by psychologically castrating the men of those groups. This message is as salient today as it was back in the day.

Guard your jugulars, minority boys. At times it can feel as if the entire world is out to emasculate you. Still, the bottom line is that Black men must do more to save the Black family. You cannot afford to wait for the system or your woman to make needed changes. Take control of your family by making the first step. She will follow if it is done right. In Beulah's case, the King of Ghosts was not the most faithful husband, nor was he an effective family leader. Most of the time, he was absent. Even the few times he was present, he was emotionally absent. Beulah's volatile temper and unpredictable behavior may have had a little to do with his omissions.

Church Mouse had just finished the third grade. He sat on the edge of his bed one day to eavesdrop on a conversation that Beulah was having with her girlfriends about men who cheat. The discussion was not politically correct, nor was it PG-rated. It went something like this:

Gullah Girl 1: Honey chile, I thought I seent yo no-good-ninja da utha day all pushed up against dis one stank-ass bitch ova at the Sweet Shop. [81]

Gullah Girl 2: Oh yeah? Who be dat bitch?

Gullah Girl 1: I heard she be da one girl from James Island who be sportin' Diana Ross wigs all da time.

Crazy Beulah: Iffin I eva catch da bitch, I'm gonna snatch dat wig off her head and let da entire world see her real shit!

Gullah Girl 1: Nah, girl, lee da bitch alone. She no different than yu and me. She just following James Brown's advice. She be "usin' what she got to get just what she needs," hey girl (with fingers snapping in the air)!

Crazy Beulah: Forget James Brown. I'm gonna do like Jr. Walker say and "shoot all dem ninjas before dey start running after dees skank ass hoes!" (The three women click their wine glasses in agreement.)

Gullah Girl 2: Seriously now, what is a girl 'pose to do when her man cheats? I really do luv my no-good-ninja. And I belee deep down inside eee luv me too.

Gullah Girl 1: Yeah, dat's what dey all say when dey wants da poontang.

Gullah Girl 2: There yu go again callin' all ninjas no good . . .

Crazy Beulah: Girl, yu know it be true. Un-lessen a boy be raised tied to eee mama's apron string, he gonna grow up to be a skirt chasin', no-bill-payin', punk-ass ninja—just like they daddies.

Gullah Girl 2: Is I'm da onliest one who got a no-good-ninja?

Crazy Beulah: Ah hell no, girl! Shoot, my punk-ass ninja is definitely of the no-good variety.

Gullah Girl 1: Well, dat might be true—but still my broke-ass ninja is mo broker than yo broke-ass ninja.

Gullah Girl 2: Wait a minute, ladies. While it might be true that y'all's ninjas is broke, at least dey ain't a dog like mines is!

Crazy Beulah: Girl, whatchu talkin' bout?! Ain't nobody's ninja is worser dan my no-good ninja.

Gullah Girl 1: Don't nary one-a-y'all know nutin' bout no broke-ass ninjas, un-lessen y'all studies da no-money ninja who calls eeself my man. Girl, now dat's a fo real no-good, broke-ass ninja!

Gullah Girl 2: Du yu 'pose all da ninjas in Four Mile is no good? If so, maybe we might hafta travel to anotha state and scout out some betta ones.

Gullah Girl 1: Beulah's ninja is from Nebraska, and he sho nuff ain't about shit.

Crazy Beulah: Oh, yeah? Well, what about dat crusty-ass ninja yu got from Columbia? He ain't worth a piss in a bucket!

Gullah Girl 1: Dat's what I been trying to tell boff y'all all dis time! We gotta darn near go to another planet just to find a better crop of ninjas!

Gullah Girl 2: Dat might be true, but if I can at least get mines to hand ova eee small check, den he be alright by me. I done told y'all many times da boy knows how to rock my world. Sometimes a girl can put up wit a half-ass ninja if eee at least pay da rent and perform well in da sack.

Crazy Beulah: Cum to think of it, my no-good-ninja is pretty gifted in bed, too.

Gullah Girl 1: Mines be makin' me scream, girl. And I ain't too proud to beg fo mo! (Playfully, all three girls laugh and high five each other.)

Gullah Girl 2: So, there it is. All y'all need to just settle down and admit it. Our broke-ass ninjas might be no good, but we'd be sum sorry-ass women if dey were to up and just leave us.

Crazy Beulah: Sista girl do have a point, yu know.

Gullah Girl 1: I guess what dey say is true . . .

G-Girls in Unison: All of us Black women needs our ninjas, even if dey is all no good!

The above conversation is written with a dangling electric wire. The topic is hotter than fish grease, and both the writer and Church Mouse will probably get crucified for including it. It is the most controversial of all the inclusions in this book. The conversation is real as dirt.

Some readers will complain that this account airs too much dirty laundry, and that Church Mouse should have kept this one in his back pocket. Considering its incendiary nature, maybe he should have. But there comes a time in life when you must keep it real and ditch the politically correct approach. Here is an important question: Should Black people duck theirs heads underground and hide when certain controversies arise, or should they rise up and fight against the evil that was done to them so they can recapture their former glory? Should they slip slide and pontificate, or should they follow Malcolm X's sage advice and take back their full physical, emotional, and cultural freedom? If you gain the freedom to live where you want but continue to refer to Black women as bitches and hoes, is that true freedom? Should African Americans co-opt or drop-kick the N-word? You decide.

To be sure, the above scenario should not be applied to all Black women. This was strictly a Crazy Beulah foray into her own personal love abyss. It would be inaccurate to say, however, that she was the only one who felt this way. Because of racism and economic stressors in the Deep South, the Black family was broken. Ignoring much needed fixes is nothing less than irresponsible. To be fair, once Beulah passed the 1970s decade, she no longer subscribed to the "all Black men are dogs" philosophy. She was able to evolve her thinking and rightly conclude that females did relationship wrongs too.

Unfortunately, her four boys caught the brunt of her ire during their formative upbringing years. As a result, they all had relationship problems that can
be traced back to Mom's early venom. June Bug was the most successful at
canceling the effects of Beulah's anger towards males, while Church Mouse
and Slim Jenkins struggled the most.

To successfully get to the bottom of problems related to social dysfunction in the Black family, we must not be afraid to grapple with uncomfortable
truths. Black people will never be totally free if they only deal with housing,
education, and jobs. Addressing the material side of freedom is OK, but that
approach is incomplete. We must deprogram and reprogram by not only
dealing with the physical side of racism, but also addressing a need for psychological, emotional, and spiritual healing. Too often, we walk on eggshells
trying hard not to offend anyone while helping no one. Conservatives fall
short because most choose to ignore the problem and/or they attempt to
fight the enemy with a Styrofoam bat. They rely on magic-pill solutions like
"just say no to drugs." Well-meaning liberals, on the other hand, are too busy
promoting emotional and guilt-based-only solutions that end up missing the
larger picture. Sometimes you don't sound like a conservative at all, Church
Mouse. Sometimes you sound like an alien from another planet.

The glory of Black love begins with the woman. The Black woman is the
most desired of all females in the world. When you find one of the gorgeous
ones, there is nothing and no one that can measure up. She is beyond comparison, and she knows it. She can take your breath away simply by the way she
walks. Men of all colors desire her. Makeda, the Queen of Sheba, buckled the
knees of King Solomon. Emily Morgan, the Yellow Rose of Texas, captivated
the minds of cowboys of all races. Josephine Baker set the boys of France on
fire with her sultry stage routine. The beauty of the Black woman makes a
blind man talk about seeing again. If you need examples, think Toni Braxton,
Paula Patton, Janelle Monae, Beyoncé, Laila Ali, Kenya Moore, and writer
Chimamanda Ngozi Adichie, and then let your bottom jaw hit the ground.

Likewise, the strong, sexy, and handsome Black male takes the American cake. He is hero glorified and king personified. He exudes a confidence that makes females of all races feel giddy and excited. When he adds the role of provider and protector to his good looks and charm, he becomes a superhero like Iron Man. At the sound of his voice, women start screaming and shaking. A few might begin to disrobe. He does not have to beg, because he conquers. He is both sexiness and security captured in a bottle. Women, if you need examples, think Lenny Kravitz, Denzel Washington, Michael B. Jordan, Terrance Howard, Rick Fox, Idris Elba, and Boris Kodjoe, and then swoon and faint. When you put a Black goddess together with a Black knight in shining armor, you get an incredible love explosion of the fifth dimension. Kapow!

Something is not right here. How can a race of people have daylight and darkness all at the same time? How can Black lovers have both a mountain-top and a valley-low experience all in the same breath? Oxymoron overload. In some circles, the Black family is in serious trouble. Black love is one of the most powerful synergies on planet earth, and yet, African American women have the highest divorce rate in the nation. [82] Blacks overall have the highest single-parent family rate at 64% compared to 34% for the general population. For Nebraska, the Black single-parent rate is 69%, and for South Carolina it is 71%. [83] These twenty-first-century numbers are real and cannot be ignored or sugarcoated. Readers cannot simply take a spoonful of sugar and wish them away as if they don't exist.

Left-leaning Black intellectuals espouse an explanation that lays the root of the broken Black family at the feet of slavery and Jim Crow practices. It theorizes that Black male and female tensions were purposely induced via racist Whites who set out to disenfranchise the entire race by breaking up the family and by singling out the male for special ridicule. Church Mouse believes the residual effects of that practice are still with us today. He is no radical theorist, but he agrees with them on this point. White men do not fear women of any color, but they do fear their men. The way to kill a snake is to cut off its head. If you damage the male, you weaken the race. Could it be that Black females aided the fiendish plan, albeit unknowingly so? Call this theory a quasi-academic hunch. Call it a stretch. Call it black and blue.

Divide and conquer. The ole slave master knew exactly what he was doing. Split up the Black family, and you disenfranchise the entire race. Give the Black woman an ounce of power, and then convince her of how weak and worthless her man is. The "better slave jobs" and a few crumbs that fell from the master's table all went to Black women and a few suck-up males who agreed to sell out. Confident and purposeful Black men, however, were physically and symbolically castrated. Many were killed. Could it be that too many Black females bought into criticizing their men without understanding the larger consequences of their actions? The impact of that practice did not end with slavery and Jim Crow. Any chance of reclaiming the glory of the Black race must first begin with healing the family. Men are a part of that solution. *There is no true Black family without a father in the home who is loved and honored.* Reestablishing our roots within the Black Church might also help repair that shattered foundation. Just because the discussion seems old-fashioned and oversimplified does not mean it is not relevant.

Without reservation, it can be said that way too many Black men are guilty of bullying and underappreciating their women. No matter how badly Black men have been treated by society, they should not take it out on the very group that historically held the Black family and the community together. It makes no sense for Black men to make their women scapegoats. Put some respect on your funk, G. Even when the woman is clearly at fault, the buck for fixing a broken family must stop with the man. Again, society will consider this a sexist statement but when considering the job of raising children, you must go with what works. Black men, stop whining and crying about what is wrong with the world; help change it one child at a time. Stop whoring around with other women. Take your ass home, and care for your wife and kids that you brought into the world. Set aside the skirt chasing, partying, smoking da chronic, and all the Mack Daddy bullshit that can so easily distract you. Why be a slave to things that are not even real? Think, don't drink. Vote, don't smoke. Pro-activate, don't procrastinate!

It is also true that the "innocent angel in heels" media image that some (though not all) women like to portray is seriously flawed. Please do not misinterpret the message. There are many women who never say the types of things quoted in the aforementioned Gullah Girl conversation. Crazy Beulah does not represent all Black women. Still, membership in the wretched male-bashing club is larger than some might want to admit. Likewise, a belief that the man is automatically at fault if a couple breaks up needs serious investigation. Unfortunately, there are women out there who browbeat their men, promote double standards, cheat on their mates, send incredible mixed messages, and turn away good men simply because "they lack that special spice or pizzaz." Black men of America, never forget the dating rule: If it looks like a duck, smells like a duck, walks like a duck, and quacks like a duck—it is probably a turkey. Sometimes it is better to marry an average-looking humble woman who is not full of herself and addicted to reality-show-style drama. Flashlight eyes, big tits, and tight thighs are not everything. Love comes in many flavors other than "booyah" and "hot sizzle." You get what you chase after.

There are several reactions one could take away from reading the Gullah Girl scenario: (a) In a politically correct world, vignettes such as these should never be printed. Cultural etiquette states that Black people should never air their dirty laundry. Individuals who share these kinds of secrets should be considered enemies to their race; (b) In a reactive world, rules are altered to make men look 100% guilty and women to look innocent. Unfortunately, this is a storyline that has been handed down through the ages. This approach has only a 10% chance of solving tough family problems; (c) In a chauvinistic world, the whole affair is often mishandled when bubble-headed men turn their noses up and say something stupid, like "It must be your time of the month or something." Sadly, this is an option way too many men choose. It dooms any chance for males of any color to be taken seriously as a true leader.

And, then there is option (d)—an interpretation of the problem from a sociopolitical and critical pedagogy perspective—the kind of answer that does not sell very well with today's language police. The ultimate answer goes like this: The White Man created the problem, while both genders of the Black race are equally guilty of sustaining and feeding it. It will take sincere compromise and hard work on the part of both males and females to come up with a workable solution to a problem that was forced upon them via racism. Translation: Set self aside and do what is best for the children! It would be nice if all that Black people had to worry about was the physical and economic consequences of slavery and Jim Crow. Sadly, the mental, spiritual, and family-health portions of the Black restoration equation have not been given equal attention.

Unfortunately, too many Black folks are waiting for the government to do it for them. Yes, the concept of reparations is as valid today (if done correctly) as it was during the times of Reconstruction. But if you are waiting on the White Man to do what he should do, you can bet that nothing will get done. Listen to an important message from Malcolm X: The Black family and the race must save themselves by circling the wagons and controlling their own destiny. Self-sufficiency and adopting a "brothers for others" perspective is the key. The lives and struggles of Black people who navigate racism and the culture of poverty are a complicated affair that the typical American does not fully comprehend. This treatise attempts to shed light on that complexity, with the hope that educators, policy makers, counselors, and pastors can help nip the problem in the bud before it blossoms into a full array of dysfunctional behaviors.

Not all Black and poor families were dysfunctional like the one Church Mouse grew up in. We can even say that most are not. Nevertheless, too many were during the 1960s. Blame cannot be hoisted upon the shoulders of Black women without men and other guilty parties accepting their fair share of the problem. She held down the Black family during a time when racist psychopaths went after her men. She should be rewarded for her faithfulness. Still, she may have taken one too many sips of her captor's brew. In all her brilliance and through all the hell that she endured, she may have neglected something of significant importance—the build-up and support of the males in her home and community—the cultivation of her own salvation. In the Black family, a woman's brilliance glows brightest when her partner's light shines like a beacon. The underlying problem? Real Black men are as scarce as hen's teeth. Thus, the carousel continues to spin. Black love is stronger than kryptonite, but it requires constant pruning, cultivating, and nourishing by both partners (including traditional or nonbinary relationships).

Young Church Mouse sat on the edge of the bed feeling chicken-fried and honey roasted. Even if the men verbally castrated by Beulah and her caustic crew were guilty of the charges leveled at them, how was a budding fourth-grade honor student supposed to compete with the "all men are dogs" designations the women spoke about? Swollen with a wry face, Church Mouse grappled with the idea of someday carrying the burden of the Black male gender on his slender shoulders. With great humility and a sense of genuine concern for his people, Church Mouse whispered to himself, "If I can just show Black women that all Black men are not bad, then maybe an open door to more trust can be established between the two sides. Maybe I can be the conduit for healing to take place within the Black family." It was during this time that overly serious, people-pleasing Church Mouse first began to grow ancient with sorrow.

———————————————————————

Earlier that year, Church Mouse experienced an episode at school where Beulah came to his rescue. During the second semester of his third grade year, he encountered taunting from his classmates at Jenny Moore Elementary School, so he put his head down on his desk to avoid making eye contact with fellow classmates wanting to ask mean and hurtful questions. For most of the 1962–1963 school year, the challenging economic times Beulah fell on prevented her from sending her children to school with lunches. Few kids in the poverty-ridden community of Four Mile could afford to buy hot meals every school day, but most were at least able to bring a sack lunch. June Bug found "creative ways" to deal with the problem of hunger. He was a master at making sure he had food to eat, even if that meant coloring outside of acceptable legal lines. His sticky fingers kept him from starving. He was more of a "by any means necessary" survivalist than a true thief. Sometimes he shared his spoils to help feed his siblings. Church Mouse was too religious and law abiding to think outside of the box. Was this a good decision? They say June Bug was the dysfunctional child, and that Church Mouse was a good boy and the honor student. But why was it only Church Mouse that needed professional help once they reached adulthood? Why was he the only one taking anxiety medication and pills to counter depression?

Beulah had just spent what little extra money she had to replace a worn-out pair of shoes that Church Mouse had been putting cardboard flaps inside of to help cover up holes in the bottoms. The new shoes were boss. They also gave Church Mouse much relief from severe foot pain that was caused by the old pair being too small. There was ample room along the top ridge of the new pair to accommodate a band of gauze to soak up the foul-smelling puss that oozed from the half-inch crater carved into the boy's foot by the old pair. Peroxide helped keep the odor down. Being called White Boy was bad enough; the insecure child did not want to add another moniker such as "Funkenfoot" to the collection of his many pseudonyms. To this day, there remains a scar along the top of his right foot to remind Church Mouse of his poverty roots.

Church Mouse's classmates snickered and whispered about their class-mate being on his third week without lunch. Sometimes charity begins at school. A few days earlier, a student showed mercy by sharing a portion of his lunch with Church Mouse. Classmates thought a day or two without lunch could happen to anyone. They figured that their classmate would soon be back on his feet. They were wrong. Because it now appeared that Church Mouse was more of a long-term charity case, they began to laugh, point, and snicker. This prompted the hungry child to put his head down so he could avoid eye contact with them.

Noticing the finger-pointing and whispering, the teacher asked Church Mouse to come to the front of the class. He shook like a leaf at her request but was obedient, nonetheless. What could she possibly want? When he arrived at her desk, she looked up at him and asked, "How is it that your parents can't provide you and your brothers with lunch? I don't get it. Doesn't your father work for the government? Surely, he makes more money than most of the parents who have children in this school. Can't your parents do better by you?"

Stunned and aghast, young Church Mouse ran out of the classroom to the restroom. He dashed into an open toilet stall, put his head between his knees, and assumed a familiar position between the wall and the bowl—a familiar place. It had a familial feel. How could the teacher embarrass him like that! Now his classmates will surely make fun of him. Not caring if he ever went back to class, he remained in the restroom for a while. The janitor ran him out and sent him back to class. During recess time, students teased him and echoed the teacher's remarks about the lack of proper parenting at home. No one played with Church Mouse at recess that day. Murphy's Law has a way of piling on.

Beulah was livid when her son told her what had transpired. If she had gotten hold of the teacher's home address, she would have driven straight over there and beaten the crap out of her. Beulah's mother, Queen, advised against that action. She made her daughter promise to cool down and find a more diplomatic way to address the incident. Beulah reluctantly said she would, but don't bet your mortgage on it. It was a Friday, so Beulah had a little time to think it over. She gathered herself and began formulating her strategy. On Monday morning, Church Mouse was given a rare personal escort to school by his mother. He knew it was going to be a special day.

Beulah was hotter than a chili pepper dipped in Tabasco sauce. Beulah was like a laser-guided missile. At four feet, ten inches tall, she was an imposing figure to most school officials. Once the teacher was summoned to the principal's office, she called the lady every kind of hoe-bag-bitch and shithead she could think of. So much for obedience to Queen's directives. Beulah warned the teacher that if she ever again referenced her family's personal business, she would "cum up to dis mutha fucka and kick your highfalutin ass in front of your boss and your co-workers." Then she added, "And my son betta be given the best education this school can offer. He'd betta bring home an excellent report card, or my foot will be all the way up yo candy ass." Intimidated, the teacher apologized, saying whatever it took to make the angry woman go away.

For the rest of the school year, the teacher barely spoke a word to Beulah's boy other than roll call and things regarding routine classroom matters. It was as if Church Mouse had carte blanche to do whatever he wanted to do. Luckily, the kid never took advantage of the situation, but he did snicker about the sudden turnaround in the teacher's attitude. Just when he was about to throw his stepmother away, she came through in grand style. Church Mouse was never a big Crazy Beulah fan, but on this day, she proved herself to be "the bomb." No, Church had no intention of joining his mom's "mutha-fuck-bitch" linguistic club, but for the moment, he was never prouder of how she put the pompous educator in her place.

At the semester's end, your boy brought home a report card that had straight A grades and all superior marks in citizenship. Because Church Mouse was an honor student, one would like to think the high scores were legitimately earned. Family members were never 100% sure about that conclusion because Beulah took a lot of the credit. Although Church Mouse was one of the top five students in the entire school building, it was hard to ignore the Beulah effect. Since the beginning of time, there was never a woman alive who possessed her moxie. The teacher ran into a buzz saw and got chopped to pieces. It was gratifying to know that the arrogant educator got a sample of what real power tastes like. Seeing the report card, Beulah responded with a sassy "Hot damn! Now dat's what I'm talkin' 'bout!" Sista Girl was an enigma for all time. Her funk was as potent as sassafras moonshine.

If the reader, like the teachers at his school, ever wondered what role the King of Ghosts played in the family's life during this time of financial turmoil, the answer to that question is: your guess is as good as his kids.'

Some people say that Daddy "hoed around" and drank up all the money, but that reasoning was not properly vetted and may not be conclusive. There is a slim chance that the father did provide sufficient financial assistance to the family, but that Beulah squandered it away via gambling and risky business and real estate investments. It is possible that the Ghost did provide sufficient assistance, but don't bet the mortgage on it. He was not the greatest example of seeing an important task through to fruition. If in fact he did take care of his financial responsibilities, there is also the possibility that funds may have evaporated in a vortex called Hurricane Beulah.

─────────────────────────

Post-chapter mentoring tips for parents: Impulsive decision making without thinking about long term consequences is a prime example of "piss-poor" parenting. There is no such thing as pure democracy. It does not exist. You cannot make all the people happy all the time. The best you can do is to build a solid foundation under the feet of your children, so they do not stray too far from their foundation when they go off on their own. It is also important that parents become more other-centered. It is not about you. It's about the entire family unit. In addition, we must heal the Black family and promote Black love. A large part of that healing comes only after we collectively agree to deprogram and reprogram what was done to the Black race by a sinister scheme. If you wait for the government to do it, it probably won't get done. Take charge of your own destiny. It would be nice if Black males and females met halfway regarding their differences. That would be the fair and sane way to solve the problem. But, if that doesn't happen, it is up to Black men to make the first, second, and third steps. Ignore comments that might call that mindset a sexist belief. Men of all colors be brave, don't be a slave. Think, don't drink. Walk, don't talk. In the words of Mahatma Gandhi "Be the change you wish for."

Post-chapter survival tips for children who hurt: One of the prime resiliency research factors that help Murphy's Kids cope with the tough realities of life is *a person's ability to put emotional and psychological distance between themselves and a messed-up situation they have little control over*. To be sure, this is not an easy thing to do. It takes an incredible amount of focus and staying power. If you can concentrate and learn how to free your mind, then your body and soul will follow. Yes, you may be in a hostage situation now, but your mind does not have to be trapped. Focus on your goals and keep your eyes on the ultimate prize of freedom and self-actualization, even when others around you have lost their minds. Find the strength to save yourself. If YOU do not do it, it may not get done.

CHAPTER 12:

ANANSI THE SPIDER AND THE BOO HAG

Drawing on memories from the past as a stimulant to help keep him awake for the nine-hour drive from Denver, Colorado, to Omaha, Nebraska, was working better than Church Mouse had first anticipated. Wide-eyed and charged, he was wired from the effects of his own adrenaline rush and the caffeine from drinking Mountain Dew and black coffee. Each anecdotal memory fueled his determination to succeed even more. No one ever said growing up would be easy, and memories of his past clearly reminded him of that truth. Thus, the drive across Nebraska became the pinnacle experience of the young man's quest to find the true meaning of life. Church Mouse was a fighter, but he also knew he was only a middleweight champion searching for heavyweight status. The brass ring was still out there to secure. This was no time for whining, quitting, or indulging in preliminary celebrations.

Wrestling with the ebb and flow between the effects of testosterone and caffeine, Church Mouse had not paid attention to the fuel gauge in the King's gas-guzzling car. When he realized he was low on fuel, he contemplated whether to continue to the next major city, Kearney, NE, or pull off to one of the smaller villages nearby. Since he had his father's wallet, there was no need to awaken the ole man. Ma Dear, still sick with the flu, was down for the count. Church Mouse decided to pull off the interstate onto a local road leading into a small hamlet. He spotted what seemed like a friendly gas station. As Church Mouse filled the tank, the White store clerk watched his every move as if the attendant "was wanna be startin' somethin'." Disappointed, the youngster shook his head in disgust. Most people nervously look away hoping not to make eye contact when you catch people eyeballing you, but not this guy. This Nebraskan seemed like he was Mississippi bold and bred. When he leaned over to spit into his tobacco can, he never lost eye contact with your boy. A blind shot it was, but the juice landed dead center. It went in like a Pistol Pete Maravich half-court basketball shot. It was nothing but net.

Church Mouse made a few faces at the guy and stuck his tongue out. Suddenly realizing he may have gone too far, Church Mouse quickly gathered himself and returned to a more conservative demeanor. Ornery behavior was not only risky for a Black teenager to display in the middle of rural Nebraska, but also not the image that God wanted him to portray. A moderate image was something he was willing to embrace once he realized that Colorado liberalism did not always deliver as it promised. He needed to get in character if he were to have a chance at succeeding as an emancipated youth in Omaha. Why wait until you arrive before you make that change? Might as well start your new life while the sun is still shining on a drunk man's ass. Especially if he is out cold. Church Mouse paid the man for the gas, some chips, and a soda pop. The redneck could not resist getting in a little dig before Church Mouse left. "Don't get too lost around these parts now, boy," he said. "Yeah, right. I got your boy right here," responded Church Mouse as he yanked on his family jewels. So much for embracing a conservative approach.

Before pulling off, Church Mouse decided to wash the bug stains from his windshield. Halfway through the task, a group of teenage boys in a pickup truck drove by and yelled, "Get out of our town, nigger!" The King suddenly woke up from his slumber and said, "Get in the car and drive off right now, son!" Church Mouse, being a young civil rights warrior full of revolutionary vigor, wanted to hurl back a few verbal insults of his own. The King rudely interrupted. "I said drive off right now!" he demanded. Church Mouse, suddenly struck by the conviction in his father's voice, decided it might be wise to obey. It was not often that he witnessed his father take charge of a situation. The bigots jeered and applauded the family's departure. "Yee-haw!" one of them yelled. Church Mouse did the yanking of the family jewels routine again, but the rednecks missed the full effect of the gesture with him being seated in the car. Puzzled, the son turned to his dad and asked, "Why did we give up so easily? I could have at least called the police." With a voice as clear as crystal, the King responded, "Remember what almost happened to us when we pulled over for gas in Kentucky," the father said. The father's reminder led to an important flashback moment for his son.

February 1961:

Church Mouse, his older brother June Bug, their father, and his new bride were traveling from Ohio to relocate to Mt. Pleasant, South Carolina. Church Mouse was only five years old, but he remembers an unfortunate incident very well, for it was one of the many times he came eye-to-eye with pure evil. A quick stop in the remote hills of Eastern Kentucky to fill up on gas almost proved fatal for the family. It began with a bigoted station attendant who did not like Black people. The features of his face were blurred as if a foul spirit had possessed his soul. His body was contorted like a zombie whose spirit had departed, leaving only flesh to dangle from bones hollowed out from the poison of bigotry. He pulled a rifle from under his trench coat as he approached the car.

"You fucking niggers better move yer asses on down the goddamn road. We don't take too kindly to serving yer kind in these parts," the man growled. Stunned, the King hesitated for a moment. Then, the creature pointed the barrel of his weapon through the window near his wife's head. "If you're not gone by the time I count to ten, yer ass is grass. One, two, three . . . ," the hillbilly started counting. He cocked the firing pin and continued his countdown. "Honey, do what this ignorant-ass cracker says!" cried Beulah. "Yes, sir; yes, sir. You'll get no trouble out of us," the father quickly responded. He put the car in gear and sped off in a cloud of dust.

Beulah used every curse word in the Ebonics dictionary to describe her indignation. The King, however, remained eerily silent. He gripped the steering wheel so tightly that it seemed he could have ripped the leather fabric from its metal base. It was the hardest thing for the proud soldier to accept—letting his wife and his boys see him "tuck his tail and run." In all the years serving his country in the Armed Forces, it was hard for him to understand why African Americans were still treated as third-class citizens. After faithfully serving his country, the King was now being denied the right to gas up his car. "Piss on these peckerwoods!" he grumbled.

Locating a more progressive establishment in a larger town several miles down the road, the King pulled over so his family could use the restroom and restore everyone's nerves to calm. "Some White people aren't worth a shit," Beulah snarled. The King responded by saying, "I could have taught that idiot a thing or two, but it's not worth losing my family over stupidity. And it is not worth going to jail for. Besides, the sheriff is probably one of his relatives. I bet they are all members of the Klan anyway," the father commented. Prophetic words.

The boys were super proud of their father. Although he came in and out of their lives as if he were a wandering spirit, they never viewed him as a weak man afraid to stand up to racism and injustice. Rather, he was a wise man who understood his responsibility of getting his family out of harm's way. All praises go to parents who do not shirk their responsibilities. Special props go out to fathers who fill that special role. You are sorely needed, Black men, more than you know. And let's give thanks to the proud father for handling his business, even though there were other times he was not able to sustain the effort. His leadership was sporadic at best.

Better a temporary savior than none at all.

A strong correlation exists between poverty in the Deep South and the lack of physical development of poor Black children. Although Church Mouse was a poster child for the media poverty look, younger brothers Slim Jenkins and the Marvelous One were even more so. From the moment the boys stepped onto the Gullah scene, it seemed as if their modest body frames were altered at the genetic level. Many Black males in South Carolina sported a wire-thin look, but it is difficult to pinpoint the root cause. Was it a genetic predisposition that dominated the Four Mile male gene pool? Poverty, hunger, and the environment were the main culprits. More perplexing is that other poor kids in the neighborhood were noticeably overweight. Both conditions appear to be connected to hypertension and a poor diet.

Any insinuation that Beulah and other parents in Four Mile did not feed their children would not be a fair assessment. On the contrary, most parents took the responsibility of feeding their families seriously, so much so that many of them went without food themselves so that their children could eat. Although food portions were small and seconds were unheard of, southern parents clearly did not neglect their children. A minimum of two small meals, and many times four, were provided. For example, many southern mothers customarily served an early dinner around 4:30 p.m., followed by a fourth lighter meal called "supper" around 8:00 p.m.

And yet, Beulah's boys, along with other neighborhood children, looked undernourished most of the time. Although the quantity of food was fair, the quality was seriously lacking. Pig by-products can only do so much to jump-start healthy growth. Maybe it was the high volume of starch and fat that most southerners ingested. An example was a foodstuff called "butt's meat" that was supposed to be like bacon, but it was mostly 85% salty fat. Then again, it could be the water that people drank, although one would suspect well water to be quite rich in mineral nutrients. For whatever reason, food appeared to flush right through a child's system as if it were a liquid. Or maybe southern Black kids were thin and sickly looking because someone put a "root" on them. [84]

By the time young Church Mouse arrived in the Deep South, a belief in spirits was beginning to fade among the younger generation, but elderly Blacks insisted that certain legendary spirits were not to be taken lightly. Even the religiously faithful were known for buying into the mystic beliefs of their Caribbean neighbors to the south. Those who did not subscribe to full-blown mystic phenomena still held pseudo-practices dear to their hearts. Beulah indulged in the practice of not proceeding across the path of a black cat. She would put her car in reverse and take a whole different route home. She also threw salt over her left shoulder to avoid bad luck. Or, if by chance a child accidentally touched her feet with a broom, she would "undo the root" by spitting on the broom three times before setting it outside the back door. Depending on the potency of one's spit, some brooms required longer airing-out times than others.

Some southerners believed that children born with a small hole near their ear grow up to have special psychic abilities. Referred to as "seers," these children are said to have had life experiences in the womb that allowed them to foresee the future. Gullah citizens gave these children special treatment. Adults even consulted them for advice. Then there is the issue of infants enduring teething pain. The cure for that malady consisted of taking the whole skeletal remains of a fish and drying them out. After a string was attached to it, the concoction was then placed around an infant's neck. The ritual is not as popular now as it once was back in the 1960s, but there are still a few believers today. Beulah was certain that the fish charm had powers to ward off demons that vexed babies. Although totally unscientific, at times the practice actually appeared to work. Good grief!

The grandmother of all Gullah spooks took the form of a success-robbing spirit known as the "Boo Hag." According to legend, if the Hag sucked a person's breath from their soul or jumped on their back and rode that person like a mule, all manner of misfortune—including death—could befall its victim. Mercy, Lord. Another pesky troublemaker was Anansi the Spider.

He was a devious trickster and mischief-maker. His job was to steal and rob good people of their joy. Church Mouse viewed the southern superstitions as a bunch of nonsense. Even if the spirits were real, he believed that no power could match that of the Holy Ghost. Why call on Jesus to save you if deep down inside you believe He is only a paper tiger? Might as well boycott church and consult the stars, right?

Anansi the Spider and the Boo Hag. WTF! What are we talking about here, folks? Speak to the writer in Gullah tongues. Who knows, maybe there really were a few goofy spirits left over from slavery and Jim Crow times that lived in the bushes and trees of South Carolina. Or could it be that so-called spirits were real human beings wearing white sheets and a hood parading around as spooks? Do they bleed? Kick them in the rear and see if they yelp. Be careful with things you do not understand. As the Gullah saying goes, "Don't let that Hag ride ya!"

June Bug tackled the ghost of hunger in his own way—he simply raided the fields of local farmers for foodstuffs. As ornery as June Bug was, his ingenuity was heroic. Beulah's kids had strict orders not to leave the yard once she had left the property, but June Bug seldom followed her or anyone else's instructions. As soon as her car was out of sight, he was on his bike and out of there. At first, Church Mouse thought his brother was plotting an escape back to Ohio, leaving him abandoned and alone in the Jim Crow South. After an hour or two, though, June Bug would return with a burlap bag full of corn, cucumbers, tomatoes, or a watermelon. The boys would hide under the big oak tree behind the barn and feast.

June Bug would rig these funky-looking Bunsen burner contraptions made of scrap materials. Church Mouse was charged with gathering sticks and leaves for fuel. Slim Jenkins was the one coaxed into sneaking into the kitchen to smuggle out various spices and cooking utensils. And how do suppose Christian children reconcile their religion with eating stolen food? Simple. You justify your funk so that it does not stink as much. Only uncut funk tends to give a brother away. Sanctified sin only lands you in Purgatory. All hail the inventive June Bug.

During the first year the boys spent in Four Mile, the family was bundled up with Queen's family, who lived in a three-bedroom house that was only one step up from being classified as a shack. Somehow, the family found a way to sleep ten people in this abode. Because respect for elders held foremost importance in the Deep South, Queen's ailing mother, Ethnography, occupied one of the bedrooms all by herself, while Grandma Queen occupied a second bedroom along with her youngest daughter, Efficiency. June Bug, Church Mouse, Slim Jenkins, and Uncle J-Bird shared a third boy's room located in the back. It held one double and two twin beds. That left a living room couch and the floor for Beulah, Nefertiti, and a young foster child to find sleeping accommodations. Arrangements were elbow-room tight.

Beulah decided to alleviate the overcrowding by building a small wood-frame house at the back of Queen's one-acre lot. Although the new structure was simple and unfinished inside, it was, nonetheless, the best house in the immediate neighborhood. It was important to Beulah to demonstrate publicly that she was a well-traveled person who set lofty goals for her family. In the South, poverty was three times worse than what the average northern Black family of that time experienced. This was Beulah's big chance to distinguish herself from the local citizenry she grew up with. She made sure that the outward symbols of progress were always in place, even if it meant that the family had to do without other important necessities.

Local norms dictated that by the fourth grade, kids became too old to believe in childhood fantasies such as the Easter Bunny, the Tooth Fairy, and Santa Claus. Being the ultimate romantic dreamer, Church Mouse ignored the blasphemous words of his skeptical peers. The second grader was wide-eyed with anticipation as he awaited the coming of Santa Claus. It was the holiday season of December 1962, and the thought of a magnificent and wealthy bearded White man taking the time to visit a poor Black community filled the fragile youngster with awe and excitement. Even if there was no possibility of receiving toys and new clothes, he welcomed the coming of the frozen wanderer. Come, Saint Nicholas, and touch poor children with the gift of life. Happiness and cheer were a rural Black child's placebo of rescue.

Bedtime was 8:30 p.m. for the younger set of children in the home, but tonight the lights went out at eight. It did not matter because Santa Claus was coming to town. Church Mouse had done everything necessary to please His Royal Jolliness. His grades were tops, and a full year had passed with good behavior both at home and at school. He performed his house chores and yard duties exceptionally. He was especially good at pleasing the women of the family. Church Mouse was the ultimate suck-up. He had the best "yes, ma'am" routine in all of Four Mile. The words sounded like gospel harmony when he spoke them. No one could kiss up as well as Church Mouse. So, there you have it. Come, Saint Nick.

The excitement of the day caused the child to expend more energy than he needed to. By 8:15 p.m., Church Mouse was out cold. He dreamt about reindeer, elves, and sugarplums dancing in the sky. He dreamt of sleigh bells ringing and Santa Claus bouncing him up and down on his knee and doing the Warner Bros. routine that his father would sometimes do. It was a perfect night for fairy-tale dreams and storybook endings. Suddenly, around 3:00 a.m., the child was awakened by an intense need to use the restroom. The anticipation of Christmas must have affected his biochemistry. Modern science would say that bad nerves caused him to have a bout with diarrhea. Those who believed in Gullah folklore, however, had a different answer—they said the local spirit known as the Boo Hag jumped on the child's back and started punching him in the gut. Either way, the child's stomach was about to explode like a bomb.

This was the wrong night to get hijacked by a fricken ghost. First of all, Church Mouse did not want to displease Santa Claus by accidentally running into him placing gifts under the tree. Secondly, he was deathly afraid of visiting the outdoor facility all by himself in the dark. Just like in Queen's home, the newly built economy home had no indoor plumbing facilities. But at least Beulah had electricity. Candles and kerosene lamps also provided inside lighting for Beulah's family, but neither were allowed after midnight. Family members used a flashlight to navigate their way to the outhouse, but the batteries were dead on this particular Christmas eve night. There were no streetlights outside. Darkness was all around, with only a sliver of the moon dangling in the sky. Sometimes Murphy can be a big tease.

At the age of seven, Church Mouse did not understand that a large part of the Gullah stories he heard were mere fantasies. The belief in Santa Clause would soon fade away, but what about the Spider and the Hag? Those two had staying power. Part of the folklore might contain a sliver of truth. If a person looked Beulah dead in the eyes, one could easily conclude that strange spirits sometimes live among us. Regarding the outhouse option, running into a stray possum or wild boar was surely cause for pause. Even grown folk feared stepping on a snake they could not see crawling on the ground. Visiting the rancid shack in the broad light of day was frightening enough without also having to contend with strange sounds emanating from animal and insect nightlife. Young Church Mouse was certain the place was haunted, and he feared that a monster would rise to bite him on his butt when he sat down on the spider-infested wooden stool.

With his stomach gurgling and intestines about to pop, Church Mouse contemplated using the white galvanized pot that women and toddlers in the household were allowed to use when ridding themselves of bodily waste. The "pot" was a rural necessity in a home that lacked plumbing. It was customary to put ammonia in the pot, as well as a lid over the top to help control odor. Church Mouse was very acquainted with the utensil, for it was his job to empty its contents daily. Older males, however, were not allowed to use the pot. It was their responsibility to go behind the barn for a number one, and to the outhouse for a number two.

The decision was a tough one to make: stay inside and use the forbidden instrument of release, or make that trek outside, hoping that Anansi the Spider and the Boo Hag were asleep. Because Church Mouse understood that his bout with diarrhea was of the variety that would splatter, he decided on the latter. Even if he were successful at aiming everything into the pot, he might blow everyone out of their beds with just the smell alone. Southern cuisine and a nervous stomach can be a lethal mixture. The tough decision suddenly became easier to make when his stomach suddenly doubled over and howled like a wolf.

As the lad jumped to his feet and ran toward the kitchen door, the Boo Hag jumped on his back and began riding him. Your girl could have at least waited until he got outside, but she was a bully. The pot was customarily placed inside the small bathroom area, a wooden shell with empty holes where a tub, vanity, and toilet fixtures would someday fit. But tonight, the last person to use the pot had inadvertently set it in the hallway against the wall. Chances are the Spider put it there. He was such a prankster. Because Church Mouse was using the wall to guide himself in the darkness, he ran straight into the pot and spilled its contents onto the floor. WTF! Could it be that Murphy is related to the Boo Hag? While quickly reaching down and setting the pot upright, hoping that not too much of the contents had spilled, he contemplated cleaning it up immediately, but the atom bomb about to go off in his gut did not allow him to linger.

Scurrying to the outhouse, Church Mouse was scared shitless, err—scared shit-filled. Fear had given him a quadruple dose of the shakes: one for his mother's impending anger regarding the spilled pot, a second dose for the fear of running into a wild animal that might be lurking in the dark, and a third for running into Anansi the Spider. The outhouse was rife with a full network of spider webs as if Anansi and his cousins were holding a family reunion there. The child also feared that he would disappoint Santa Claus if they came face-to-face. But, boy, oh boy, did the relief in his digestive system feel ever so good when he released it all! Like a plumber's pipe that gives way under two hundred pounds of pressure, Church Mouse's system flushed out with a mighty "swoosh," and for a moment, he thought only of the sweet sensation of finally being relieved.

Back to reality. Young Church Mouse gingerly made his way to the house, making sure not to break the code of childhood ethics by spying under the Christmas tree. The pitch-black night would have made it a fruitless endeavor anyway. Although animals and ghosts never materialized and your boy's stomach cramps quickly disappeared, the problem with the spilled pot did not magically go away. The young child decided to use the T-shirt off his back to clean up the spilled urine and feces. It was the right thing to do, the smart thing if he wanted to stay in Beulah's good graces. "This problem can be fixed," the child convinced himself. Because it was so dark, he believed the spill was much smaller than it actually was. He threw the soiled T-shirt out his bedroom window with plans on ditching it the next morning. Convinced that the problem had been averted, he climbed back into bed. With a false sense of completing the task and the pressure in his stomach gone, he slept like a baby for the remainder of the night.

The next morning, the shit hit the fan, or in this case it hit his mother's slippered foot. Beulah accidentally stepped on a "dookie" that Church Mouse failed to recover. Traces of urine also remained on the floor. That morning, Beulah became Mrs. Funkenfoot. Livid, she gathered up her children for interrogation. The other kids were baffled. At first, Church Mouse acted like he had no knowledge of what had happened. "Who got up last night and knocked over the pot?" Beulah scowled. No one responded. Intimidated by his mother's take-no-prisoners persona, Church Mouse could not force the words from his mouth. Then she threatened, "No one will open a single Christmas present until the guilty party steps forward. If I have to, I'll take every toy and piece of clothing back to the store tomorrow," Beulah warned. Her children moaned and looked at one another. Then with a sudden burst of courage, Church Mouse stepped forward and admitted, "I did it. It was me, Mama, but it was an accident." She looked at him and smirked with a fiendish grin. The other children sighed in relief.

Nothing Church Mouse said or did could convince Crazy Beulah that the spilled pot was an accident. Even well into adulthood, she remained confident that her son lied about the episode. In her stubborn archaic mind, Church Mouse got up to spy on Santa Claus and get an early peek at the gifts under the tree. No way in hell was she going to buy the story about him needing to use the outhouse. As punishment, Beulah decreed that half of his gifts be given to his brothers and the rest of the items save one gift, a fancy spinning top, would be returned. In addition, he was grounded in his bedroom for the day.

The punishment sent Church Mouse into an emotional tailspin like never before. For the first time, the child began to entertain the idea that there truly was a crazy she-spirit that rode him like he was a pony. This incident was also the beginning of the child's fascination with suicide ideation. What is the use of living when you are constantly hungry, your mom is always angry at you, your older brother plants you into the ground on a biweekly basis, your classmates call you White Boy, and southern crackers refer to you as a nigger? Why hang around a community that you do not seem to fit in? And how can a simple country boy ever hope to battle powerful spirits that he cannot see? What are his options for survival? Should he run away from home? Should he become a deviant child? Or he might channel his frustration in a negative way and become a terrorist that buys an automatic rifle and shoots up his school one day. Maybe it was time for young Church Mouse to consider a different option. Maybe he was the root of the problem and just needed to disappear.

Fight the power, my son. God loves you, and the opera is not over until the "fat lady" sings. You must continue searching for a sliver of hope to grasp on to. One day you will be able to ride that ray of hope into a bright future. One day you will shoot the moon. One day—someday—daylight and darkness will meet and form a circle of love. On that day, heaven and earth will rejoice. But until then, concentrate on the few things that are good—on the things you can control. Think about the good ole days of roaming free in California and Ohio. For any chance of survival, you must tie a knot in the rope they supply you and hang on for dear life.

Beulah did not back down from the punishment she doled out. She believed her son was untrustworthy just like his "hoe daddy," and that her actions were totally justified. In her mind, she was saving her second son from becoming like his father and his older brother. From that day forth, Church Mouse was never again the same innocent child. The dark angel put his foot so far up young Church Mouse's ass that your boy's breath smelled like spent charcoal. There was no pardon. There was no rescue. There was no respite. There was only guilt and shame with icing stacked on top. Being unjustly denied Christmas joy over a bullshit incident left the boy emotionally scarred for life—not because of missing toys and clothes, but because of being misunderstood. It was an early pattern that curiously became a lifetime norm.

This was not an isolated incident for Church Mouse. Eerily, the pattern of being hit with a false charge or a sucker punch from left field—and seldom receiving acknowledgement that he was innocent—continued to take place well into his adult years. Whether it was a job, a love relationship, a break-through opportunity, a budding music career, or even during a roller-coaster political stint, the pattern of almost making it to a mountaintop and then swiftly tumbling backward kept happening one astonishing time after another. It was uncanny and surreal. Like clockwork, Murphy kept his foot up your boy's ass. The only difference is that when Church Mouse came of age, he learned how to effectively "clap-back" and apply foot pressure "where the sun doesn't shine." He learned how to deliver an effective counter blow, and yet he was careful to adopt an "only-in-defense-of-himself" posture. Spiritually, Church Mouse refused to pout or complain about the road he traveled. He would simply press through all unfortunate mishaps one incident at a time. Each time he overcame a trial, he gave God the praise and glory for his survival. Here is a special tip for readers: If people want to make light of you being too "churchy" and relying too much on God's grace to help see you through the trials of life, plug in your radio, find a nice R&B station, turn it up as loud as it can go, and then funk them.

Never once did the Lord fail Church. He did not forsake His child, nor did He leave him stranded in the streets to beg for bread. Throughout his life, people bailed on Church left and right. It was brutal. But God never left his side. And it drove detractors crazy to witness your boy succeed despite the many snares and traps people set for him. Never once did Church Mouse cry about his fate. He simply took the lemons given to him and turned them into a fine wine. The Lord served as a blocking fullback when haters mounted campaigns against him. And God did not allow the fat lady in the opera to sing her last note. She tried often, but angels kept plugging her pie hole with slices of lemon meringue treats every time she would wind up for a crescendo.

Church Mouse did not fold or crumble when the heat was on. He did not throw in the towel when Lucifoot came after him—when others chose to abandon him. He simply dug deep and heroically fought back one incident at a time. This is the main message Church Mouse wants to impart to young at-risk readers: *Even when you do not receive the mentoring or the credit that you deserve, you can still win. You can beat the odds and overcome obstacles in life if you believe in yourself and adopt a refuse-to-lose demeanor.* Like Church Mouse, you, too, can become more than a conqueror. You can become self-sufficient. That might mean getting far away from people who do not have your best interest at heart. Relatives hold a special status, however. They are like a boomerang. No matter how much you try to throw janky relatives away, they will find a way to circle back and hit you up again. Occasionally, they ask for forgiveness, but mostly they ask for a large loan they have no intention of ever paying back. With relatives, love them and serve them even when they cut your wings. Well, at least . . .

Pressing his tiny face against the windowpane in his bedroom, young Church Mouse watched his siblings outside, wearing his clothes and playing with his Christmas toys. "Would somebody please tell that Boo Bitch to take her boot off my neck?" the young boy cried. "And if I ever catch that spider mutha-fucka, his ass is grass," the religious child uncharacteristically snarled. A large tear traced his face and evaporated before it left its place.

Love him or hate him, Church Mouse turned out to be what they made him to be: A super confident, self-made man who grew up in a silo with little or no help from others. A fighter. A survivor. An enigma. A recovering Murphy's Child. His storyline began one Christmas morning in 1962 when his mother stepped on a piece of Gullah girl dookie that was accidentally spilled onto the dancefloor of rural poverty life. Witness the birth of a solo dancer.

So low? Solo!

Beulah continued to zealously pursue her desire to demonstrate to the local citizenry that she was a leader in her neighborhood. It really was not because she thought herself to be superior. It was more of a thing where she was one of the first women from her era to assert the spirit of the new independent female. She was a strong Black woman who traveled to various parts of the country and sought to break out of the domesticated second-class role many of her female peers had fallen into. She brought a new mindset with her when she returned to Four Mile. Two years earlier, Beulah had her first house built behind her mother's abode, and now, she was masterminding the building of a second home up on Venning Road.

With the new home being constructed of concrete block instead of wood—this time with indoor plumbing and electricity—Beulah's reputation took several leaps forward. She also went into business for herself and started the most popular juke joint in her community. At first the establishment was housed out of her living room. She rented a jukebox and purchased spirits from the local liquor store. On weekends, she would send the kids to their bedrooms to watch TV. Patrons from far and wide visited her make-shift establishment. Later, she purchased a building off Highway 17. Both establishments were jumping to the popular music of the day. Beulah was the ultimate host and socialite. The party did not start until she showed up. For the period between 1963 and 1967, sista girl was clearly queen bee of the poverty community.

The new house boasted three bedrooms, but Church Mouse still had to share a twin bed with younger brother, while June Bug had his own. Church Mouse was at the head of the bed and Slim Jenkins took the foot, while their little feet met in the middle. Although the boys' comfort level slightly improved, it did not mean life was all good. Poverty was still very real, and bills were hard for Beulah to pay. During this time, the father of the home was curiously absent, and other men were starting to come around and flirt with Beulah.

The boys were still adapting to a strange new culture. Peaceful sleep came sporadically. Reoccurring nightmares plagued all three boys. Night after night, Church Mouse woke up to marble-sized drops of sweat seeping through his pajamas like fluid funk celebrating the birth of a new mildew scent. Coastal smells emanated from within the urban prince now turned country bumpkin. The transformation was complete. The boy wonder could no longer resist the lure of Gullah traditions and culture. The northerner was quickly becoming a "Geechee Boy."

Imagine seeing small trolls patrolling the bedrooms of frightened little kids. We're talking irritating little goblins who gave each other high fives every time they got a child to wet the bed. Some of them even helped themselves to food in the refrigerator. Better tell them critters to lay off the red Kool-Aid, the Black man's official drink. Country folk go ballistic if plain water is all they have left to consume. You can take a man's wife, kids, dog, and even step on his blue suede shoes, but you better not leave an empty Kool-Aid pitcher in the refrigerator. While you are at it, you'd better hide the pork skins and the bottle of hot sauce too. Psyche.

Night trolls, aka Boo Hag pickaninnies, with an unquenchable thirst ruled the new home. Oh, the writer understands this all sounds foolish, but how else does one explain a reoccurring nightmare Church Mouse had about a giant human-faced horsefly trying to eat his arms and legs? Many nights, Church Mouse struggled in his sleep to rid himself of the beast's torment. Occasionally, he won the fight, but most of the time, he barely escaped. Right before the beast was about to devour him, he would find enough strength to awaken and break free from the nightmare. Drenched from head to toe, the child had to peel off layers of funk-soaked clothing. Sometimes, he was falsely accused of wetting the bed. Once, Jenkins thought he had gotten up in the middle of the night to take a swim in a neighborhood pond. Beg your pardon, Slim? Church Mouse was not that fond of hanging out with cotton-mouth moccasin snakes.

One day, Church Mouse confided in Grandma Queen about the recurring dream. She looked deep into the boy's eyes, briefly paused, and then calmly said, "Da Lawd is done touched yu. Eee fidna to do a mighty work in yu." Without uttering another word, she returned to her knitting. Come again, sista girl? What about the big-assed fly monster that vexes your grandson? What about the nighttime trolls? The boy does not need parables and riddles. He needs a revelation. Can a brother cop an intercessory prayer? Can you throw in a Reverend Ike prayer cloth for added security? Shouldn't you be anointing the boy with oil? How about sprinkling some holy water on his feet? Will somebody slide dude a crucifix? Can a nigga get a fly swatter?

Grandma Queen began humming a gospel song while she knitted. Like most Gullah church folk, she was unimpressed with the devil's antics. Unlike her carnal daughter, Queen was into the Bible and undaunted by the feeble threats of Gullah ghosts and goofy spirits. Knowing Jesus personally, she understood that His Father worked in mysterious ways. "You'll understand it more clearly when you grow older," Queen told her grandson. She continued with her duties while singing the song "Jesus is on the main line." Church Mouse staggered back home.

That night, Church Mouse carried June Bug's pellet gun with him to bed. "Mess with me tonight, and I'll pop dis gun off in ya boonkey," the emboldened child warned. And boy, did he ever have a smile on his face that night! You would have one too if you were hiding a gangsta gun under the covers. The decisive moment came soon after Church Mouse wandered off into dreamland. Like clockwork, the fly monster showed up. The frantic child vigorously worked the pump action on the rifle, took aim, and blasted the creature as it advanced. The monster went down several times but kept getting back up. Church Mouse splattered the creature against the wall but it peeled itself away and kept coming. "I'm gonna eat dem yams wit some hot sauce," reveled the cantankerous fly. I guess even demon spirits have jokes. Whatever, dude.

Tearing the weapon from the lad's hands, the monster flung it against the wall, grabbed the young lad, and put him in a headlock. Church Mouse struggled to break free, but the harder he tried, the tighter the monster squeezed. Pop, pop, pop went the child's second weapon, a cap pistol that he had tucked under his shirt. It was all to no avail. The child's toy was no match for the foul spirit from Hell. Maybe he should have chosen Bible verses instead. Sometimes you have to reach for that uncut funk when you deal with street hoods.

You know that horrible feeling when your mind says move, but your body cannot put itself into motion? Mentally aware of what is going on around you, your limbs are trapped in a time warp, and you struggle just to move an eyelash. Church Mouse felt like a runaway slave not knowing the local terrain well enough to plot an intelligent escape. Claustrophobic and constraining is that feeling. Spastic. Numbing. Familiar. Familial. Focusing his concentration and summoning a great surge of energy, Church Mouse finally broke free from the nightmare and sprung to his feet. With eyes ghost-wide-open, he gagged to clear mucus that was lodged in his throat. Enough of this mess. Either teach the kid how to effectively plead the blood of Jesus or give him an Uzi with hollow-point bullets. A can of insect aerosol spray might also be useful. Either way, the pesky creature had to go.

The exhausted child sat on the edge of his bed trying to make sense of the recurring dream. Stop and think about it for a moment. Giant flies with human faces that sprinkle pepper sauce on the thighs and arms of little kids. Hmmm. The thought can be both frightening and comical at the same time. The fact that funny-looking trolls smacked their lips and say, "Yassa, yassa, I sure likes crispy little knuckleheads" also does not help to clarify the situation. What is a person supposed to make of this foolishness? Was it a sign from the Lord, or a warning from Lucifoot? Maybe the nightmares were caused by the way the child combined his foods. It takes a special digestive system to mix exotic southern foods such as cow tongue, pig ears, and chicken feet, with grits. You know what they say about Black folk eating spicy meals late at night.

Well into his adult years, Church Mouse continued to have bad dreams about being attacked in one form or another. Both his first and second wives would have to shake him to free him from his nighttime struggles. Sometimes he would cry out for help in his sleep. Banana Babe would anoint him with oil and pray over him before sending him back to sleep. To this day, Church Mouse has been unable to decode the meaning behind the nightmares, other than the possibility that someone or something wanted him dead. Maybe the Boo Hag jumped on his back in Four Mile and rode him up north to Omaha. Or perhaps Grandma Queen was right. Maybe the Good Lord was preparing Church Mouse for something special—something to be revealed at a later time. Or maybe the bad dreams were a predictable reaction—a carry-over effect from the pillow-smothering episodes and other early bullying attacks he endured from his older brother June Bug when he was a toddler. Trace it.

———————————————

Church Mouse was not the only child afflicted by nightmares. The unfamiliar terrain, wildlife, exotic insects, and strange new culture had a huge impact on all three boys. Younger brother Slim Jenkins was the most superstitious of the three. Jenkins bought into the existence of Gullah spirits hook, line, and sinker. He felt he had entered a strange world of enchanted creatures and voodoo spirits. Large oak and sycamore trees with gray moss hanging from each limb swayed in the coastal breeze, making them appear like ghosts that came to life at night. At any moment, you might expect Tarzan to bellow out his famous rescue call. In addition, the thought of a snake dropping from a tree right into your path was enough to make a young child crap his/her pants. A rattler once did that to Church Mouse, and it scared him senseless.

Unlike his two younger brothers, June Bug's fears did not center around mystical spirits but rather the everyday garden variety of stick-and-bush demons such as neighborhood bullies who picked fights just to prove their manhood. He always met their challenge head-on, but sometimes the fights got out of hand. Sometimes he went out of his way to prove his manhood. Poverty was another spirit that vexed June Bug. As the oldest male child, he was expected to help ease the family's financial burden. While Slim Jenkins and Church Mouse did chores around the house and yard, June Bug was allowed to do heavier duties, such as working in area fields picking corn and cucumbers for pay. It was not unusual for Four Mile's fifth and sixth-grade boys to spend their summers picking produce to help feed their families.

One chore June Bug truly dreaded was going into the thick forest to track down Pinky the pig, whenever he got out of Queen's "inescapable" pen. Church Mouse swears Pinky was more human than swine. When the animal grunted, it almost sounded as if he was saying the N-word. Wonder if the animal meant it as a racial slur, or was he affectionately referring to the kids as his "home boys"? June Bug hated going into the woods after Pinky because ticks and other exotic insects would bite him and leave huge welts all over his arms and legs. Coming out of the thick bush tugging a defiant pig by a rope, with seven mosquito bites, an attached lizard, and a couple of wood ticks solidly clamped onto your ankles, was hardly a walk in the park.

One day, the boys were called to the dinner table for a treat: BBQ ribs, candied yams, black-eyed peas, cornbread, red Kool-Aid, and peach cobbler for dessert. In a rare move, Grandma Queen went all-out as if she were preparing a Christmas or an Easter meal. The boys wondered if there was a special occasion. But it was the dead of summer and there was no special holiday. There was no funeral. No wedding. No birthday. The normal food offerings in Four Mile were your typical beans and rice, with maybe some okra on the side. But today was more celebratory. Church Mouse and Slim Jenkins smacked their lips in gospel harmony. They also licked their fingers after every bite so that meat juices and sauce would mix in well with the protein. You didn't have to wonder were Queen got her funk from.

Then June Bug dropped the ultimate bomb on his siblings. "How do you guys like eating Pinky?" he asked his two brothers. Wha, wha, what?

Come again? June Bug went on to explain that, yes, Pinky the pig was sold to another man not as a pet, but rather to be butchered and carved up for fresh meat to eat. Church Mouse and Slim Jenkins started coughing and spitting out the half chewed meat in their mouths. They began acting as if the meat suddenly tasted like doodoo. Church Mouse's face was contorted. Slim started spitting and gagging. June Bug laughed his head off. The privileged city boys had no idea where meat came from. They made themselves believe that meat products grew on special trees and were already pre-packaged ready for the supermarket. Never in their wildest imagination did they think people ate their pets.

Feeling a little on the devilish side, June Bug told the boys that if they continued to eat Pinky that the pig would visit them that night and bite them in their sleep. Very much afraid, Church Mouse rapped the rest of his ribs in a paper napkin and stuck them into his pants pockets. When he got outside, he refused to feed Pinky to the dogs. The naïve child had too much respect for the animal, so he threw the meaty bones into the deep bushes across the nearby winding dirt road. That night when he dozed off to sleep, June Bug got up and started making hog noises in his ear. Church Mouse jumped out of bed and started yelling and frisking himself to avoid getting bit. Jenkins followed suit. June Bug rolled on the bed with a belly laugh so hearty you would have thought he was Santa Claus. Church Mouse cut his eye at the blasphemous brother and said, "It ain't that funny, dude!" "I don't mean any harm. I'm just funkin' wit cha," June Bug replied. No, it wasn't funny then, but now that you look back on it, it was pretty hilarious. June Bug got his brothers really good that night. For the good times.

As time progressed, the boys gained a better understanding of farm life and living in a rural area. The boys had particular difficulty watching Grandma Queen butcher chickens and ducks for food. She was an old pro at it and desired to pass on the tricks of the trade to her oldest grandson before she grew too old to continue the family tradition. June Bug lived for new experiences, so he accepted the challenge. The process began with sending the youngster into the pen to catch a hen—a science in itself. Once June Bug secured the fowl, Queen grabbed it by its neck and began swinging it in a circular motion above her head. With a sudden jolt, she thrust the animal forward to break its neck before severing the head from the body with a sharp butcher knife. The bloody, headless body of the chicken was left to jump, twist, and contort in an old washtub until all the reflex life was drained from its body. The boys watched in horror.

They stood in shock and awe each time the process unfolded. Although June Bug was gangster-tough, he never really got used to the break-neck routine. He, too, experienced nightmares that kept him up all night. He often dreamt about headless chickens wishing to exact revenge by chasing him around the yard. He also dreamt about the snakes, boars, wild animals, and huge insects he encountered when he had to fetch Pinky the Pig. Sometimes he would awaken screaming and jumping up and down on the bed, frisking his clothes as if to rid himself of animals and critters. Beulah eventually took him to see a doctor about his bad dreams.

The coup de grâce of scary experiences came one night shortly after the family had moved into their new brick house. The night started out serenely but did not end that way. A substantial-sized black bear wandered into the backyard looking for food. June Bug, the first to notice the creature, figured the animal would eventually wander off. When it became obvious this was not going to happen, he woke his siblings, and together they went to peek out the window. When the bear spotted their little faces pressed against the glass, it flew into a rage and lunged toward them. Luckily, the windows were built with reinforced glass, anchored in a series of metal frames that cranked open into several smaller rectangular sections. Had the window been constructed in traditional style, the bear surely would have come crashing through.

The boys did what most scared children do—they jumped into bed and hid under the covers. Church Mouse was so scared, he thought he saw Slim Jenkins transform right before his eyes. Much like scared negro characters in Reconstruction-era movies, the younger brother's hair stood straight up from his head and his eyes bulged out like inflated balloons. When the bear growled, Slim turned White! [85] When Church Mouse rubbed his eyes, his younger brother looked like he was Stepin Fetchit in the flesh. Church rubbed his once again, and Slim looked like the bear! To be sure there were no drugs ingested that night—only chicken feet.

All night long, the bear camped outside the window. It used a nearby sycamore tree for an occasional back scratch. Wicked groans accompanied the bear's hunger pangs. It may have been that the bear was also injured, but the boys were not about to investigate. At least, not when covers were available to hide under. This was no time to be brave and adventurous. An hour passed, and still, all one could hear were the sounds of howls and hungry bowels accompanied by the chattering of tiny teeth in three-part harmony. Beulah and the rest of the family were out cold during the incident.

Mom, a heavy sleeper, only became aware of the situation at daybreak. She immediately telephoned Mrs. Steed, a neighbor, to tell her family that the bear was headed toward their property. The two Steed boys, well trained in the use of firearms, took aim at the bear, fired, and hit their target. It is hard to say if the creature died or not, but it scampered off into the forest mortally wounded, never again to be seen or heard from.

Word of the incident spread quickly throughout the neighborhood. It became the talk of the school for a whole week. Beulah's boys became instant heroes. With each retelling of the story, it grew gorier and more gruesome. None of the boys could resist the urge to exaggerate facts and embellish accounts of their personal bravery. The way June Bug, Slim Jenkins, and Church Mouse told it, the bear had flames shooting out of its mouth and bat-like wings that allowed it to fly. For the good times.

The bear episode elevated the social status of Beulah's boys, and like magic, they grew into overnight sensations. They became folk heroes of sorts. It was as if the locals were saying, "You are one of us now. You've gone through an important initiation rite that has transformed you from city slickers into country kids." The boys finally earned their Geechee culture cards. Like hot sauce on grits. Like Crisco-fried funk and hog maw philia, it was a Gullah metamorphosis of the third kind. Can the reader Ebonically say, "We fidna do dis ting?"

220 | DR. FRANKLIN TITUS THOMPSON

———————————

In a surrealistic world, one that is permeated with smoke and mirrors and inundated with a strange kind of love that bends and conforms to enigmatic idiosyncrasies, a child can believe that the putrid smell of natural gas is really an exotic perfume. She can believe that love is a commodity to be bought and sold at the drugstore, that children can navigate upstream in shit without a paddle, that war is peace, and that God is a capitalist entrepreneur. This is the way of the world when the devil is in his moon. A histrionic demagogue, he is. His breath is cold, and his song is silent. His message is death. Look at his underbelly. His womb, swollen from pregnancy, is about to give birth to an era of pure nonsense. A time of dark shadows and inverted images is upon us. Revelry and misery. Callousness and conceit. Turmoil and tears. This is how the world looks when doves cry. A cap gun will not do you any good now, Church Mouse. It is a Junior Walker–style shotgun blast or bust. Shoot 'em for eee run, now.

Buffalo chips. Death can never be a sweet-smelling temptress. That sentiment has got to be the biggest lie ever told. Something is wrong when we allow ourselves to be fooled by a dastardly ghost dressed in a negligée. Scooby-Dooby-Doo, where are you? No. The stench of gas will never pass for the sweet smell of perfume. Its odor is much too rancid for such adoration. Let it be known that the writer says the devil is a liar. His punk-ass ain't worth a shit. Suck on this gun barrel, D-Money. The Spider is also a liar, and his Boo Hag Bitch better be glad the Lord did not make us in the image of lawn mowers! And, no matter what they say, one plus one will never equal three, and a sugar tit will never taste as good as the real thing. It did not yesterday, it does not today, and it will not ever.

Forever and a day, Lucifoot will never flourish in the light because that is not his nature. Darkness is where he finds his delight. Fear is his drug of choice. His drink is the blood of uncritically thinking adults, even from the few of those who attend church. Alas, we concede that sometimes our children serve as his dessert! It is a revelation of the most grievous kind, for it only takes one knuckle-headed parent to start a downward chain reaction within a disadvantaged community. Like a whirlpool, kids turn on each other until they turn on themselves. Yes, the banished angel may snatch a couple of rebounds off the rim of life, but I have read the back of the Good Book, and it says that in the end, that SOB gets slam-dunked.

Death dressed in thong panties descended upon Beulah's household one night, bearing the scent of a strange-smelling perfume. For whatever reason, death had a thing for young Church Mouse. Saturating and dense she was. Like a seductress in heat, ultra-surreal was her love jones. The devil wears Prada. Exhilarating and exciting. Powerful and attractive. "Kiss me," she said. "I want to give you ecstasy. I want to offer you a life of uninterrupted rest. Do not fight it, for it is your destiny. Sleep forever and a day. You shall be with me in paradise," she whispered. Shhh! Set this manuscript down and close your eyes for a moment. Imagine the steamy temptress rotating her hips and calling out your name. Check out that funky little reverse thang she does with her hips. Can you experience the moment? Can you feel the rush?

Church Mouse knew something was terribly wrong that night. You can only listen to the Boo Hag's call for so long before you realize you need to slap yourself into reality. Wake up, sleepy child. Throw on some James to help you get funked up. It can be any kind of James: James Brown, James Cleveland, Etta James, Skip James, Rick James, Boney James, King James—any kind of funk is better than elevator music, especially when the elevator is going down. Church Mouse knew what to do. He may have been one of the weaker physical specimens in the family, but he had the strongest will. Who says brawn is mightier than the spirit?

Church Mouse struggled to his feet. Groggy, ill, and unable to walk a straight line, he staggered and knocked over a few things as he groped around to find something to help support his weight. The cops would have booked Church Mouse and thrown away the key had the child been asked to take a sobriety test that night. Drunk with the sins of the culture of poverty, he beckoned to his mother, but she could not discern his call. He called out to

June Bug, but he, too, was in another world. *Why is everyone moaning and groaning?* the young boy thought to himself. And why was Beulah calling out to the name of the Lord? "Oh, Jesus, sweet Jesus, help me, Lord. Father God, please forgive me," she cried over and over. Had Beulah seen a vision of her maker? Was she trying to make amends before the death angel took her away? If so, amends for what? Was there something deeper, something more revealing about her plea? Does death use her tongue when she kisses her prey?

About to explode from the pressure of diarrhea, Church Mouse stumbled to the bathroom and perched himself on top of the stool. At least it was an indoor facility and not a spider-infested outhouse this time. Swoosh came generations of ghosts and family demons from the bowels of the semi-sanctified one. Their scent filled the air as they permeated the house. "Victory, victory," they cried. "It is finished. We have won," the demons shouted. Church Mouse's eyes rolled back into his head as he struggled to remain conscious. "June Bug!" he cried. "Augh," responded the older brother. The elder sibling could do little more.

The pressure began to rebuild in Church Mouse's gut. Churning. Gurgling. Boiling. Swelling. He braced himself for yet another cleansing. Flush those suckers, C-Money. We don't know who the hell they are, but let them know they do not own you, son. They don't even know your name. They are indiscriminate. Swollen with a sense of cockiness, the spirits popped the corks from their wine bottles and began serving one another. Champagne on the Gullah rocks. As they raised their glasses to propose a toast, Church Mouse leaned forward and gave up resistance. There he remained slumped over, seated atop a familiar throne, and unconscious for more than an hour. Church Mouse estimates that it was about 4:30 a.m. when he passed out on the toilet stool. "It is finished. We have won," the demons reveled.

Not so—6:00 a.m. rolled around, and the Lord decided that enough was enough. It was time to intervene. He may not come when you want Him to, but He is always right on time. Hallelujah somebody! In a rare move, the boys' father made a surprise visit. I guess angels come in all shapes and sizes. Apparently, some even drink Jack Daniel's whiskey, smoke cigarettes, and bump and grind with young ebony side-chicks. Thirty minutes more and it would have been too late, but God stepped in right on time. Praise the Lord, lightbulbs! [86]

The King of Ghosts was aghast at what he came home to—his wife and two boys were nearly dead of asphyxiation. He quickly turned off the gas, got his family out to the back yard, and opened all the doors and windows to air out the house. He later commented that it luckily was one of the few times he entered the house without a lit cigarette in his mouth. Beulah, Church Mouse, and June Bug were terribly ill, to say the least. As soon as they hit fresh air, Church Mouse vomited what little food remained in his digestive system. Unable to steady himself, he laid down in the grass with his eyes closed, trying to rid himself of the intense throbbing that was radiating in his head. "Just take slow, deep breaths," the King told his sons. Neither the boys nor Beulah went to the hospital for treatment. Maybe it was a Four Mile mentality; you suck it up and tough it out like a Geechee gangster.

The King demanded an immediate explanation. Beulah told him that because the home's regular furnace was broken, she substituted the kitchen stove as the heating source for the night. When the pilot inadvertently went out, propane gas continued to leak, creating a deadly situation. The King checked the furnace, and just as Beulah said, it appeared to be defective, even though it was a newer unit. The whole incident was Boo Hag strange. The husband proceeded to preach and lecture Beulah about safety, but by and large, he accepted her explanation, and within a couple of days, the incident was forgotten.

Local youth were not as kind, however. Whisperings about the incident bolted through the neighborhood built of dirt and mold. A few kids pounced on the opportunity for cruel and divisive gossiping. "I heard yo mamma tried to kill y'all the other night," one boy said. "Betta watch your back. Crazy Beulah gonna take boff you niggas out," cracked another kid.

Giggle, giggle, giggle went the tormentors. Church Mouse defended Beulah with vengeance. "Shut up, punk, before I pick up a stick and knock the Boo Hag outta ya boonkey," he shouted. For the most part, June Bug and Church Mouse chose not to respond to the neighborhood taunting.

The episode is seldom spoken of among family members. There exists no official ban against doing so or any threat of sanction should someone decide to bring up the topic, yet you will not get much conversation about it even if you tried. It is one of those unfortunate events that quietly gets assigned to pilot light status—quiet, out of sight, and yet explosive.

A few bothersome questions remain regarding the incident, however. For example, why didn't Beulah just get out of bed and turn off the stove once she began feeling ill? Surely, she must have remembered that it was she who had turned on the gas in the first place. A clear-thinking adult would easily put two and two together and intervene. Secondly, why was she crying out for the Lord to forgive her? Forgive her for what? Raising too much hell? Cooking too much pig feet? Using extension cords as a weapon to whip her children? Thirdly, why were Church Mouse and June Bug the only children chosen to sleep in the new house with Beulah that night, while the other four children slept in the family's other house located behind Queen's abode? Even to this day, it seems like an odd arrangement. It was the first time Beulah had done so, and she never did that arrangement again. Perhaps it was all coincidental. Nevertheless, the incident was sent to the inactive file. It became an open-and-shut case, and the family moved on.

In the final analysis, the family was saved, and once again, the fallen angel received another pie in the face for his failed efforts. Boo Hags and other false-face demons simply do not have power in places where God reigns supreme. The incident also served to strengthen Church Mouse's spiritual faith. Keep on praying, son. Keep holding onto Grandma Queen's dream for your life. It is one of the few things that has not failed you down through the years.

———————————

It was Friday, November 22, 1963, a day forever etched in the minds of freedom-loving Americans of all ethnic backgrounds. On the local Gullah scene, Church Mouse had just defeated the last remaining classmate, a sassy classmate by the name of Miss Know-It-All, in a class spelling bee contest. School was one of the few things friends and siblings allowed Church Mouse to excel at, so he took his time savoring the moment. He was the academic king of Jenny Moore Elementary School, and he was feeling higher than a Carolina kite.

On occasion, Church Mouse was still sent to school without lunch, but his male homies grew less concerned with his family's poverty and more interested in other things like writing nasty notes and looking under girls' dresses. Despite his Ohio introduction to the topic of sexual awareness, Church Mouse still had some catching up to do in understanding that pursuit. Summer vacation tends to awaken the dormant urges of boys entering puberty. Church Mouse was getting older and starting to see the world through a new lens. The pursuit of pretty girls provided a new motivation for Church Mouse. Just keep it wholesome and clean, C-Money. Diminished teasing from classmates, a new teacher who treated him as someone special, as well as an attractive female classmate who thought he was cute were exactly what the doctor ordered for a child with less-than-zero self-esteem. What more could a loser ask for? All throughout the school halls, something special permeated the air with positive promises for the new year.

Enter a cruel reality check. An announcement came across the school intercom system at around 1:45 p.m. EST that John F. Kennedy, the 35th President of the United States of America, had just been assassinated. Like a hungry raven descending upon baby chicks, the mood of the school suddenly turned dark and sullen. School children witnessed the wailing and shrill cries of female teachers as they gnashed their teeth and pulled at their clothing. Three male staff—the principal, the janitor, and a sixth-grade teacher—tried desperately to console their female colleagues. Tears flowed like rivers of cool velvet blood. Despair drifted all through the school building, seeping into cracks in the walls. Students tried to console their teachers, but it was all to no avail. In their failure, they, too, started crying, most of them unaware of the full ramifications of the disparaging news. America had just snatched the heart out of the Civil Rights Movement. Now it was time to weep in gospel harmony.

To most African Americans in the Deep South, John Kennedy was a hero. He was not a saint and by no means was he perfect, but he was the best thing the Black man had since Abraham Lincoln. The fact that JFK was not your typical Jim Crow, lynch-happy democrat was inconsequential. A leader needed to emerge. Because of their bigotry, most southern democrats of that time hated both the Civil Rights Movement and the Kennedys. Common folk had waited for years for a republican to make a move, but most of them sat on their hands. Republicans seemed to have forgotten the freedom movement they had invented one hundred years earlier. Citizens had high hopes for President Eisenhower, but he proved to be too cautious and lukewarm on civil rights. The nation was ripe for a paradigm shift. Earlier, on June 11, 1963, a renegade democrat (JFK) stepped up to the plate and delivered a speech about the need for civil rights that turned into a home-run hit for Black folk. Finally, a modern-era White man had the guts enough to step forth and tell the truth about America's treatment of its under-citizenry.

Northern Black activists may have concluded that both Lincoln and Kennedy were more political strategists than they were true change agents. In their eyes, the two were nothing more than White opportunists in sheep's clothing. But to many Black southerners—to the people who daily swam upstream against a fierce racist tide—pure or not, God used Kennedy to set Black people free a second time. Like Moses crossing the Red Sea, JFK stood up to the devil, and the hooded one blinked. But now they shot him down and stilled his voice as if he were a common criminal. They laid him on the altar of human indifference and cut open his bowels to appease the under-gods. The Boo Hag and her trick-ass spider cousin struck with vengeance. The cold-hearted duo caught a Greyhound bus all the way to Dallas, Texas, and cut the President down.

Theories about Cuban-based conspirators and angry American mob bosses wanting revenge against Kennedy never took root in the mind of the typical Black citizen from the greater Charleston area. Those beliefs are more accurate than what people wanted to admit, but to the average Black citizen of that time, it was the KKK that killed their prince. Simply put, racist White Americans did not want a nigger-loving, Catholic, Benedict Arnold running the country. As unacceptable as this answer may be to readers, it is a truth (real or perceived) for the many citizens who call themselves Black and Blue. It is their reality brought on by centuries of having to endure brutal racism and stark poverty.

Beulah looked with great compassion upon a teary-eyed Church Mouse, who was watching the evening news. What a weirdo child. Most fourth graders were outside playing cops and robbers. Cowboys and Indians. They were not sitting in their living rooms following the evening news and "acting White." Hmmm. Beulah put her hand on the boy's shoulder and gently rubbed it. "All is not lost, my son. At least we still have the President's brother," she said.

———————————

Once upon a time when the planets were not in Aquarius alignment; when the country was caught in an "everything is groovy" dreamland; when Black families were forced to eat the remains of animal body parts that White people threw away; when ten cents could buy you a soda pop; when mothers boiled water in a cast iron pot over an outdoor flame to wash clothes in a chemical called Borax; when kids used a galvanized tub outside to take a bath one right after the other using the same water; when Black toddlers preferred playing with White dolls over Black dolls; when Black folk embraced *both* ideological and cultural diversity; when Black women were not considered sexy and beautiful; when Black men used a chemical called conk (congolene) to straighten their hair; When Gullah people showed disapproval by sucking their teeth; when Black men and women who played golf were considered

Uncle Toms; when TV portrayals of Black people were mostly maids, but-lers, chauffeurs, criminals, pimps, hookers, and hoes; when TV shows such as *Father Knows Best* and *Mayberry R.F.D.* had no resemblance whatsoever to the lives of Black folk; when cartoon and comic book superheroes were all White; when Black parents made their children rush inside the house to witness a rare celebrity Black person on TV; when poor people used a Sears and Roebuck catalog for outhouse toilet paper; and when children really believed that eating spinach would make them instantly strong like Popeye—back in those days, there lived a skinny little country boy who they say was devoid of funk. He had a passion for integrity and fair play. Chances are, he was not the only one.

It was during a time when neighborhood kids gathered up pop bottles to exchange them for money to buy candy; when a person's word was his/her bond; when truth and common sense carried more weight than style and emotion; when the N-word and the B-word were viewed as unacceptable; when non-related adults in the neighborhood were encouraged to discipline other people's children; when kids sent money home to support retired par-ents; when Black people did not send their elderly parents to an old folks' home; when talking to yourself was frowned upon, and answering yourself was forbidden; when scientists were 99% confident that there was no such thing as extraterrestrial beings; and when White folks called young Church Mouse a Jungle Bunny, and Black folks called him White Boy. On the strength of a magic pair of shoes and a stubborn refusal to lose, this Black child sur-vived to tell a story of how he fought against odds that were heavily stacked against him. He grew up to provide hope to other at-risk youth that they, too, can overcome the problems of life. There were good times for Church Mouse—not everything from his past was bad. Still, there was a plethora of reasons for him to throw in the towel. Instead, he chose to stay the course and become a role model for kids who hurt.

Although living in the rural South with poverty and racism was a tax-ing experience, it nonetheless instilled in Church Mouse character traits he would not have gotten had he been raised up North, or with a silver spoon in his mouth. Having to navigate the mixed signals of living in the Jim Crow South helped him to better understand true Black history and the concept of service to others. Likewise, having to endure child abuse helped him to become an effective counselor and master educator later in life. Child abuse, poverty, the various forms of racism, learned helplessness, and polemic politics all pulled at young Church Mouse like a vampire in heat. Yes, it was difficult, but in the end, the experience made him a stronger Black man.

Resilience is a wonderful survival tool that Murphy's Kids can rely on when parents, teachers, churches, and government officials do not do what they should. Unfortunately, resilience is often touted by "selective amnesia" republicans as a panacea. Quick-fix conservatives would rather give vague speeches about pulling oneself up by the bootstraps, as opposed to questioning the existence and the quality of said boots and matching shoestrings. We can all do better. Saving children is a full-time job that must come from multiple sources and different political and social angles. Unfortunately, trick-ask is forever and when we play games, kids lose. Resilience is the antidote for both forgotten children and adults who hurt.

Church Mouse was not the poorest nor the most abused child to survive the ghetto. In fact, at least five of his own siblings had it worse than he did. While they chose not to speak up, Church Mouse decided to let her rip. Pity and revenge was not his motive. Rather, his goal was to properly heal, and then stand in the gap so that other hurting children can be saved. Still, let us not forget that homeless kids living on the streets in Kolkata would gladly trade places with Church Mouse or any of his siblings. Most Americans do not comprehend the global definition of hunger and disadvantage. And yet, the US brand of poverty and abuse can be debilitating in its own right. Moreover, the problems that Church Mouse faced were not just family and poverty based. He wished it were that simple. By street standards, Church stuck out like a virgin at a hooker's convention. He was a Strange Bird, a Sell-Out, a White Boy, an Oddball, and a dreamer who did not earn his "Black Card." Or at least a few trick-ass folk told him so.

Under normal circumstances, most children would have folded, and yet, our curious son was able to overcome his obstacles and wrestle his demons to the ground. We should package his formula for success and market it to all hurting kids. And let us cross our fingers and hope that he makes it through follow-up iterations of this saga. Are you ready for the next episode?

———————————

Post-chapter mentoring tips for parents, educators, counselors, and law enforcement: It is important that we establish in children the values, beliefs, and practices that help them rebound when society comes along to knock them to the ground. In a sense, we must "rubberize their rumps" so that when others knock them down, they bounce back up, as opposed to crashing to the ground like broken glass. We must teach them how to rebound—how to make lemonade out of lemons. Parents: Do not wait for the schools or churches to do what you should be doing. Finally, don't you be the reason why kids fail or lose hope. There is no sin in you admitting that you need to attend professional training or counseling yourself. Do it, if only for the survival of your own future. We know that senseless shootings by angry and confused kids at places such as Columbine HS (1999), Virginia Tech University (2007), Sandy Hook Elementary School (2012), and the Von Maur shooting in Omaha, NE (2017) could have been avoided by adhering to a policy of working with high-risk kids BEFORE they reach a boiling point. The shooters in those tragedies were not born wanting to harm others and themselves. Something dreadful happened along the way to drive them to the dark side. We must help steer them back to the light!

Post-chapter survival tips for children who hurt: It would be quite easy for hard-luck children to assume that unforeseen forces and bad spirits haunt them and determine their futures. You must resist believing in such talk. You are the master of your destiny. When the entire world has lost their minds, dig down deep and summon the strength needed to forge your own path. Do not conclude that you are cursed with bad luck. Claim yourself to be an overcomer! And do not wait for others to give you what you need to survive. Rather, adopt a mindset that says *you will legally take what belongs to you*. Learn how to orchestrate the environment in a way that puts you in the driver's seat of determining what your future will look like, even if life is pouring rain on you at the moment. And if by chance you get caught in a Boo Hag trap, throw on Stevie Wonder's song "Superstition" and dance until your shoes say, "enough already, G!"

A Special Message for Courageously Independent Thinkers of the World: Although there is not a perfect correlation between being at-risk on one hand and living outside the traditional box on the other hand, these two realities can and often do overlap. If you are an individual who is unappreciated for the way you think and live, that can be cause for either celebration or severe depression depending on how you manage your truth. When free thinkers choose a course of action that does not conform to the popular norm, there is bound to be a measure of skepticism and unfair critique that goes along with that choice. More than likely you will be misunderstood, and you will not receive the validation that you deserve. Unfortunately, this is an unfair reality that will probably not change. It is the way of the world. If you make the decision to navigate *a certain road that is less traveled*, you must also be willing to accept the pain, sorrow, and criticism that goes along with your choice. Translation: It is possible to be totally right about a situation, and still be isolated, ridiculed, and misunderstood. This is a sad statement, but it is real. Give people time to catch up to you. Oftentimes, your views and conclusions are genuinely lost on those who are not as gifted or insightful as you are. People cannot acknowledge what they do not know. Some people actually know better, but don't care. Please make sure, however, that you do not double up on your sorrow by looking for pity. One of the worst things you can do is purposely go against the grain, and then play the "woe is me" card when people do not understand you. In reality, you probably are a victim, but try hard not to play that card. The alternate choice is much healthier: Maybe your mission in life is not to be liked, but to introduce a new paradigm for the world to consider. To help stretch the way people see truth. If so, God bless you for your much-needed service, albeit it will often be an unfair and lonely journey. Although your feelings of being unappreciated are valid, becoming distraught over people not understanding you has the potential to cause serious mental illness. Yes, you deserve love and support, but not at the expense of magical thinking. Borrowing from Albert Ellis' Rational Emotive Behavioral Therapy (REBT) research, *we must take careful steps not to "disturb ourselves."* Learn to accept your calling however atypical it may be. Bear your cross and do the best solo dance routine that you can, while also blocking out the slings and arrows that come your way. And do not let the haters see you sweat. At the end of your journey, throw a huge "I-told-you-so" party and dance until your magic shoes say, "enough already!" Don't forget to take care of you. What good is it to save the world, but you personally end up looking like death warmed over? In addition to being right, it is also important for you to be persuasive. Effectively sell the whole package and not just the content of your message. Whatever you choose, do not break inside, and do not turn to the dark side. Fight both the urge to exact revenge and the urge to give up. Lucifoot (aka, Ole Trick Ass) might win a battle or two every now and then but stay in the game and don't let that mother function win the war. Continue to fight the powers that be—both those that are seen and unseen! Although I can't always be there with you in person, I am with you in spirit.

CHAPTER 13:

FAT LADY, PLEASE TAKE A PIE BREAK

WINDING DOWN BEFORE A MUCH-NEEDED LUNCH AND RESTROOM BREAK, the writer observed that Church Mouse was unusually swollen with a wry face. "What is your plan to move forward?" he asked his guest. "Will it be about forgiveness and healing or has there been too much negative water that has passed under the bridge?" the writer questioned. "To err is human, to forgive is divine," responded Church Mouse. [87] "My wish is to leave the pain and sorrow in the past and move on. At the same time, I have a duty to help children who are currently trapped in situations they cannot control. I want to prepare a path for kids who follow me in the struggle. I can do that best by detailing how I survived the madness. Hiding behind a happy-face façade is not the answer. I would feel like a failure if I didn't provide meaningful guidance for children who hurt."

"The story of overcoming odds is not pretty. Yes, it is true that as a victorious adult I need to celebrate more and learn how to smell the roses. I realize that there is more to life than looking backward and engaging 24/7 in heavy conversations about the past. More laughter and fun in my life would increase my joy and improve my health," Church Mouse said. "I am working on that as we speak. But I refuse to sell out. If God brought me through the storm so that I can be a blessing to others, then so be it. There is plenty time to work on being popular and cool. The bling, the ching, and all the styling and profiling is just fluff. The in-crowd and the club scene will still be there tomorrow. That stuff isn't going anywhere," he assured the writer.

"Some of your scars appear to be deep. How hard will it be for you to forgive the people who have cut you past the white meat all the way to the bone?" the writer probed. Your boy's response was as caustic as it was iconic. "First, I clap back strong, and then I hug them," Church Mouse responded. "I have learned how to assertively exercise my rights without being a bully. I have also learned that forgiveness is not for the other person. Rather, it is mainly for me. When a person does not forgive, they tend to wallow and fester in their sorrow. They slowly die from within. There was a time when I held on to my pain like it was a security blanket. It was all I had—all that I knew. It gave me a warrior's identity, but it also consumed me from within. Holding grudges made me ill physically, emotionally, and spiritually. I finally came to realize that the people who I was angry at were sitting somewhere on a beach drinking a Bahama Mama and not even thinking about me. I called myself 'fixing them' by feeding an ulcer that grew inside me. I became a vigilante with misguided anger."

"As a race and human relations professional, I am now requesting that members of the dominant group take their knees off the necks of People of Color. It is not right for a person to get the life choked out of them for spurious reasons at best," Church Mouse continued. "For far too long, White Americans have been guilty of throwing rocks at their own creations. When you throw that rock, oftentimes you are aiming it at a mirrored image. And let it also be said that wayward parenting is not the only cause of problems in the Black family. Neither is the White man nor racism the sole cause of America's problems. Other forces such as selfishness, the abuse of power and privilege, unwillingness to share scarce resources, idiot consumerism, societal ambivalence, learned helplessness, and trick-ask politics have also played a major part in the dismantling of the Black race. Yes, my worldview may not be popular, but it is real. And while it is true that my perspective might reveal a few cracks, it has helped me to survive and overcome."

"The main contribution of my story comes by way of challenging dysfunctional societal norms. While we live in the best nation on planet earth, not everything American is good. Despite our brilliance, we need to find a better way to interact with one another and strive for greater balance. It is all about collaboration and compromise," Church Mouse firmly said. "And we must be willing to ask the tough questions of one another, while remaining positive. That includes at-risk children asks, American asks, Republican asks, Democrat asks, and White asks. Naturally, some of my questions will be of the 'Black-ask' variety. Even if my asks (i.e., my worldviews) have a few cracks in them, I promise to be fair and balanced. I promise to make critical-thinking my close confidant. I will look at all sides of a debate before making decisions."

"The line between love and hate is razor thin. Unfortunately, when child abuse, racism, and poverty band together and collide with trick-ask ideology, the fate of our children splatter like sweet dreams hitting a high-speed fan," Church Mouse reminds the reader. "My default setting will always choose love and forgiveness, but sometimes family ducks fly off the farm and it takes a significant amount of wisdom and energy to regather them. Once I get them back on property, getting them lined up can become quite the task; but at least they are not cats. And as long as the opera lady does not sing her last note, Black people have a real chance at success. Let's keep an extra lemon meringue pie on deck for your girl," Church Mouse quipped.

"If parents will agree to put the interest of children first, then not only will God curtail his judgement—He might even prosper them. If my Black brothers and sisters return to their historic culture and stop all this insane crab-in-the-barrel, hating-on-each-other BS, not only will I forgive them—I will sing their praises. Conversely, if White people will respond that they are open to engaging in more rigorous research and reconsideration of

HIS-story as it is currently taught, as well as studying power and privilege issues at a deeper level, then my questions might have a real chance of not being asked in vain. [88] If these things happen, I will shower my critics with love and respect. If, however, Whites and Blacks continue to ignore legitimate inquiries about reaching our collective human potential—if democrats and republicans continue to go down the selfish paths and slippery slopes they have chosen—I just might have to request that my oppressors and the haters *kiss all the cracks of my Black asks."*

To Be Continued . . .

ENDORSEMENTS

"Unfortunately, the actions and sins of adults and society in general often fall on the shoulders of children. We must find a better way to live. Fortunately, stories like this demonstrate that faith in God and a stubborn refusal to lose can help neutralize the poison that radiates from child abuse, racism, poverty, and learned helplessness."

DON BACON (R), U.S. CONGRESSMAN

"This retrospective biography, told in third person, offers a unique and true story of how to live, learn, forgive, and look past negative circumstances and reach out to the good and the positives in life. There are many lessons in this fascinating fourteen chapter read, the most important being the protection of vulnerable children. Dr. Franklin Thompson (aka, Church Mouse) is my kind of conservative thinker, and yet readers from all political persuasions will grow in perspective from this must-read book."

HAL DAUB (R), FORMER U.S. CONGRESSMAN,
OMAHA MAYOR, NE REGENT

"I have always perceived Dr. Thompson as having a unique personality, and now I know why. His candid, revealing, and unfiltered story helped him become an independent thinker who has used his talent and skills to serve the community. I also appreciate the grit, resilience, and perseverance that he has demonstrated to help him beat the odds of living in a society that was, at times, stacked against him. In addition, his post-chapter tips provide valuable guidance for the survival of today's at-risk youth."

THOMAS WARREN (D), RETIRED OMAHA POLICE CHIEF

"From family life to community life, Franklin Thompson discusses a myriad of cultural experiences and challenges of Black life in America, and creatively takes the reader on an arduous, cross-country odyssey with him. This epic and intimate look at one Black man's journey tackles cultural stereotypes and illustrates that Black people experience and respond to both Blackness and anti-Blackness in a variety of ways.

DR. CYNTHIA ROBINSON (I), UNIVERSITY OF NEBRASKA - OMAHA

"This inspiring and unapologetically raw story is a masterful treatise on overcoming various obstacles in life. It made me both laugh and cry. It also challenged me to think more critically about race and human relations in a way that I had not previously done. I can't wait to read the next installment of the Church Mouse saga."

AIMEE MELTON (R), OMAHA CITY COUNCIL

A COMPANION MUSIC PROJECT

Apple iTunes	Amazon Music
Spotify	Deezer
Tik Tok	iHeart Radio
Napster	Pandora
Shazam	Sound Cloud
7-Digital	Omahachangeagent.com
Hearnow.com	And other digital media outlets

END NOTES

[1] The urban phrase "chronic" was coined by Rapper Snoop Dogg (an entertainment genius) to describe marijuana. Although I don't smoke, I no longer deny the medical benefits that come from ingesting marijuana and its chemical derivatives. My own uncle, a conservative Air Force veteran ill with a mysterious disease, clearly benefitted from marijuana as a treatment. I also do not deny that the ingestion of cannabis appears to amplify the abilities of musicians and entertainers. Apparently, it enhances their creative juices, and we are better entertained by their drug-induced state of mind. I respect a person's right to smoke. Nevertheless, I believe marijuana is a gateway drug that can potentially lead to more addictive drug usage for some (though not all) individuals. As an educator of 45 years, I have witnessed scores of high school and college students who have not done well on tests and homework assignments because of marijuana usage. Many a student grade point averages and job opportunities have been negatively impacted by smoking "da chronic." Yes, marijuana has a legitimate place in society, but the drug is not for widespread consumption. I also personally believe that the KKK wants to keep Black people high on drugs and distracted by in-fighting and the pursuit of materialism. I acknowledge that my worldview may need further vetting. The main point of this notation is that measuring a person's "cool factor" or deciding if they are worthy of a cultural "Black Card" based on whether or not they smoke and slip and slide through life—a view that was dominant during the 1970–1995 time period, is a faulty and ignorant worldview to adopt. Please, please get that funk out my face.

[2] The Blaxploitation film producing era of the late 1960s until the late 1970s was not the most shining moment of pride for Black people. Some of the films were OK, but many portrayed Blacks in demeaning and stereotypic ways. Black media portrayals included con artists, pimps, hoes, criminals, and super-bad private eye detectives who didn't always have the best morals. Even the heroes in the films were still lacking in positive character traits compared to their White counterparts. The super-cool character "Goldie" from The Mack, for example, may not have been the healthiest portrayal for Black males to emulate. Although some progress was gained by giving Black actors much needed work in Hollywood, the era was generally a time of racism and cultural imperialism on the part

of unscrupulous Whites who made millions of dollars by perpetuating Black stereotypes. Unfortunately, too many Black citizens drank the Kool-Aid.

[3] Unfortunately, both races and both political parties utilize peer pressure and guilt to co-opt and control the way a person votes and thinks. While Black democrats use terms like Uncle Tom or Aunt Jemimah to control and co-opt conservative Black people, republicans use the term RINO, which is an acronym for "republican in name only." The end result of the pressure that emanates from the right-wing moniker is to try and make all republicans think and act alike. While it is true that republicans do have some positives to offer the nation, the practice of shaming a Black conservative person for promoting civil rights and social justice causes is not one of the party's strong points, especially in light of their Abraham Lincoln roots.

[4] The word "crunk" is an urban slang term that not only describes a subgenre of rap music made famous by artists such as Lil Jon, Lil Scrappy, and the Ying Yang Twins, but also the word includes a certain survival mindset, as in – "I am really turned-up and laser-focused to manage a demanding situation that I am facing. The musical era prior to rap and crunk is known as "funk." During the 1970s and 80's, the term funk also applied to a certain lifestyle and mindset of inner-city people, which allowed them to better handle problems such as police brutality, poverty, and miseducation. While the funk of a corrupt system held a Black person down, the funk music of musicians such as James Brown, Parliament-Funkadelic, Sly Stone, George Clinton, and Bootsy Collins had the power to set people free (well, at least in your mind it did). In summary, crunk and funk were more than just music genres. They were utilized for the dance floor and for helping people cope with the daily stresses of life.

[5] The Ebonics translation for "Yah Mo" is Yahweh, the Old Testament name given to the Jewish God. The catch phrase was made popular by singers James Ingram and Michael McDonald via a hit song entitled Yah Mo Be There, which was released in 1983.

[6] Source: Schimelpfening, N. (2021) Why do people commit suicide? VeryWellMind. About, Inc., Dotdash publishing, pp. 1-8.

[7] Source: Knoll, J. L., & Pies, R. W. (2019) Moving Beyond Motives in Mass Shootings. PsychiatricTimes.com, Vol. XXXVI, No. 1, pp. 1-3.

[8] The phrase "one last swig" is 1970s Ebonics for "give me one last drink or one last shot at (x) before I acquiesce . . ."

[9] The term "Casper the Holy Ghost" may appear blasphemous to religious readers and perhaps it is to some extent. In this context, however, the reference is to an actual song and music character created by P-Funk musician Bootsy Collins. During the 1980s urban music scene, the song and the caricature of Casper the Holy Ghost was a big hit in the funk and urban community.

[10] The term "Lucifoot" is a 1960s Deep South dialectal translation for "The Devil." It is a combination of the two words "Lucifer" and "Slew foot" – names given to describe heaven's fallen angel. Older Black preachers who have Deep South roots still use various versions of the Ebonics term. Many of those unique language speakers, however, are starting to die out as time passes.

[11] The art form, imagery, and philosophy inherent in the music of R&B singer James Brown is often quoted by many middle aged and older African Americans. In the 1960's, this was standard practice among Blacks because James Brown was seen not only as an entertainer, but also as a spokesman for the Black community. Later generations have forgotten about the influence Brown had on the worldview of Blacks. But even the younger generation must pay homage to the Godfather of soul music who wrote the Black anthem Say it Loud, I'm Black and I'm Proud.

[12] The phrase "Yo smack is whack" is 1970's urban slang for "Your thinking is messed up and your talk is nonsense!"

[13] The Ebonics translation for "hoopty" is "a broken-down used car that barely works from week to week."

[14] The phrase mentioned here became a popular saying among partygoers during the 1970-95 nightlife scene. Much to the writer's chagrin, the phrase also represented a broader worldview by which some (though not all) people actually lived by. It is possible, however, that most readers are not as conservative or as sensitive as Church Mouse is about the potential negative impact of such verbiage on youth development. Yes, it is possible that he is being overly sensitive, but please be careful. Words are powerful even when we mean no harm.

[15] The phrase "Cook dem chillen (children) some hominy grits so they can xyz" is Deep South language and philosophy for "We must properly prepare Black children to deal with the White Man and his hard-to-navigate system."

[16] The word "Jitney" describes the 1950-80 system within most urban areas to provide taxi

service for poor people. Jitney drivers may or may not have been properly licensed. They used their own personal cars and were often able to provide the same service for up to 50% less the cost of more established companies.

[17] Mad Dog 20/20, Boone's Farm, and Ripple are brand names for cheap bottled wines that became popular in the 1960's and 70's ghettos of America, due to affordability and easy accessibility. These products were dubbed as "the poor man's high."

[18] The author uses the title of the famous jazz song "What Did I Ever Do to be so Black and Blue" to express the saga of sorrows that many Black people are continually subjected to in this country. The original authors of the song are Fats Waller (music) and Harry Brooks (lyrics). It was introduced in the Broadway musical Hot Chocolates (1929) by singer Edith Wilson. Louis Armstrong later did a popular remake of the song. Although social conditions have improved since the song's inception, some Black people in the 21st century continue feel the sting of racism and poverty, as if they are still Black and Blue.

[19] Rudy Ray Moore was one of the founders of the X-rated form of Black comedy. He utilized an imaginary character known as the Signifying Monkey to deliver punch lines full of sexual and repulsive language. For example, one of his albums is entitled The Pussy Belongs to Me. In the 1960s his products were seen as obscene and over the top. Over the years, however, people have become desensitized to Moore's controversial approach, and increasing numbers of comedians have copied his style. Moore's approach is now considered by many (though not all) as an acceptable form of comedic art.

[20] Trap music a subgenre of hip-hop that originated in the Southern United States during the early 1990s. The genre gets its name from the Atlanta slang word "trap," a house used exclusively to sell drugs. Other trap lyrical topics include street life, acquiring wealth, violence, American vehicles, and life experiences that artists face while navigating hard times.

[21] An urban Don Juan styled character by the name of The Mack was made popular in a 1973 Blacksploitation movie by the same name. The movie glamourized drugs, street life, pimps, and prostitutes. In many senses it was harmless entertainment not meant to be taken seriously, but unfortunately it had a devastating impact on the minds of impressionable Black boys who wanted to get rich quick and emulate a pimp's lifestyle.

[22] The usage of the N-Word throughout this book is not done out of malice. Rather, it is more of a cultural/historical thing. It started as a racist word bestowed upon Black people by racist Whites, but over the years African Americans have co-opted the word to mean several different things at once. Usage of the word by black boys during a pick-up game of

basketball almost becomes a rites of passage deal. For some kids it is not a negative word at all, but rather a term of endearment—as in my best friend. Many researchers feel Blacks have earned the right to use the word in any manner they choose because this is their way of detoxifying and recapturing a negative word that was originally meant to harm and degrade. Conversely in 2007, the NAACP attempted to discourage usage of the word by giving it a church funeral and a casket burial. This action was ignored by most urban styled comedians, however. The usage of the N-word by Black people in general and Black comedians in particular is a very explosive topic that everyone does not agree on.

[23] During the 1940s, 50s, 60s, and 70s older grandmothers (Black and White) used the word "pill" to describe a person who was "hard to swallow" as in, "She's a pill!" The younger generation, however, used the term to describe a basketball. In addition, the term "the rock" was also used as an urban metaphor for a basketball.

[24] The phrase "handing out snaps" is urban terminology for issuing "verbal insults." The inner-city game was also known as "playing the dozens" and "selling wolf tickets." In 1939, Yale researcher John Dolland posited that (a) the practice was a survival technique held over from slavery times. He theorized that Black males used verbal brinkmanship as a way to mark territory and establish their manhood without crossing a certain line and coming to physical blows. Fighting was seen as unacceptable to the slave master. Fist fighting was also a show of non-solidarity, something Black women did not allow amongst their men. Hence, Black males learned to "fight within safe rules." Dolland stated that the practice was a manifestation of frustration aggression theory – i.e., blow off steam in a safer way before you harm or kill someone due to pent-up aggression. (B) Folklorist Alan Dundes was able to trace the American practice back to rites of male passage practices found in Nigeria and Ghana. (C) Another theory derived from Dr. Mona Lisa Saloy's work says the verbal practice was encouraged by Black parents as a self-defense mechanism for crippled and deformed relatives and close friends. Twelve deformed or crippled slaves were often traded by the slave master for one good slave. The practice of "cracking on one another" was a method parents used to make their children psychologically tough. Playing the dozens (or handing out snaps) taught young children to take a negative situation and turn it into a positive. How does one deal with someone making fun of your crippled hand? You laugh and make a joke about your own infirmity, and you also celebrate when others do it to you. But you don't stop there; you load up your gun and fire back with an insult of your own! It was verbal warfare at its best. If in fact any one of the above explanations are true, it would be just one more example of the incredible resourcefulness and resiliency of African American people living in a hostile land. In addition, contemporary TV producers

such as Nick Cannon, has found a way to cash in on the phenomenon. His hit TV show Wild-N-Out is based on the historical art of "playing the dozens" (handing out insults) and not getting angry about it.

[25] The term "diss" is urban slang for disrespect.

[26] The phrase "you threw up a brick" is an insult given to an inner-city basketball player who launches a hard, flat shot that has no chance of going through the net. "At least draw some iron" refers to the need to avoid shooting an air ball—at least hit the rim! A shot that misses the entire rim and blackboard (an air ball) is the ultimate basketball embarrassment to endure for urban ball players.

[27] John Shaft was a 1970's Black hero from the Blaxploitation era. Richard Roundtree played the initial role of the person who cleaned the ghetto up from drugs and thugs. Samuel Jackson played the reprisal role in the 2000s. John Shaft never made it to White Lone Ranger status, however, because writers and producers made sure that he came up a little short in certain character traits. Namely, he was loose with women. While the White hero was 100%, the Black version was 80%. But he was bad-ass and he carried a big gun that sounded like a canon. Dig it?

[28] It was popular for Blaxploitation era movies to perpetuate a myth that Black and Asian martial arts heroes had special abilities to catch a bullet with their teeth! One such movie character was Leroy from The Last Dragon (1985). Other martial arts producers have also toyed with this silly yet entertaining myth. It was all done in jest.

[29] The phrase "knock a hog in da head" is and endearing Ebonics phrase used in states like Louisiana, Mississippi, and Arkansas. It refers to a practice where older southern Blacks saved their best hog for times when special guests came to town. The head of the house would "knock a hog in the head" (i.e., kill it), and lay out a big feast for the individuals they were trying to impress.

[30] The phrase "Soul looks back and wonder how I got over" is a standard line used in the Black community. It's meaning is both religious (i.e., how I made it into heaven), and historical (i.e., how did Black people ever survive the institution of slavery and Jim Crow?" The phrase equates to a cultural battle cry for some Black folk.

[31] Joe Clark is the name of the teacher (played by actor Morgan Freeman) highlighted in the Hollywood Blockbuster film "Lean on Me," which details the problems educators had with getting disadvantaged and high-risk urban students to focus on non-violent solutions

and academic improvement.

[32] Jaime Escalante (played by actor Edward James Olmos) was featured in a film entitled Stand and Deliver. The educator is best known for not throwing at-risk students away as was popular in the 80's and 90's, and for proving that barrio and ghetto students had the ability to do higher level math. Many of his so-called low-performing students went on to become college students or successful tax paying citizens.

[33] Prior to 2020, the state of Nebraska suffered an inaccurate reputation for being a place where only conservative White farmers and ranchers lived. The overriding inference is that no Black people could possibly reside in an agricultural dominated state. It was not unusual for Black citizens visiting other parts of the country to have to endure public ridicule for living in an "all-White state." On the other hand, outside of the Omaha and Lincoln metropolitan areas, Nebraska is predominantly White (smile).

[34] Whereas the word "homie" is 100% a positive term (as in my best friend), a "hood homie" could either be a good friend or a hater depending on that person's motives for wanting to hang around you. It is not a perfect correlation, but you are more likely to get robbed by a hood homie, as opposed to a true homie who's got your back.

[35] Child actor Ron Howard (aka, Opie) played the happy-go-lucky son of Sheriff Andy Taylor in the 1960s weekly sitcom The Andy Griffith Show, which used the rural town of Mayberry RFD as the storyline setting. The show was about an all-White town where people trusted each other to the point where they would leave the doors of their homes unlocked. Opie symbolized an innocent child devoid of the problems that most kids from the inner-city faced. He was an all-American poster child. During the 1970s and 80s, if any male – White or Black – was called an "Opie," it was similar to calling them a naïve, out-of-touch person who needed to be educated about what was happening in the real world.

[36] The cited phrase used here is one of singer George Clinton's Parliament/Funkadelic euphemisms that became popular during the 1975-90 P-Funk music era. Its translation is: "Give a soul brother some room to breathe. Don't be so hard on a struggling person who is just trying to survive!"

[37] Dolomite was a popular stage and media character in the Black comedy scene during the 1970s. Comedian Rudy Ray Moore was the architect of the Dolomite comedy routine, which included risqué and controversial material for, not only that time, but even by today's standards. Dolomite was the ultimate bad-ass from the ghetto who went on to

influence a bevy of Black comedians that followed him.

[38] The phrase "Ace Boon Coon" is Ebonics terminology for a person's best friend. The friend is assumed to have gone through the trials and tribulations of racism and inner-city life and understands the games that are played. It is interesting to note the phrase is a testimony to how Blacks historically take negative things (i.e., the word coon was a racial epithet used by Southern Whites to put down Black people) and turned it into a positive thing (i.e., this is my very best friend who I trust).

[39] The term "smelling oneself" is an Ebonics, as well as a general southern colloquial, term used by older parents to describe a teenager who was "getting too big for his/her own britches."

[40] The cited phrase was made famous by heavyweight boxing champion Muhammad Ali and his cornerman Drew Bundini Brown. It was a rallying call to succeed despite the many obstacles and hurdles a person faces in life.

[41] For the sake of honesty and transparency, I can only vouch for a portion of this account. I have struggled for years trying to string together what took place the rest of that evening. I am 100% sure I did not go home. I am also 100% sure I did not sleep outdoors or at a local gas station. I may have went to a friend's house. My gut tells me that I hung out at school overnight, but I am only 50% sure about that. I was a hurting child suffering from a major mental and emotional meltdown, and I honestly cannot fill in the details of how the remainder of that night went. I apologize to readers for utilizing "creative assumptions" to help fill in the missing blanks. Brave and strong survive the best way you know how.

[42] The term "beeyotch" or "biatch" is urban, hip-hop slang for "bitch." Some people joke that it is the French version of the word. Some people give credit to famed rapper Too-Short for coining the alternate pronunciation of the word in the late 1980s. After the turn of the twenty-first century, the word bitch was often viewed as a positive thing much in the same way that the N-Word was co-opted by Blacks.

[43] The phrase "cock strong" is street language referring to a teenage male being a virgin, and as a result he is gifted with a testosterone bump in physical strength and stamina. It is believed that boys who have not experience sexual activity possess extra strength due to bottled up libido. Is it reality or a myth? Many professional boxers are ordered by their trainers to abstain from sexual activity a month before an important fight. Despite urban folklore, science has not yet established a substantial relationship between sexual abstinence and physical strength for athletes.

[44] The Ebonics translation for the well-known urban catchphrase coined by comedian Rudy Ray Moore is: "The superstar can no longer be accessed." It is a play off the popular saying that "Elvis Presley has left the building." Sometimes the signifying phrase can also mean: "The boy with the big talk is a humbled man and must now eat crow."

[45] These are various song titles and related subject matter from the 1960s and 1970s Black Power Movement, many of them having to do with the advancement of African Americans during the Civil Rights era.

[46] The phrase "all that and a bag of chips" is 1990's urban slang used to describe "a person who really had their stuff together."

[47] The phrase "snow bunny" is a pejorative urban term to describe a White female, especially those who dated Black men. Today, interracial dating is not that big of a big deal. In the 1970s and 1980s, however, Black women viewed it as the Black male's ultimate betrayal to their race.

[48] The original poem written in early 1971 was about 70% of how it reads today. Over the years, I have modified and amended the original creation another 30% to help capture more of the true essence of what I felt as a child.

[49] The 2000s urban slang translation of the phrase "the shiz-nit" is: I am, or you are the shit!

[50] The urban phrase "mo fo" is a softer substitute for the more caustic "mother fucker" descriptor. Bernie Mack and other comedians were known for using this safer phrase during their routines.

[51] The movie character known as Stepin Fetchit was made famous by actor Lincoln Theodore Monroe Andrew Perry. His characterization as a lazy, slow-witted, jive-talking "coon" offended progressive African Americans at the time he was a major attraction in motion pictures (primarily during the 1930s and 40s). It still offends African Americans more than 60 years after he has faded from the screen. Despite strong criticisms he received during the early civil rights era, in later years Perry was praised for his part in opening doors for Black actors, notably receiving the Special Image Award by the NAACP in 1976. He was also elected to the Black Filmmakers Hall of Fame in 1978.

[52] Candid Camera was a popular prime time television show during the 1960's and 70's, which thrived on capturing people authentically and unaware that a camera had been filming them.

[53] Leave it to Beaver was an early 1960's popular television sitcom, which chronicled the life of a typical, successful, White suburban family where things perfectly worked themselves out. The show has been used to describe the American Dream. In the eyes of Black, Brown, and Red people, however, the lifestyle portrayed in the show is an idealistic fantasy world that never existed for them.

[54] Eugene Curran Kelly was an American actor, dancer, stage, and television, singer, film director, producer, screenwriter, comedian, and choreographer. He was known for his energetic and athletic dancing style, his good looks, and the likable characters that he played on screen. Both his voice and his dance moves were widely emulated far into the 21st century.

[55] Chuck Berry is a legendary singer and guitar player from the 1950's and 60's who is often credited as being a co-founder of rock-n-roll music. He also made the gooseneck dance motion while playing the guitar famous.

[56] Little Richard is a legendary singer and piano player from the 1950's and early 60's era, who is not credited enough for his role in co-founding rock-n-roll. Also noteworthy is the fact that his dress, look, and general showmanship have heavily influenced many Pop and R&B performers of later decades. His signature "shut up" verbal routine was popular with late night talk show hosts such as Johnny Carson.

[57] Although singer James Brown is most often credited as being the father of rap music, The Last Poets must also be credited for their contribution to the political and social consciousness portion of the rap and hip-hop music scene. In particular, they borrowed from the West African Griot tradition of storytelling.

[58] The phrase "bust me a slob" is 1970s urban slang for give me a kiss.

[59] The phrase "gimmie sum-a-dem-yams" is 1980s urban slang used by Black males when they lusted after a female's thighs. It's mostly a playful bantering type of thing between men and women. The phrase is not necessarily a request for actual intercourse, but more of a flirtatious request to be frisky. All of this would fall under the category of today's definition of sexual harassment if it were done outside of consent.

[60] The term "boonkey" or "boonkay" is the Gullah word for rear end or booty.

[61] The term "Knock a few boots" is urban slang terminology for having sex. It can also mean being unfaithful to one's committed partner.

[62] The term "player hater" is urban slang for a person who is always trying to embarrass or front you off because they are jealous of what you have. The term is also applied to those who do not easily succumb to peer pressure.

[63] The term "Gank me again" is 1980's urban slang for "Be careful how you go about disrespecting me. I won't let it slide a second time!"

[64] Cujo is the name of a rabid dog – a character in a 1983 blockbuster movie with the same name. Cujo, at one time a good animal, became dangerous when he was bitten by a diseased bat, which caused him to spread holy terror on an unsuspecting mother and her family.

[65] In 1974, Lockbourne Air Force Base was renamed to Rickenbacker AFB.

[66] The phrase "Ming Dynasty" is twenty-first century Gullah slang for females who are a part of "the pretty girl club."

[67] The following publications from the Equal Justice Initiative - EJI (122 Commerce Street, Montgomery, AL, 36104, 334-269-1803, www.eji.org) serves as some of the better sources for understanding the Jim Crow era and how Blacks were forced to navigate Black Code and other exclusionary laws and practices: (a) Lynching in America: Confronting the Legacy of Racial Terror, (b) Reconstruction in America: Racial Violence after the Civil War, 1865-1876, and (c) Segregation in America.

[68] Source: The Oxford English Dictionary.

[69] Source: The various EJI resources previously cited in #67 above.

[70] Source: https://www.abhmuseum.org/

[71] Source: Education Trust (2014). The state of education for African American students. https://edtrust.org/resource/the-state-of-education-for-african-american-students/

[72] Source: Ziegler, Brett (2021). The states with the highest poverty rates. U.S. News and World Report (online). www.usnews.com/news/best states/rankings/education.

[73] Source: Davis, Elliott (2021). Education rankings. U.S. News and World Report (online). www.usnews.com/news/best states/slideshow/ us-states-with-the-highest-poverty-rates.

[74] Most people don't know that the first organized Christian religion was the Coptic Church founded in Ethiopia and Eritrea in the year 42 A.D. by Apostle St. Mark. This was

long before the establishment of the earliest version of the Catholic religion around 110, which was still not officially recognized by Rome until 380 A.D. The Protestant Church did not form until 1517 A.D.

[75] The oldest university in the world was the University of al-Qarawinyyin located in Fez, Morocco (859 A.D.) Black African leader Mansa Musa established the world renowned University of Timbuktu in Mali in 1100 A.D. Algebra was introduced to the world in the ninth century by Muhammad ibn Musa al-Khwarizmi. Abu Al Qasim Al Zahrawi (Albucasis) from Saudi Arabia relocated to Spain and taught modern surgical practices to Europeans until he died at the age of 77 in 1013 A.D. The history of Black and Brown peoples include a rich combination of higher learning, math, science, and family values from both a liberal and conservative perspective. While the 1960s American activist piece of the puzzle is a legitimate focus, it only represents 10% of Black history. People of Color need a 360 degree view of their full history and culture in order to properly heal from the racism that was done to them by racist Whites. Yes, intelligent revolution and reparations are legitimate topics to discuss, but there is so much more to the Black experience than just 1960s and 1970s events and rhetoric.

[76] Here is the standard English translation of Grandma Queen's Gullah message to Church Mouse: "Stop throwing rocks before you hit your brother in the eye. If you make me repeat myself, I will give you a spanking you won't forget. Do you hear me boy?" If you are a new visitor to the coastal areas of South Carolina, it can take a little adjustment to understand the local dialect.

[77] A full description of Gullah history and culture would take some time to unfold. A quicker (i.e., a Cliff's Notes) description of Gullah people and culture, however, can be obtained by watching various videos produced by Queen Quet. Quet is known as the official ambassador of the Gullah Nation for the state of South Carolina. She can be viewed on You Tube and is one of the better contemporary representatives of the art of code switching, as well as demonstration of a culture that is starting to rapidly disappear right before our eyes.

[78] Source: https://worldpopulationreview.com/state-rankings/black-population-by-state. (2022).

[79] A cultural practice in the traditional Black Church is for a preacher to use the phrase "amen light bulbs" when they perceive that the congregation does not get the main point or when the congregational response is viewed as unresponsive.

[80] The empowering axiom is taken from the 1969 song entitled Stand by Sly and the Family Stone. I believe Sylvester Stewart wrote these lyrics as a form of therapy for children who hurt, and for people who are misunderstood and underappreciated. Thank you, my brother, for your healing words!

[81] Obviously, the word used in the scenario was nigga and not ninja. When the word nigga is used in succession, over-and-over like a machine gun, however, it can tend to have a killing effect. I may be a hypocrite here, but sometimes you have to use a viable substitute for caustic and controversial words and phrases. Thus, I made the decision to substitute in the word "ninja" because it is a softer term to use in rapid succession. Another important side note is that when some (though not all) Black women used the N-word, they were not always talking about a person's skin color or race. The word can sometimes be substituted for "my boyfriend, my husband, or my homie." Even in contemporary society, the word can have multiple meanings. The original racist spelling of the word (nigger) is never used among Blacks, however. The two spellings have opposite meanings. In addition, rapper Ice Cube has gone on record as saying "nigga" is the African American ingenious way of capturing a negative word, regurgitating it, and spitting it back out as a badge of honor. Not all Black educators and authorities agree with Ice Cube and other apologists like him on this view, however.

[82] Source: https://www.itsovereasy.com.

[83] Source: The Anne E. Casey Foundation (2021). Kids count data book: 2021 State of trends in child well-being. Retrieved from www.aef.org. Baltimore, Maryland: Casey Foundation Publishing.

[84] The phrase "put a root" on somebody is southern Ebonics language for "casting a spell on a person." Historically, the Gullah people of South Carolina have borrowed heavily from both African and Caribbean cultures.

[85] The description of this particular reaction to fright is greatly exaggerated although the overall scenario is true. It is one of those times when the writer used his wild imagination to add coloring to the script. White southern racists perpetuated the myth that Black people turned White when they saw a ghost or when they were frightened by a scarry animal. The Reconstruction era films made during the 1915 thru 1955 time period were fraught with these types of stereotypes. Sometimes southern Black kids co-opted White foolishness in such a manner as a way to show just how ridiculous the stereotype really was.

[86] Similar to what was mentioned in chapter 10, when Black ministers do not get the amen

response that they think their preaching deserves, they will often say something like, "Praise the Lord lightbulbs!" It is a contemporary takeoff of Jesus telling the Pharisees that if the people were made to be quiet, the rocks and stones would start to cry out (Luke 19: 39-40).

[87] The well-known quote by English poet Alexander Pope has been an inspiration to many people down through the ages. Love and forgiveness is a rock upon which the future of our world rests.

[88] The phrase HIS-Story is a way of advancing an interpretation of history that is told from the viewpoint of the dominant ruling (White) group only. That kind of history is not accurate nor healthy because it only gives one perspective, and it lacks a 360 degree cultural and political perspective.